SIBERIA AND OTHER PLAYS

Studies in Austrian Literature, Culture and Thought.

Translation Series.

Felix Mitterer

SIBERIA

AND

OTHER PLAYS

ARIADNE PRESS

Ariadne Press would like to express its appreciation to the
Austrian Cultural Institute, New York and the Austrian
Ministry of Education, Vienna for their assistance in
publishing this book.

Translated from the German ©Österreichischer Bühnenverlag
Kaiser & Co., Vienna.
Performance rights for all plays by Felix Mitterer must be
acquired from Österreichischer Bühnenverlag Kaiser & Co.,
Vienna.

Library of Congress Cataloging-in-Publication Data

Mitterer, Felix, 1948-
    Siberia and other plays / Felix Mitterer.
        p.   cm. -- (Studies in Austrian literature,
    culture, and thought. Translation series)
    Translated from the German.
    Contents: Siberia -- Stigma -- Visiting hours --
    Dragonthirst, or, The rusty knight, or, Black and white,
    money and bread, the living and the dead -- There's not
    a finer country.
        ISBN 0-929497-68-6
        I. Title. II. Series
    PT2673.I79A27   1994
    832'.914--dc20
                                                93-34857

Cover design:
Director and Designer: George McGinnis

CONTENTS

Siberia

A Monologue

Translated by

Margit Kleinman and Louis Fantasia

The author wishes to express his thanks to
Magdalena Stöckler (Pro Senectute Österreich),
who worked as a nurse in a Senior Citizen's Home
and provided information for this piece. Her experience
is documented in *Arbeit mit alten Menschen*, Pfeiffer
Verlag, Vienna 1985.

The translators would like to thank Joel Kleinman for
his assistance and contributions.

I.

(An OLD MAN stands on two crutches, in pajamas and bathrobe.)

> Family!
> What kind of family is this?
> What kind of family is this
> that would plot
> against me?
> What kind of family would do this
> to plot against one of its own?
>
> I know!
> I know!
> I know, Frau Daughter-in-Law!
> I know I've injured my hip!
> I've injured my hip a little.
> So what?
> Is that any reason to condemn me?
> Is that any reason to put me out to
> pasture
> like an old nag?
> See?
> I can walk.
> I can get around.
> I'm still pretty lively
> for a man of my age.
>
> Even I'm starting to use those words now,
> those disgusting words:
> "pretty lively for a man of my age."
>
> Sorry, old boy,
> for using those words!
> Those terrible words:
> "for a man of my age."
> Man! Man your battle stations! To arms!

The knight arms himself.
Well, that's still okay.
The root is okay.
The root is okay:
the knight arms himself.
The knight arms himself with his armor.
With his armor he arms himself for the
battle.
For an honorable death.
But not in this context please.
Not when you talk about
"a man of my age"
still being able to put one foot in front
of the other.
The aftertaste is disgusting.
The aftertaste of the word "man"
is just disgusting.
I won't take that.

Same story with the word
"lively."
Lively.
Disturbing!
Of sound mind.
Disgusting!

Dear Senior Citizens.
Disgusting!
These announcements over the loudspeaker
drive me nuts!

Dear Senior Citizens
we warmly wish our beloved resident
XYZ
a sound mind and a healthy body
as he celebrates his 86th birthday!
Disgusting!
What don't you understand?

What don't you understand about it?
Of course you don't understand anything
about it!
You don't understand anything!
None of you understand anything,
otherwise, you'd never have brought me
here.
Otherwise, you'd never have had me
deported.
Yep. That's right, deported!
My second deportation.
The second deportation in my life.
The first was to Siberia.
As a prisoner of war.
The second was here, to this "home"!
Just like Siberia!

What do you mean I'm exaggerating?
Don't tell me I'm exaggerating!
You didn't know the other Siberia,
and you don't know this one either!
It was cold there and it's cold here!
At least there I learned something!
At least there I was allowed to learn
something!
Chess and Russian!
Russian and chess!
Zhat' tebe, drug moi!
Here, you're not allowed to learn
anything.
Absolutely nothing!

Lie down and die!
Those are the orders!

Care!
What do you mean, care?
Huh? What kind of care?

There isn't any care here!
Stuff it in!
Shit it out!
Clean it up!
That's care?
Not for me!
I don't need it!
I don't belong here, you understand?
I don't need this kind of care!
I don't need this Siberia!
You see how I can walk?
You see?

(*He throws one crutch away.*)

With only one crutch!
You see?
Soon I won't need any at all.
I can get dressed by myself.
I can feed myself,
wash myself, I can even
go to the can by myself!

You won't have any trouble with me.
Absolutely no trouble!

(*He reaches for the other crutch.*)

Leave me alone, damn it!
I can pick it up by myself!
I don't need help from anyone!
That should make you happy!

(*He picks up the other crutch with great
difficulty.*)

Upsy-daisy!
You see that?

I did it!
Proof!
Satisfied?
No, you're never satisfied.
You want me to do somersaults?
Want me to jump up and touch the
ceiling?
What kind of proof do you want?

I was thrilled!
I was so thrilled!
Finally to get out of that hospital!
Finally to get out of that drafty corridor!
You saw it, you know what I'm talking
about!
I pay for social security my entire life
and that's what I end up with?
They put me in a drafty corridor!
With athletes!
With all those stupid athletes!
You know, they break their legs too,
those stupid athletes,
did you know that?

They can tear their tendons, they sprain
their joints.
But an old man
who injures his hip,
who injures his hip just a little,
he's condemned to Siberia!

I used to be so happy!
Finally to be home!
Finally to be in my own room!
Finally to be with my own dog!
And what happens?
What happens?

In some cloak and dagger operation—you heard
me—
in some cloak and dagger operation
I'm deported here, to this "home."

And because I'm outraged,
because I'm upset,
and rightfully so,
they threaten me with the psycho ward!
They give me a couple of shots
and I'm out for three whole days.
And I wake up,
I wake up,
and I'm strapped to this bed.
That's right, strapped!
Strapped down like a lunatic!
Even in Siberia
they never strapped me down,
Frau Daughter-in-Law.
Not even in Siberia!

But that's not all of it!
That's just the beginning!
They've turned me into a baby!
I lie strapped in my bed
wearing diapers!
Do you believe it?
No, you don't believe it,
and you don't care!

At first, I thought I was going to go
through the roof,
symbolically speaking, of course;
I was strapped down, wasn't I?
But then I came to my senses
and told myself to be reasonable.
Calm down, old boy,
I said to myself,

if you rebel, if you scream,
they'll give you a couple more shots
and then you're done for.
Not me!
I didn't survive Siberia for nothing!
You have to get up pretty early in the
morning
if you want to catch me!

Excuse me, Frau Head Nurse,
have you got a moment?
No, no, there's no hurry!
Thank you! Thank you!

I'm really sorry if I've
made any trouble for you!
It won't happen again.
I can see you've got a lot of work to do.
And with such a small staff.
You're overworked.
You won't have any trouble from me.
I promise.
Could you please unloosen these straps?
Thanks, thanks a lot.
Could I please go to the bathroom?
Thanks, thanks a lot.
No, no, I can do it by myself.
Just the crutches.
The hospital gave me these crutches.
Thanks, thanks a lot.
Would you be so kind as to inquire
where they've put my little bankbook,
Frau Head Nurse?
I'd love to be able
to give you a small contribution
to use as you see fit,
for some charitable cause,
or the coffee fund,

or the annual staff picnic,
or whatever you think best!

What?

Of course!
Of course I had my bankbook
with me in the hospital,
what do you think?

It was in the inside breast pocket of my
sportcoat,
like always!
An old man needs his money, Madam;
it's a question of survival!
Without money you don't exist!
Nothing is free,
absolutely nothing.
Have you by any chance
looked for this little bankbook yet?
What?

No?
You didn't?
Isn't that amazing!
It wouldn't have done you any good,
anyway.
It won't work without the password.
Do you know the password?
No, of course you don't!
And you know what, neither do I!
I forgot it!

Yep. I forgot it.
Sorry!
Too bad!
These things happen, right?
It could even happen to a trained, young

athlete,
right?

Yep. And so the Head Nurse invites me
down to the staff cafeteria
again and again into the inner sanctum
reserved for staff,
where patients are strictly forbidden!
Of course it only happens
when none of her colleagues are around:
I get a cup of coffee and a little glass of
brandy
and a good cigarette
as we try to refresh my memory.
Is it a name?
Is it a thing?
Is it a day of the week?
It's really touching how much she cares
for me,
this Head Nurse!
Nobody else knows about it.
It's our secret.
Secrets bind.

What?

Of course she wants my money!
I know that!
I'm not stupid!
The little bankbook, Frau Daughter-in-
Law,
is my life insurance policy.
As long as I can never remember the
password
I have a free life insurance policy.
Understand?
And by the way,
I wanted to give you that little bankbook

as a gift.

Yep. I wanted to give it to you as a gift,
a kind of homecoming present.
In the hospital,
in that drafty corridor,
with all those athletes,
I said to myself:

Old boy,
when you go home to your family
you can give your son and your
daughter-in-law
a homecoming present.
They can certainly use the money.
You don't need it.
There's nothing else you need to buy.
What do I need to buy?
There's absolutely nothing else that
I need.
Absolutely nothing.
All those glitzy things,
I don't need them.
It was comforting.
Yep. That's what I thought.
And then comes the cloak and dagger
operation!
The "family"
didn't want me any more.
The "family"
didn't want me around any longer.
So you lose
all that lovely money!
But that's not all,
not just the little bankbook
that had a nice little sum in it, oh no,
you lose my pension, too!
My pension, most of which you used

up anyway,
if you recall,
for room and board
for me and my dog.
Right?

I didn't expect something for nothing,
you know.
I paid for everything!
Now my pension goes here, to this
"home,"
right to the last penny.
Was that smart of you?
Answer me!
You don't want to answer me?
Fine!
No answer!
You don't want to answer me?
Fine!
No answer is already an answer.
Who's in my room?

Of course!
That was the reason
for my deportation, wasn't it?
So that each of them could have their
own room?
The old must give way to the young.
There were five of us in a room,
Frau Daughter-in-Law.
Five!
But we didn't have a cassette player.
We didn't argue over
who would listen to what music.
Music!
That's not even music!
It's intimidation!
Acoustical intimidation!

They intimidated me, your children.
With their constant racket
throughout the entire house.
My dog suffered from it.
Really suffered from it!

He used to crawl under my bed,
whimpering.
What kind of music is that?
Blows to the brain!
Blows to the brain is what it is!
In my house.
It is my house,
remember?
I bought the house!
I worked for it my entire life!
And what happens?
What happens?
They kick me out
of my own house.
It's disgusting!
There'll be consequences!
You'll see!

What?
I'll put the ball in the other court.
That's right!
I'll put the ball in the other court!
I'll give you notice!
I'll have you removed from the premises!
I'll have you evicted!
Evicted! Understand?
Then you'll be out in the street!
Homeless!
You can move into a homeless shelter
and be inmates, too!
Either you get me out of here
or I'll have you evicted!

Is that clear?

That's right, go on.
Tell him!
Go tell my son!
I'll have you evicted!

II.

(*The OLD MAN stands, leaning against a walker, in pajamas.*)

They're building a new skyscraper over there.
It gets bigger and bigger every day.
Nothing but glass and steel and concrete.
Sometimes the cranes swing around in the wind.

How's the dog?
All right?
Tell me, how's he doing?

Yep. He's old.
Like me.
We're both old.
But he's all right, huh?

I hope so.
"To love my dog, such as I do,
mankind calls a sin.
But my dog in tempests is ever-true,
while mankind shifts with the wind."
You give him something decent to eat, don't you?

I hope so.
Plenty of water?
Water is important!

It's cleansing,
it cleans out the system,
stops hardening of the arteries.
Stops the drying out.
I sent you the money,
expense money for the dog.
(*He holds up a photograph of the dog.*)

He's a clever mutt.
You don't appreciate that.
You don't understand animals.
Except for your kids' stinking guinea pigs.
I'd love to see him.
He always slept
at the foot of my bed.
Against your will.
Like a hot water bottle.
God forgive me, but this dog
was the most important thing in my life, next to
my wife.
The most important, really.
Complete love.
Complete trust.
Complete fidelity.
Without conditions.
You don't understand?
No, you don't understand anything.
His look.
That look.
I don't see it anymore.
And I miss hearing his happy little growls
when he'd curl up at my feet.
He misses me.
He misses me terribly, I know it.
Am I right?
I ask you, am I right?

I knew it.

I miss him, too.
Why can't you bring your pets
to a "home" like this?
I'd take care of him,
with pleasure!
Then I'd have something to do,
I'd have a purpose.
He felt sorry for me,
lying on the steps when I'd fallen down.
He whined,
and licked my face,
and tried to help me up.
He wanted to jump into the ambulance,
but you held him back
as they slammed the door.
And for the longest time,
as the ambulance drove away,
I could still hear his desperate whimpering.
I can still hear it.
What's he doing?
Tell me, what's he doing?

What do you mean, nothing?
What do you mean, nothing?
How's he behaving? Where does he stay,
in my room or somewhere else?

No? Uh-uh!
And why not,
if I may ask a rhetorical question?

Of course!
I knew it!
That's just what I thought.
That's Angela's room.
No dogs allowed.

Of course he sheds.

A teenage girl's room with dog hair!
It's not possible!
It'd be a catastrophe!
So where does he stay,
I ask you?

In the corridor.
That's what I thought.
In the corridor to my room, right?
In the corridor outside the door to my room.
He sits there and waits,
waits for me to come home.
When he hears the key in the front door
he runs to see if it's me.
Right?
Right?
I knew it.

I know everything.
I'd do the same thing.

(*He puts the photo of the dog away.*)

Listen!
The password,
the password for the bankbook,
I just remembered it.
They forced me to go to bed!
I fell down.
Just once.
I fell down just once.
Just a little bruise.
Not even worth talking about.
In spite of that,
without mercy,
into bed!
And I know,
as soon as I'm lying there,

that I'm finished.
Just like the others.
I can see it.
But I'm not ready to give up yet!
Not yet!
That's why I asked for this!
For this walker.
For this stupid walker.
So I can walk.
So I can exercise.
At first they didn't want to give it to me,
they didn't want to be responsible!

Simply wouldn't be responsible.
So I bribed them!
All of them!
From the Head Nurse on down.
Except the little Filipino girl,
to tell you the truth.
Asians respect their elders.

How?
How did I do it?
With my little bankbook, of course!
I told the Head Nurse
the password.
Inspiration! Inspiration!
I remembered the password!
Oh what joy!
Oh what joy!
Finally!
She had just about given up.
She was getting suspicious.
She's not stupid.
She pressured me.
Not openly, of course,
but I could tell by the way she treated me,
by the way she dealt with me,

the way she talked to me.
Oh, what joy!
The way her face lit up
when she ran to the bank to get the money!
Naturally, she took a nice little chunk for herself.
I had to talk her into it, of course.
Please, Frau Head Nurse, I beg you,
for the coffee fund,
of the staff picnic,
or whatever charitable cause
you like!

Listen!
About the eviction,
I didn't really mean it.
I'm temperamental, you know.
I take it all back.
I'm sorry
about the whole thing.
I know it wasn't easy.
Up all night,
pacing about my room,
rearranging things, puttering about,
muttering to myself,
talking things over with the dog
about Heaven and earth.
It's not easy, I know.
You warned me enough times.
And sometimes I was difficult,
I admit that.
I criticized you.
I criticized the way you brought up the kids.
I should never have
stuck my nose in,
I admit it.
I apologize for the whole thing.
Accepted?

Good. Good.
A step in the right direction.
You let me come back,
you let me come back to my house,
and you can have my bankbook.
There's still plenty in it.
You can still buy a lot with it.
Of course, you'll get my pension, too!
And I swear, with all my heart,
to be a well-behaved, quiet, unobtrusive
Senior Citizen.
I'll let the kids have their way,
and you, too!
I'll be a nice, friendly grandpa to them,
one that likes every idiotic hairstyle,
and every silly piece of clothing,
and all that noise they call music.
Because we were all young once!
Don't forget that, old boy!
I'll be absolutely one hundred percent
cooperative!
And, of course, regarding
your marriage,
my lips are sealed.
No advice.
No lectures.
Discretion personified.
Practically invisible!
And if my son should ever invite me
to watch football with him again
on TV,
I will never be so stupid and selfish
as to decline the invitation
but will, with the utmost enthusiasm,
sit in front of the set
and cheer my guts out
for his favorite team of
wonderful, sporty, young

athletes.

And with regard
to any problems you might have,
please,
tell me, make me aware of them,
so that I'll eat everything
on my plate without a comment,
without suggesting
that my wife's cooking was better;
and I'll try every new-fangled dish you make
with the greatest of pleasure,
whether it's
Chinese, Malaysian or Moroccan,
it's all fine with me.
I won't bother you in the least
when you're in the living room,
and most of all
I won't crush the pillows
on your sofa.
I'll keep the dog confined to quarters,
just like me;
I'll be personally responsible
for taking every last hair that he sheds
to the garbage;
I'll air my room out three times a day
in order to get rid of the stench of old age;
and I'll take a bath just once every three days
to save on the hot water bill,
just once every three days,
and all by myself,
so you won't have to
look at my old body.
How's that for a plan?
Why don't you take it up
at the next family meeting?

Ah, you've already discussed it?

I can see by the expression on your face
that the answer was no.
Then I request
that you bring it up again,
considering the latest developments.

What do you mean
it doesn't make any sense?
I said
I'd be a well-behaved, unobtrusive
old man!
Or weren't you listening?
Maybe I was talking to the wall?

Where is my son?
Where is my son?
Why didn't he come?
Why doesn't he visit me?
Why did he send you?
Is he afraid of me?
Or does he feel guilty?

So?
Angry over the threat of eviction?
I took it back!
Tell him I took it back!
I'm a desperate man,
and I beg him to understand!
Tell him that!
Tell him he'd better get himself
over here!

What do you mean, he's got too much to do?
He can find ten minutes
to visit his father!
I created him!
I fathered him!
I raised him!

Am I a criminal?
Do I have the plague?

What is it this time?
What's he up to this time?

Bookkeeping?
What's he doing bookkeeping on the weekend for?
For whom?

But what for?
Why does he take home so much work?
Why is he killing himself on the weekends?
He doesn't have to work on the weekends.
You've got everything you need, don't you?
A house,
enough to eat,
clothes on your back.
What more do you want?

New furniture? New furniture?
Why new furniture? Is the old furniture
broken?

So what if it's old!
It's my furniture
and it's good furniture!
Solid wood!
Where do you find solid wood furniture
now-a-days?
Plywood!
Pressboard!
Plastic!
It's all garbage!
Junk!
Trash!
First you rip out the beautiful old
kitchen,

then the bedroom,
and now the rest of it.
It's a waste of money!
And the fool goes along with this?

What do you mean, "it's dark"? What do you
mean, "the others"?
What do you mean, "it's dark"?

Do you want an operating room, or what?
Throw away those stupid catalogues
that are always jamming up the mailbox.
And as for your neighbors, your
colleagues, the "others,"
why do you worry about keeping up with them?
You don't have to have everything
everybody else has!
You'll go to Hell
if you throw away my old furniture!
To Hell!
It's my room!
You've already done it, haven't you?

Of course!
I knew it!

Of course!
A teenage girl in an old man's room
is just not possible!
Not a trace of me?
Not a trace of my existence?

What do you mean, promised?

Yep. You're right.
I'm starting up all over again.
I can't help myself.
Sorry.

I know, I know what I promised!
I can't help myself!
I'm an old man,
so have a little compassion!
I can't change overnight!
You know me, I get angry quickly!
I just don't get it, why he's slaving away
for nothing.
He does all right.
And you work part-time.
You make enough to get along
without overtime and weekends!

Vacation!
You and your vacations!
I never went anywhere.
Except in the war.
And then unwillingly!
Staying home is just fine.

You think you'll see different faces
on the Riviera?
Vacation.
What a joke!
Just another new-fangled idea.
Go to the park!
Or go down to the lake!
It's more tranquil than the Riviera.
And you won't get stuck in traffic!

I know, I'm giving you advice again.
I can't help myself.
I admit it!
I know I'm hopeless.
I'm just pig-headed.

A pig-headed sonofabitch.
It happens at my age.

We all get that way here.
It's frightening.
We all look alike.
We reflect each other.
But no one sees himself in the mirror.
That's the worst part of it.

Nothing but old folks.
Nothing but old folks.
A ghetto.
This can't be good.
And if I get angry sometimes
with the kids, or the two of you,
it's because you mean a great deal to me!
Youth!
Young people!
I always enjoyed
being with young people.
And here there are only old folks.

You should have my little bankbook.
I'll give it to you.
Without condition.
Without prerequisites.
Just do me one favor:
be good to the dog.
He deserves it.
Take him for a walk
every now and then.
Let the children take him to the park
every now and then.
They can take turns doing it.
Pay them for it.
You know, my dog loves going to the park.
We used to go walking
through the woods there.

No!

Don't bring him here.
Then he'll know where I am.
Then he'll scratch at the door
and whine and look for me.
They won't let him in here.
I couldn't stand that!

Come on. I'll give you my little bankbook.
I hid it in the broom-closet.
The password is my dog's name.
What else?

III.

*(The OLD MAN sits dangling his feet from the edge of the
hospital bed. He is wearing pajamas and a hospital
gown.)*

Who is it?
It's my son.
Hello!
They let me sit side-saddle now.
They call this side-saddle.
They wanted to force me to lie down.
But I spoke with the doctor
when he came to visit.
The others hesitate to say anything,
because they're afraid
of the staff.
They lie in their beds like corpses,
with the covers pulled up, nice and neat.
Only once a week, of course,
when the Director comes to visit—
then the covers are pulled up nice and neat.
They're like corpses.
Freshly washed and combed.

Nobody moves.
Like in the army.
At attention.
Well, how are we? All right?
No, everything's wonderful, absolutely wonderful.
We thank God and country
and the entire human race,
and anyone else as well,
that we've got it so good!
Then he's gone.
Red-carpet treatment!
He doesn't even have to
open the door for himself
on the way out!

If he'd only look under one blanket!
Just one blanket!
Then he'd get an eyeful!
Foul, festering, black boils
on our backs, our behinds and on our legs!
From enforced bed-rest!
From lying in bed!
From lack of care!
Just slap on the cream,
everyone with the same spoon!
I have one.
One of those boils.
It's like the plague.
Believe me, it is the plague!

But I don't give in!
Not yet!
I never said
everything was wonderful!
I've insisted
that they let me sit side-saddle.
I said that to them.
Naturally not in that tone;

I'm not stupid!

I restrained myself.
I restrained myself in Siberia, too.
Only with self-restraint can you survive
an institution like this.

I was the enemy then, you understand,
the enemy
who invaded their homeland.
Considering that, they treated me pretty good.
Better than here.
Amazing, isn't it?
Why is it like that?
Am I the enemy here, too?
No. No.
It doesn't matter.
Look at us.
Do I look like the enemy?
No.

It's just the total indifference.
Indifference.
That's the worst of all emotions.
No, it's not an emotion.
It's the total lack of an emotion.
Cold.
A thousand times colder
than the biting cold of Siberia.
Moreover:
the indifferent regard the rebellious
only as a nuisance.

Therefore I restrain myself here
the best I can.
I can't always do it.
You know me.
I'm temperamental.

You, too.
You got that from me.
You blow up in the same way.
You blow up at your kids
the same way I blew up at you.
Sometimes it really embarrassed me
when I heard you from my room.
You blow up just like I did.
Just like I did.
It hurts to hear your own echo after so many
years.

Once—
you were four years old—
I screamed at you so loudly
you almost passed out from fright.
You started to cry.
I was really sorry,
and I said:
Everything's fine, stop crying.
But you didn't stop.
And so I said it again, only louder this time:
Stop it, everything's fine, it's okay!

You caught the tone in my voice
and you wanted to stop crying
but you couldn't.
You wanted to leave the room
but I stood in your way:
Stop it, now!
I want to, Dad, but I can't,
you said, crying.
And suddenly I started yelling again:
Stop it!
And you stopped,
stopped crying.
Then all of the sudden
came this strange sobbing,

a constant, repeated sobbing,
like an uncontrollable hiccup.
I looked at you
and was suddenly terrified;
I saw how you tried
to restrain
this uncontrollable sobbing
so as not to upset me anymore,
but you couldn't do it;
then you began gasping furiously
for breath
as if you were having an asthma attack;
and suddenly I had
this unbelievable pain
in my heart,
and I picked you up
and held you in my arms
and hugged you
and carried you around the house
and out onto the balcony
and tried to talk to you,
tried to calm you down,
all nice and quiet,
as never before in my life:
It's all right, everything's all right!
I'm sorry, I'm so sorry!
Please forgive me!
And finally, finally, after an eternity,
you stopped sobbing.
That was the only time
I ever said that to you:
Please forgive me.
But I still yelled at you a lot after that.

I don't make any excuses.
But it still hurts me today
when I think of it.

No, I never hit you,
but the screaming wasn't any good, either.

You don't have to feel sorry for me.
I yelled at you,
not the other way around.
You were stubborn, all right.
Do you remember
how you refused
to go to college?
I'm willing to sacrifice
and support you for a few more years,
I want you to have
what I never had,
and what did you do?
You refused.
What followed was my final temper tantrum.
But it didn't have much effect on you.

I know that you regret it, today.
Too late to change.
You wouldn't have had to yell at me;
I would've loved to go to college.
It wasn't possible.
So I became a civil servant.
An unimportant civil servant.
But I kept studying.
I took classes.
I expanded my horizons.
I didn't do it for the money.
I did it because
I didn't want someone stupid over me.
But maybe that was foolish.

At the end of my career
I became Department Head.
The day after my promotion
when I came to the office,

my new office,
and sat all alone
at my new desk . . .
You have to picture it,
all alone in the office.
I always was a loner, you know.
I got in very early,
I wanted to enjoy it,
I was really excited.
I opened the door,
they'd already put my name on it;
it was really a wonderful feeling,
a wonderful feeling
just to look at my nameplate
and open the door,
and go into my own office.
But somebody was already in there.
Somebody else was already at my desk,
asleep,
or so I thought;
in any case he had his head down,
resting on the papers.
So I went in,
curious,
to see what he's doing
in my office,
in the Department Head's office.
And I see
that his head is lying in a pool of blood
covering the whole blotter,
right up to the edge,
exactly to the edge,
covered in blood;
he had this little black hole
in his temple,
and the blood running down his cheek
had already dried;
his ear was the color of wax;

his right arm on the desk
was bent at the elbow,
not disturbing the blotter
with the shiny red-black lake on it,
a pistol in his half-opened hand.
My dear friend and colleague Reiter,
who, just the day before, had congratulated me,
toasted me,
and wished me all the best
on my promotion,
sits at my desk
and kills himself.
And at the funeral
his wife comes up me and says:
Would you please leave?
And, dumbfounded, I turn and leave to avoid a
scene.
She was very disturbed
and all my colleagues were watching.
He wanted my job.
He wanted to be a simple Department Head.
I liked him.
Really, believe me.
You pay for everything.
Yep. You do.

What?

No, you don't need to talk to the doctor.
What for?
It won't do any good!
I can speak up for myself, you know.
I'm allowed to sit side-saddle in bed now,
and when the nurses aren't watching
I exercise and try to walk.

*(He slides down carefully from his bed and takes a couple
of steps, while holding onto the bed.)*

No, no help!
I have to do this myself!
I had crutches.
And one of those walkers.
They took everything away from me.
No more privileges.
Because there's no more money.
Because I can't bribe them anymore.
Because I gave my little bankbook to you.

No, please don't talk to the doctor.
Otherwise, they'll say I'm a troublemaker.
The nurses will take it out on me.
Then they report it higher up.
How's my dog?

Fine! Fine!
You took him to the park?
Terrific! Terrific!
Did he run around, huh?
I can see it!
Terrific!

Have you noticed how small I've become?
I used to be relatively big, right?
No giant, true,
but relatively big.
You, too.
You're relatively big, too.
I'm shrinking.
I'm shrinking!

That's right, I'm shrinking!
The bones shrink,
the body shrinks,
even the head shrinks!
I'm getting a shrunken head!

(With his back against the end of the bed he reaches behind him, and holding onto the bars of the bed, begins to sing.)

> I had a little Dachshund once
> and the little mutt got sick.
> The vet came and saw and
> said,
> your little Dachshund's dead.
> He didn't want his milk or
> water
> and that is why he died.
> I said to myself, what can it
> hurt:
> I'll give him a sip of my
> wine.
> Then he sat up
> and sang—sorry—barked:
> You know, this is a wine
> that I call friend;
> I pour him out,
> and he, he laughs at me.
> He hears all my woes,
> he is a friend to me,
> he laughs and cries with me;
> this is wine
> that must be addressed
> respectfully,
> he barked, he barked.

(The OLD MAN takes his hands away from the bars.)

> If I sing
> the shrinking process is retarded.
> I think , to be more exact,
> the shrinking process stops while I'm singing.
> Because the chest expands
> and the body stretches.

(Sings)

Did you see how my chest expanded?
> This is a wine
> that I call friend;
> I pour him out,
> and he, he laughs at me.

(*He sits down on the bed again and wiggles his feet.*)

I have to be on guard.
One of the nurses already
hit me on the head with a wet towel.
And she threatened to gag me.
You old shitter,
she said,
stop your bellowing!

They give us heavy sedatives,
you know.
So they can have their peace and quiet.
Look at all the others.
Lying in their beds half dead.
I won't swallow the stuff!
I spit it out on the sly!

Once, we all had the runs.
They give us pure opium for that.
And naturally they all took it willingly!
They do it all the time
because it stops the runs instantly.
As long as you can make it to the can by yourself
you've still got a chance.

Unfortunately, I get lost sometimes.
I can't find the bathroom
and I can't find my way back, either.
Because everything looks the same here!
The rooms, the doors, the corridors
all look alike!
How can you find your way around here,
I ask you?
I could find my way around the house.
Damn right.
They have all these potted plants in the corridors,
all half-dead,

I never liked that stuff!
What do they need half-dead potted plants for?
I want to go for a walk in the park!
There's plenty of greenery there!
I don't need it in the corridors!
And take a look at this bed!
It's way too high!
It's like a duck blind!
You need a ladder to get up here!
What do they think I am,
some sort of retired big-game hunter?

Pops, finish your supper or there's no fruit cock-
tail!
Who needs fruit cocktail?
The food here is crap!
I wouldn't give this crap
to my dog.
Lukewarm, overcooked crap.
Can't even tell what it is.
Tasteless.
Seniors' Diet!
Seniors' Diet they call it!
I need fat.
All my life I ate fatty things.
It never hurt me.
I was never sick.
Pops, finish your supper or there's no fruit cock-
tail!
Who needs fruit cocktail?
Dinner at five, lights out at eight!
Can you believe it?
I'm a night owl!
You know that!
If you need something, forget it.
They turn the buzzers off at night.
The buzzers!
Not all of them.

Just the troublemakers'!
I'm a troublemaker!

What?
You're going already?
Stay a little longer!
Five minutes!
Is that asking too much?
Sorry, I'm being demanding again.
I'm a little bit bitter, you know.
But I'm hanging in.

I still have my own teeth!
They took everybody else's teeth away.
That way they don't have to clean them.
More work.
Overtime.
Think about it:
cleaning sixty dentures.
No, double that, uppers and lowers.
A hundred and twenty dentures to clean!
It's not possible, you can see that.
But I still have mine, you see.
The successful outcome of my bribery.
But for how much longer?
I don't have any more money.
You've got it now.

That one over there
doesn't open his mouth anymore.
Won't say a word.
When the nurse went to feed him
he'd only open his mouth a little.
So she hit him with a spoon.
No luck.
So she hit him again!
It didn't help.
He was so humiliated.

And he's humiliated
when they have to wash him
and put a diaper on him, too.

It's not like that with me.
With me it's just the opposite.
You can't humiliate me.
I can tell you this
because you are a man.
I go to the can by myself,
I don't crap in my diapers.
But my weekly bath . . .

(Sings)

A couple of banknotes

> Give me a little bit of love,
> love;
> be a little bit nice to me!
> Do you know the little sweet
> desire,
> desire,
> that my heart is longing for?

and you begin to feel like
you're in a massage parlor in Thailand!
She showed me her breasts!
For a little extra
I got to feel them!
Unfortunately that's all over now.
I shouldn't have given you my little bankbook.
What an idiot!
What did I get out of it?

You're never going to bring me back home!
I'm warning you, you better treat my dog well!

He doesn't know the meaning of the word "Attack."

Nope.
My dog doesn't know what "Attack" means,
absolutely not!
But now I'm ready!
I'm ready and I could teach it to him:
Attack!
Attack the white uniforms!
I've written
to the Bundespresident!

Yep! Yep!
I've written to the Bundespresident!
A man from the cleaning crew
snuck it out for me.
A foreigner.
He understood immediately
how important this matter was!

All of it!
I wrote him about all of it!
About the conditions here!
I was a civil servant.
A Department Head!
And I'm treated here
like a stubborn child!
I won't stand for it!
You're an old man, too,
I wrote,
you've got to understand!
Please, more respect for the aged!
The residents are being
neglected,
drugged,
humiliated,
and beaten!
Locked in their cribs!
Stripped of their honor!
Severe shortages of staff!

Resulting in lack of care!
Stench-clouds over the entire home!
Stench of the plague!
Stench of corpses!
Stench of the grave!
Come here and
see for yourself, Herr Bundespresident!
This is an S.O.S. call!

No, I'm not kidding!
Do I look like I'm kidding?
That's exactly what I wrote him!

You're going already?
When are you coming back?
You haven't even told me anything!
Next time you have to tell me what's going on.

He was always a quiet boy.
He got that from his mother.
Me—I'm more outspoken.
Otherwise I'd rot!

IV.

(The OLD MAN sits in a safety bed with bars, dressed in a nightshirt.)

There's his bed over there,
by the wall.
They let him out.
Probably sits in chapel
and prays.
He's an old Nazi, you know,
one that always accepted the dummies
as leaders.

Not me.
Drives me nuts
with his war stories.
Stories about the Blitzkrieg.
Stories about his army buddies.
Now, all of a sudden, he feels guilty
because he's afraid
that there might be an afterlife after all.
A Day of Reckoning!
A Heaven and Hell!
He goes to Mass every day
and you know what he does there?
He's an altar boy!
An altar boy!
In one of those red and white gowns, like a girl!
And he always spills the communion wine
because he's got the shakes.
That old army-asshole!

He cries out at night.
And in the daytime, all he talks about
is the chain of command.
I'll fix him.

Chain of command.
Don't make me laugh!
I was there!
I had a buddy there!
I stod there holding his bloody brains in my
hands.
A buddy.
I had a buddy.
The partisans did him in.
The others would have
burned the next ten houses down
and executed civilians.
But not me.
What were we doing there?

In that foreign country?
You know,
what I want for him
is a nice coffin and wreath,
that's all I said.
And they brought it right away.
No, no. There was no chain of command.
That's why I'm alive today!
Now I tell him about euthanasia!
I've convinced him
it's coming back.
For old folks!
Now he's afraid.
Now he's shitting in his pants.
Whenever he sees a syringe
he starts screaming!
Screams his guts out!

Why not?
Why shouldn't I do that?
He was in favor of euthanasia!
As a young man.
As a handsome young soldier
with a death-skull on his cap.
You don't work, you don't have the right to exist!
No exceptions!

You know what?
The Nazis scared us!
To put it mildly!
Now you'll get a divorce,
because of my heritage, right?
That's what my Agnes said.
You're crazy,
I said,
I'll never divorce you
because of those goose-stepping bastards.
Absolutely not!

We were downtown
when *he* came to town.
Thousands!
Thousands of people!
Bussed in from everywhere!
Screaming like idiots!
Heil!
Heil to the Führer!
We've got enough leaders of our own,
I said to my buddy.
Boy, did he get a kick out of that.
He's a scout leader himself, you see . . . Get it?

Agnes laughed too.
She really knew how to laugh.
We liked each other even as kids.
She knew a way through the entire city
without ever having to walk on the ground.
Over walls and fences and window sills,
through the entire city
without ever once touching the ground.
You can't do that nowadays.

Herr Aigner,
they said,
come midnight you're a soldier!
Good! Good!
And what about your wife?
We still don't know anything about her heritage!
Gentlemen please,
I said,
she was orphaned
somewhere near Moravia,
so there's no chance
of knowing what her heritage is!
And I'll tell you something else:
If you don't leave my wife in peace,

then you can have this . . . this . . .
Wehrmacht,
or whoever's running this war,
go fight it for themselves,
without me, got it?

Naturally, I admit, I was susceptible to their
ideas.
There was no work, nothing.
I was always for law and order.
For authority.
Until now.
But I could never stand to have idiots over me,
understand?

And the extermination
of the elderly had already begun.
That was a revolution of the young,
don't forget.
Down with the old!
I was young myself.
I was against the old ways, too.
But I loved my father.
I would never shout:
Down with the old!
Authority from nightsticks,
authority at gunpoint,
that wasn't for me.

The German People!
What do I care about "the German People"?
People are people!
The Jewish tailor
who always gave us credit,
why does he suddenly become a criminal?
My dear Agnes,
why should she be worth any less
because of her heritage?

It was for these pigs,
I'm ashamed to say,
that I went to war!
And now I'm sitting behind bars!
As the extermination of the elderly continues!

Oh, it's my fault?
What are you talking about, my fault?
You see what they're doing to me?
I'm trapped!
I'm sitting in a cage!

What do you mean, making trouble?
Has the Head Nurse already
convinced you of that?

Of course I was upset!
I can't walk anymore!
I asked for the bedpan.
No time, no time;
you've got to hold it.
When I've got to go, I've got to go!
So I crapped in the bed.
And they let me lie in it for hours,
lying in my own shit.
Once you've already shat on yourself
you might as well keep going.
Of course I insulted them!
I threatened to speak with the doctor!
I told them about my letter
to the Bundespresident,
that I slipped it out
right under their noses!
And what did I get?
They drug me
and lock me in this cage!
Like an animal!
A wild animal!

At the end of my life, I'm locked up
like a wild animal!

(*He gets up on his knees and starts shaking the bars.*)

Let me out of here!
Let me out of here!

(*He falls back.*)

I've had it.
I've really had it!
That old Nazi fool is afraid of dying,
but I'm not!
Not me!
Do you know what I want?
Help.
Help!
At least help me with this!
Help me to die!
Help me to die!

How would you like me to talk?
I've had it up to here, understand?
When you on the outside don't care
about these conditions,
what's left to do?
An exit!
A half-way decent exit!

I am a human being!
Think about it!
You wouldn't let an animal die like this!
Not an animal!
I've already been here too long.
Because I'm such a stubborn old dog.
I've always been like this!
The rest of them

give up after a couple of weeks.
Roll over and die.
Heart attack.
Lots of heart attacks.
They don't want to live anymore.
There's nothing left for them to do.
They can only die.
And then it comes.
One less pay-out
from the pension fund.
What a relief.
For everyone!

Two today in one hour.
The guys from the mortuary
happily bring in the coffin,
throw them in naked, one on top of the other;
they're not heavy,
these dried up old men;
they don't have to go back for a second coffin,
too much trouble,
so out they go!
This is a death factory,
Frau Daughter-in-Law.
A death factory!

Why are you crying?
You don't have to cry.
Stop it, you know I can't stand that,
or I'll wind up feeling sorry for you!
And that wouldn't be right, would it?
You don't have to die.
Not yet.
But maybe one day you'll end up here.
And then you can cry!

I'll tell you a joke;
you hear it around here all the time.

A clown performs at an old folks home.
He looks through the curtains and says:
Is everybody here?
Yes,
scream the patients.
But not for long,
screams the clown!

V.

(*The OLD MAN lies in bed wearing a night shirt.*)

This is a great honor for me,
Mr. President!
Is this your wife?
Oh, of course I recognize you!
How do you do?
Your hairdo is as unique as ever,
very charming.
Please, be seated.
The gentlemen in your entourage
can put their guns away;
I'm not armed.

And what's this?
A box of cigars?
How very thoughtful,
really, very thoughtful;
I thank you from the bottom of my heart!

No, thank you, not right now.
There's a bit of dysentery going around.
Dysentery.
It's not good to smoke cigars
when you have dysentery.
I'm not a big cigar smoker, you know.

To tell you the truth
I never was very big.
And now I've shrunk, to boot.

Shrunk.
A little man.
A little man with a big cigar
always looks a bit ridiculous,
don't you think?

If you don't mind,
I'll take these
big, lovely, good-looking cigars
and bribe the guards with them.
You must understand:
here you survive only on bribes.
You didn't have to bribe
the guards, did you?
Did you have difficulty
with the guards?
They didn't try and shoot you, did they?
I won't stand for that.
You don't shoot the Bundespresident.
And certainly not his charming wife.
I assume
you made use of
your diplomatic status?
Diplomacy is everything.
One survives by diplomacy.
By diplomacy and bribery.
But I certainly don't have to tell you that.
You know more about that than I do.

It's like that everywhere.
But especially here.
This camp is special.
No one even thinks about escaping.
Where would you escape to?

There are only the steppes.
The endless Russian steppes.
They'll hunt you down.
Like a sable.
And if they don't hunt you down
you'll freeze to death.

The ground is frozen solid.
They call it permafrost.
One meter down there's a permanent layer of
frost.
An endless underground glacier.
Cold above and cold below.
Your breath turns to icicles
that fall to the ground and shatter.
And sometimes even your words freeze
before they reach
the ears of the listener.
In the spring sun,
when the speaker and the listener
have long since departed,
the words melt
and are heard.
Without meaning.

Excuse me, Mr. President,
I don't want to lecture you.
I'm sure you're well informed
about the climatic conditions
in this part of the world.
I'm truly grateful
that you have traveled
all this way,
this long, tiring way,
to come here.
And I want to thank your wife, too.
A long journey to Siberia, isn't it?
A journey to another world.

Is your charming wife
dressed warmly enough?
This outfit,
this lovely outfit,
is so light
and airy
and summery.
A lovely sight,
Madame,
thank you.
My wife used to dress like that.
Just as summery.
We used to go walking.
With our dog.
In the park.
It smelled of springtime.
The birds were singing.

I must tell you something in strictest confidence,
Mr. President.
I believe that you never received my letter.
That it was confiscated.
Here in the camp,
or in your front office
by your secretary.
You have a secretary, don't you?
I imagine that as Bundespresident
you receive a lot of mail.
A lot of it from troublemakers, I mean.
To make a decision
isn't easy, is it?
I'm glad you didn't
include me with the troublemakers.
I'm honored you've taken this time.
A Bundespresident, especially,
must budget his time carefully.
So many responsibilities.

So many appointments.
Opening nights.
Highway dedications.
Groundbreaking ceremonies.
State dinners.
State visits.
So the Head of State has a lot to do.
And still you came here,
with your charming wife, no less.
I'm honored.
Really.

I'll show you around the camp now.
Stand next to me, please;
the guards might try to shoot me,
which wouldn't surprise me.
Take a good look at everything.
Keep your eyes open.
Don't close your eyes for a minute.
Don't let the clean floors
fool you.

Take a look
at the prisoners lying stiffly at attention.
Lift up one of those nice, clean blankets.
Your wife
might want
to hold a handkerchief to her nose;
it smells like a dead rat.
Smell the emaciated bodies.
Smell the dysentery.
Smell the black, puss-filled sores.
I know it's offensive
but isn't that why you came,
Mr. President?
Isn't it?
I wrote you all about it,
you knew exactly what to expect,

so please don't be so delicate.

With many of the prisoners
you might notice
they look like
dried flowers.
Lack of fluids.
It comes from not getting any soup or tea
or fruit cocktail or water or infusions.
And so they wilt
and dry out.

This is assisted dying.
I thought there was no more assisted dying.
But there is.
Unfortunately, it's not upon request.
It's totally arbitrary.
Not easy to think about.

It's interesting to note:
the confused and the difficult
wilt first.
When you touch them
their skin crumbles.
Like dried roses.

Please visit the kitchen as well,
Mr. President.
Smell the casserole.
Your wife should sample it.
Your wife certainly understands
good cooking.
She must always be
entertaining guests,
distinguished guests,
I would imagine.
And please eat all of it,
Madame!

All of it!
Otherwise there'll be no fruit cocktail!
Don't tell me
you don't need fruit cocktail.
Everyone here needs fruit cocktail!
Except the candidates for extermination.
And don't forget, Mr. President,
to take a look in the broom-closet.
We had another one hang himself in there.
Most of the attempts fail;
we're all too weak.
All hell broke loose.
Ranting and raving.
They drug us.
They punish us.
They put us in our cages.

Take a look in the staff cafeteria.
That's where they relax and get drunk.
The guards are all drunk.
All the time.
Because they can't stand
to look at us anymore.
Because they see their own deaths
in each one of us.
Sometimes I feel sorry for them;
they don't know any better.

That's the system,
the camp system.
One of these days we
won't need camps.
Any camps.
What do you think, Mr. President?

You have to get the whole picture first?
Do that!
I'd love to show you all of it.

I won't try to influence you.
Get the whole picture.
Make your own picture.
And if your impressions
coincide with my experience,
then the gentlemen in your entourage
might like to ask the camp guards and adminis-
trators
a few questions.

They'll deny everything.
They'll tell you how difficult it is
to put up with
the prisoners.
They'll say we're
ignorant, stubborn troublemakers!
And believe me,
we are troublemakers!
We make trouble because of the way we're
treated!
Even you, Mr. President,
would be a troublemaker if you came here!
You, too, Madame!
When you leave, please,
tell the world about our condition here.
They'll believe you,
Mr. President.

Unfortunately, I can't go with you at the moment.
You'll have to go on your own.
I'm feeling a bit tired.
Nothing serious.
I'll be there in a minute.

You never met
my wife Agnes, did you?
A pity.
A wonderful woman.

You would have liked her.
My God, how we quarreled!
Or rather, how I quarreled.
You have to understand, I'm temperamental.
Agnes never could fight.
You couldn't have a fight with her.
Awful!
But we knew each other well.
We were very close.

Funny.
It's true, you know.
The short-term memory goes first.
But you recall more and more about the early
days.
Perhaps one dies newborn.

Maybe I'll meet Agnes?
What do you think, Mr. President?
And you, Madame?
Maybe, maybe not.
Who knows what we wish for.
God?
I have a funny story to tell you,
Mr. President, and you too, Madame.
Do you have the time?
Yes?
Thanks!

I was five years old
when I wanted to know
what Heaven was like,
because I'd heard the most fabulous things
about it.
And so I turned the gas on.
A neighbor of ours had done that,
which is how I knew what to do.
I was just about gone when they found me.

Just about.

There's another funny story.
Do you have time for one more?
Terrific!

We had gone down to visit my uncle in the coun-
tryside.
They had warned me about the trolls,
the trolls in the forest.
They told me not to go in there,
that it was dangerous.
Lots of children had disappeared there, they said.
Stolen by trolls.
But I took a sandwich as bait
and an axe for protection,
and went into the forest.
But the trolls never came out.
Maybe they were afraid of me.
Maybe they were watching me
and thought I was funny.
Maybe there were no trolls.
Maybe there were no trolls there.
Maybe there were no trolls anywhere!
What do you think, Mr. President,
and you, Madame?
You don't know?
Neither do I.

Anyway, I believed in them then.
I've always been inquisitive.
I've always been inquisitive, anyway.
And I still believe that
everything happens for the best.
It's much more interesting
than believing in the opposite,
don't you think?

I must appear pretty helpless to you,
right?
It isn't easy.
I crap in my diapers
which, I hope, doesn't bother you.
Just hold your nose,
Madame.

They put my dog to sleep.
Quite some time ago.
A neighbor told me
when he was visiting me.
You didn't know my dog,
Mr. President, did you?
Or you, Madame?
A pity.
My dog was worth knowing.

Do you have a dog?
I don't believe it!
Your charming wife has a dog!

Then you understand!

Oh, he was very old.
And half-blind.
He hardly ate anything.
And he shed everywhere.
(He sings.)

        My girlfriend is only a sales
        girl
        in a little shoe shop.
        She makes only 80 francs a
        week
        but she makes me feel like a

millionaire.
On Sundays we go dancing:
she puts on her little white
silk dress
that I love so;
then she looks just like
a little princess.
The jazz band softly plays
her favorite song;
she snuggles up to me
and throws back her head.
My girlfriend is only a sales
girl
in a little shoe shop.
She makes only 80 francs a
week
but she makes me feel like a
millionaire.

Agne's favorite song.

You know, Mr. President,
Madame,
I used to sing every day
to keep
my body from shrinking.
But now I have to admit
the battle's over.

It's not death,
but the long, drawn-out process of dying
that frightens me.
Dying like this,
here,
and now.
If you don't mind
I'd like to be left alone now.
Agnes, come sit by my side;
Dog, come curl up by my feet;

it won't be long now
  till we're all together again
walking through the park.

THE END

Songs

"Des is a Wein, mit dem bin ich per Du"
from the operetta Schwalbennest
by Bruno Granichstaeden

"Schenk mir doch ein kleines bißchen Liebe"
from the operetta Frau Luna
by Paul Lincke

"Mein Mäderl ist nur eine Verkäuferin"
from the musical comedy My Sister and I
by Ralph Benatzky

Stigma

A Passion Play

Translated by

Todd C. Hanlin

Characters

MADY, maid
BEST, foreman (in his mid-forties)
LITTLE JOE, hired hand
RUPP, the Farmer's son (mid-twenties)
FARMER (mid-fifties)
FARMER'S WIFE (around fifty)
PRIEST (mid-forties)
MONSIGNOR (around fifty)
PROFESSOR OF MEDICINE (around fifty)
OLD MAID
SCRIBE
SHERIFF
OLDER FARMHAND
RICH FARMER
TENANT FARMER
TENANT FARMER'S WIFE
FAT GENTLEMAN FROM THE CITY
TWO DEPUTIES, TWO BEARERS, FARMHANDS,
FARMERS, CITY FOLK

(Translator's Note: For the three demons Schnalljuza, Saggara Taggera, and Hatzes, I have substituted their more conventional counterparts GRESSIL, BALBERITH, and VER-RIER, as found in the Admirable History (1612) of that noted exorcist, Father Sebastien Michaëlis.)

SETTING: In and around a farm in the countryside.

TIME: Long ago (As a suggestion for the staging, we could presume around 1830.)

NOTE ON MADY'S AGE: The actress who plays MADY should not be under twenty, but also not much older than thirty.

NOTE ON LITTLE JOE'S AGE: The actor who plays LIT-TLE JOE should be roughly the same age, or possibly older than the actress who plays MADY, depicting a "Joseph-Mary" constellation.

NOTE ON THE WOMEN'S COSTUMES (with the exception of the city women): The women should be clothed from the neck to the feet. Neither their bare throats nor their calves should be visible.

NOTE ON THE SPEECH: The dialogues of the original text are in Tirolean dialect. The play can and naturally should be adapted to the local dialect of the performance.

STAGE MUSIC: The use of music (possibly organ music) is left to the director's discretion.

First Station

Outdoors, evening, it is still light.

(*RUPP is sitting stage left, honing his scythe with a whet-stone. After a while, on their way back to the farm, enter from stage right: BEST, the simpleton farmhand LITTLE JOE, and the maid MADY. They are coming from haying, carrying pitchforks and rakes, as well as rolled up coils of twine that are used to tie the haybales together. MADY is wearing her hair in braids, woven around the top of her head like a crown, not unlike Jesus Christ's crown of thorns. They pass by a wayside cross. BEST crosses himself hastily in passing, LITTLE JOE pauses momentarily and crosses himself with great zeal, MADY stops, kneels down, entwines her fingers in prayer and prays softly. RUPP sees BEST and LITTLE JOE coming, looks around for MADY, sees her kneeling before the cross.)*

RUPP *(sings)*:
>Now the farmer likes to hammer,
>And the blacksmith likes to hammer,
>And the girl in the barn hammers too
>Too bad my honey won't hammer.

>Now a real sharp blade
>Needs oiling every day
>Needs lots of attention
>For work or for play.

(BEST and LITTLE JOE approach RUPP, lay down their tools. BEST looks back at MADY, upset. MADY crosses herself, gets up, kisses the nailed feet of the crucified Jesus, then joins the others. RUPP has stopped honing, puts down his whetstone, lays the scythe aside.)

RUPP: You guys finish haying the whole field?

(BEST sits down on a bench, fills his pipe, LITTLE JOE squats on the ground, looking for a splinter in the sole of his foot.)

BEST: Yeah, we're done.
RUPP: Do the upper pasture tomorrow!
BEST: Right.

(MADY approaches. RUPP grins at her, sings without honing.)

RUPP *(sings)*:
>It won't take a year,

> She's just like the rest,
> Till my sweet little honey
> Can hammer with the best.

(MADY ignores RUPP, lays down her rake and pitchfork.)

RUPP *(resumes singing)*:
> But when she can hammer
> We'll flatten the flowers,
> And just like the angels
> Seventh heaven'll be ours!

(BEST, upset, glances at RUPP, gets even more upset at RUPP'S lyrics, looks over at MADY, who acts as if she had not heard a word. MADY hangs up her coil of twine, suddenly grabs her head and begins to totter. BEST gets up, catches her, sets her down on the bench. LITTLE JOE gets up, looks worried.)

BEST: Mady!

MADY *(defensively)*: No! No! I won't go with the boogeymen! No! No!

(MADY closes her eyes, clenches her fists, is overcome by an epileptic seizure: her head flies back, the muscles on her neck bulge, her whole body quakes.)

BEST: Mady!

(BEST shakes MADY, slaps her hard twice, her fit subsides. MADY, panting loudly, as if she had just been hard at work, looks around in confusion.)

BEST: You okay now?

(MADY nods.)

RUPP *(taken aback)*: That happen to you a lot?

(MADY shakes her head, slowly gets up.)

VOICE of the FARMER'S WIFE: Come 'n get it!

(ALL exit upstage. BEST tries to steady MADY, she declines his help, but in a friendly manner.)

(Stage lights slowly dim)

Second Station

Indoors, twilight.

(Two tables. Sitting at the main table are: the FARMER, the FARMER'S WIFE, and RUPP; at the servants' table: BEST. MADY brings out the food to the main table—dumplings and a pitcher of something to drink. LITTLE JOE brings out a pan with flower paste and a pitcher of something to drink for the servants' table. MADY and LITTLE JOE then sit down at the servants' table.)

FARMER: Lord, we ask that you bless this food to our use. In the name of God the Father, the Son, and the Holy Spirit, Amen.

(ALL cross themselves. The FARMER helps himself, the OTHERS also begin to eat, but not MADY.)

MADY *(prays, in her normal speaking voice)*:
    Lord, we pray for this meal,
    Your suffering and death we shan't ever conceal,
    The holy cross is our table,
    The holy three nails are our staple,
    Your holy body is our nourishment,
    Your rosy red blood is our drink,
    Heavenly Father, we praise and thank
    For food and drink and for everything
    That you grant us,
    And for everything that sustains
    Our body and our soul, Amen.

(While MADY was praying, the FARMER first looked at her disapprovingly, then went back to eating; the FARMER'S WIFE, RUPP, and BEST also eat. Only LITTLE JOE had waited, and only now does he begin to eat. MADY be-

gins to eat also, but only a few spoonsful.)

FARMER *(after a short pause)*: You know, saying grace is still up to the farmer! Or the foreman says it. But never the maid! Don't you know that? *(MADY doesn't answer.)* Next time you're gonna get it!

(ALL continue eating silently. MADY stops eating, puts away her spoon, stares as if in a trance.)

FARMER: Do the lower pasture tomorrow.

BEST: Yes, sir.

RUPP: I thought the upper pasture.

FARMER: Do the lower one.

FARMER'S WIFE *(after a moment, to the FARMER)*: Heard the latest? The neighbor's maid had a baby.

FARMER: You don't say?

RUPP: Who's the father?

FARMER'S WIFE: One of the hired hands. *(pauses)* They tried to feed it to the sow to eat. So the baby wouldn't live. But the farmer's wife's nursing it back to health.

FARMER: Damn farmhands'll do it every time!

RUPP: What happened then?

FARMER'S WIFE: They're behind bars.

FARMER: Damn hired hands are always a pain!

FARMER'S WIFE: The neighbor wants to know if we can help him get in his hay, when the time comes. At least till he can get some new hands.

(MADY becomes nauseous, gets up from the table, exits. ALL briefly notice her leave, only LITTLE JOE watches her for a protracted period of time.)

FARMER: Sure, sure, we'll help him out. *(He puts away his spoon, ALL the others follow his example.)* Lord, we thank you for this food you've provided. In the name of God the Father, the Son, and the Holy Spirit, Amen.

(ALL cross themselves, rise from the table.)

BEST: God bless you, Farmer!
LITTLE JOE: Yeah, God bless you!
(Black-out)

Third Station

Split scene—indoors / outdoors, at night.

(MADY, her hands folded, is kneeling in prayer at the foot of her bed. She is wearing a white nightshirt. On the bed frame is a straw mattress, on top of that a dark woolen blanket as a cover, though there is no sheet and no white cover for the mattress. A tallow candle is burning on the little stool next to the bed.)

MADY: I lay me down on Christ's cross,
     I lay me down in Christ's body,
     I lay me down in Christ's torment and woe,
     To make all ghosts and evil spirits go.

(MADY makes the sign of the cross, climbs into bed, blows out the candle, pulls up the cover. She is sitting up halfway, with open eyes, thinking about something. BEST enters with blackened face, a hunting rifle slung over his shoulder, backpack on his back. He looks over in MADY'S direction, stands still, speaks with his back to her.)

BEST: Mady!
(MADY, startled, sits bolt upright.)
MADY: Best?
BEST: Yeah, it's me.
MADY: What do you want?
BEST: I want a wife. And my own children. And smoke coming out of my own chimney. I don't wanna be a hired hand for the rest of my life.

MADY: Then you'll have to marry a farmer's daughter. From a farm family that doesn't have a son.

BEST: I want ya for my wife.

MADY: Best! You know hired hands aren't allowed to get married.

BEST: I've saved almost 300 guilders over the last twenty years. And for over a year now I been out huntin' every other night. Down in the valley they pay me four guilders for a goat. When five years are up I'll have enough money put away so I can buy a piece of land and build a small place. Then we'd be land-owners and could get married.

MADY: When five years are up, you'll be long dead, be-cause the forest rangers'll shoot you. Get that idea out of your head, Best.

BEST: I've got a scar on the palm of my right hand, Mady . . .

MADY: I know, I've seen it.

BEST: You know where I got it?

MADY: You must have cut yourself.

BEST: Yeah, I cut myself all right. I took a knife and cut open the palm of my hand and stuck a holy commu-nion wafer from our heavenly Father under the skin. Do ya hear me, Mady?

MADY: Yes, I hear you.

BEST (*looking at his right hand*): Now I don't shake any-more. Every shot's right on the mark. And if some-body tries to kill me, he can't do it. A thousand bullets'd bounce off me, like bouncing off a stone. I'm invulnerable. Do ya hear me, Mady?

MADY: Yes, I hear you. You made a deal with the devil.

BEST: I don't know nothin' about no devil, Mady. The Lord Jesus Christ protects me.

MADY: The devil's got you, Best.

BEST: Things just are the way they are. And if it's the devil, then I'm not gonna worry about it one way or the other. I wanna own my own place. Now go to sleep, Mady. And sweet dreams. Dream about all those boys and girls we're gonna have together.

(BEST exits along the road. MADY lies back down, though with her eyes still open, thinking. After a while, RUPP enters from upstage, stops at the same mark on stage as BEST.)

RUPP: Mady! Mady!

MADY: Rupp?

RUPP: Yeah, it's me.

MADY: Go away, Rupp. I don't want you.

RUPP *(sings in a whisper)*:
>He'd beat me to a pulp,
>That's what Daddy used to say.
>But I thought he said
>I needed a roll in the hay.

MADY: I don't want you, Rupp.

RUPP *(sings)*:
>Hey, little girl, don't be actin' that way,
>Out of sheaves we make straw,
>Out of grain we make hay.
>The flowers only bloom for four weeks in May.

MADY: That'd be a sin, Rupp. Love requires God's blessing.

RUPP *(sings)*:
>I tried at first
>To sneak into her room.
>She said: See the priest,
>He's got a key for the groom.

(MADY doesn't answer, just stares straight ahead.)

RUPP: Mady! Love is great! How can God Almighty have anything against that? The animals aren't married! I think we're told that just 'cause the priests are jealous! *(MADY doesn't respond.)* I know you aren't made out of clay! I know you've got a warm body! *(MADY doesn't respond.)* In the middle of summer, when it's so hot and the hay's all over the place, gets in through every crack in your clothes, and you itch, and you sweat all over . . . Sometimes I just can't stand it anymore! I just want to roll around on the ground! Mady!

MADY: What about the baby? Afterwards, we just feed it to the sow. . . ?

RUPP: I'll be careful, Mady. I promise!

MADY: No, Rupp. It's a sin. (*RUPP falls silent, resigned.*) And you'd never marry me, no matter what.

RUPP: I can't marry a maid, you know that! My dad'd disown me, if I did. . . (*pauses*). . . I need you! (*RUPP approaches MADY.*)

MADY: Stop, right where you are, or I'll scream so loud everybody'll hear.

(*RUPP stops in his tracks, lets out an audible sigh, and exits upstage. MADY lays back down.*)

MADY (*softly*): Jesus Christ! Help me!

(*After a while, LITTLE JOE enters with a bowl full of blood, stops at the same mark on stage where BEST and RUPP had stood.*)

LITTLE JOE: Mady!

MADY: Little Joe! Is something wrong?

LITTLE JOE: Oh, just wanted to see if you're hungry.

MADY: No, I'm not hungry at all.

LITTLE JOE: But I've got something really good to eat.

MADY: What's that, Little Joe?

LITTLE JOE: Fresh blood!

MADY: What? Where'd you get that?

LITTLE JOE: I bled a cow, opened a vein in its neck. Got a whole bowl full.

MADY: But, Little Joe, you can't do that! If the farmer ever caught you. . .

LITTLE JOE: I'm so hungry all the time. The portions are so small and the foreman always eats so fast! By the time I eat a spoonful, he's eaten five! But I'm gonna go cook up this blood over the fire and enjoy it. You're the only one I'll share it with!

MADY: I don't need anything, Little Joe, I really don't need anything. God bless you!

LITTLE JOE: Don't mention it. Just thought you might be hungry too. (*He walks upstage, speaking as he exits.*) I'm gonna go cook this up over the fire and enjoy it! And nobody's gonna get any. Mady'd have gotten some. But now I'm gonna eat it all by myself.

(*MADY lays back. She had been overcome by the temptation of the flesh during RUPP'S monologue.*)

MADY: Stop! Don't! Don't! Go 'way! Go 'way! I don't want you! Go 'way! (*She waves her hands, trying to chase away the tempters from her sight. She pulls a small crucifix from under her pillow, holds on to it for dear life, talks to it.*) Help me, Jesus! Help me! (*She kisses the five wounds, then places the body of Christ against her cheek.*) Jesus, my Savior! Jesus, my Savior! Jesus, my Savior!

(*Suddenly she has another epileptic fit, her body convulses, she trembles all over, strikes the crucifix against her breast repeatedly. Finally, she cries out, flings the crucifix away, and collapses as if she were dead.*)

(*Black-out*)

Fourth Station

Split scene—indoors / outdoors, at night.

(MADY, sleeping in bed. Gradually a light appears, focus-ing on her. Simultaneously, a white light appears on the wayside cross. As the light becomes very bright, MADY awakens, sits upright in bed, astonished, looks into the light source, hears a voice speaking to her, she listens in-tently. After a while she slowly gets out of bed and walks downstage, the spotlight following her. Slowly, as if in a dream, she approaches the wayside cross, kneels down be-fore it, gazes up at the figure of Christ.)

MADY: Dear Lord, Jesus Christ, I can't bear to look at you! You tried to do so many wonderful things for us, and look how horribly they've treated you. And again and again, everyday all over again they nail you to the cross! You poor man!

(She reaches under her nightshirt, pulls a piece of folded linen cloth out of her underpants, stands up, unfolds the cloth, holds it up with both hands, as if offering it to Christ. The cloth is stained red from MADY'S menstrual blood.)

MADY: Look! I'm bleeding too! If it's all right with you, if it doesn't offend you, I'd like to sacrifice my blood to you, just as you gave your blood for us.

(MADY waits for confirmation from Christ, receives it, steps up to the cross, kisses Jesus' feet, places the cloth over His feet, and steps back.)

MADY: Now you are my love, Lord Jesus. And from now on, you'll be the only man in my life. And I'll do every-thing for you.

(She looks up at the figure of Christ, hears Him speak, and slowly climbs up to him on "invisible" steps—it should look as if she's walking on air to get to him—spreads out her arms, places her hands on the hands of Jesus, places her

head against his, places her breast against his chest, puts her feet on his. Now the spotlight is radiantly bright. MADY emits a cry, half ecstasy, half pain, and clings tightly to Jesus' hands or wrists.)

(Black-out)

Fifth Station

Indoors, at sunrise.

(MADY, lying in bed, half covered, is sleeping a deep, feverish sleep. The FARMER'S WIFE enters her room.)

FARMER'S WIFE: Mady! Mady! What's wrong with you? How many times do I have to yell till you finally get out of bed?

(MADY has opened her eyes, but doesn't answer. The FARMER'S WIFE looks at her.)

FARMER'S WIFE: You gone crazy?

MADY *(softly)*: I hurt all over. I hurt all over.

(The FARMER'S WIFE feels MADY's forehead.)

FARMER'S WIFE: Why, you're burning up! Farmer! Farmer! *(FARMER enters.)* Mady's sick!

FARMER: What? Now, just when we're mowing!? *(looks at MADY)* What's wrong with her?

MADY: So much pain! And I'm on fire.

FARMER: On fire?

MADY: Feels like I'm on fire inside, my body, my feet and hands, my head's burning up, my hair feels like nails, going right through my brain. And my heart, my heart hurts so bad, like a glowing piece of iron's sticking in it.

FARMER: Right now you're gonna go mow for two hours,

then you can go back to bed! (*The FARMER exits upstage.*)

FARMER'S WIFE: You've just got a fever. Hot flashes. I know what that's like. I've had that before too. You can't give in to it. Come on, I'll help you up.

(*MADY gets up slowly, painfully, the FARMER'S WIFE puts one arm around MADY'S shoulder, with her other hand she grasps MADY by the hand. MADY immediately pulls her hand back, looks down at her hand in astonishment, wondering why it could cause her such pain; she doesn't see anything. MADY is now sitting on the edge of the bed, with her feet on the floor.*)

FARMER'S WIFE: It's still cool and fresh outside, and the grass is wet. That'll help you feel better with these hot flashes. And when the sun gets too hot, then just come home. (*MADY nods.*) Now get a move on. (*FARMER'S WIFE exits.*)

(*MADY props herself up slowly, using both hands, but suddenly sinks back with a cry of pain, looks at the palms of her hands. At this point there is nothing visible, but MADY can feel the stigmata. With the index finger of her right hand, she traces the palm of her left hand, locates the pain in the middle of the palm, presses down and immediately pulls her left hand away, wincing with pain.*)

MADY (*whispers*): What's happening? Jesus!

(*MADY looks at her hands for a second time, shakes her head, then stands up and, crying out in pain, grabs her left breast. She unbuttons her nightshirt, reaches under her left breast, pulls her hand back out of the nightshirt, looks at her hand, sees blood on her fingers.*)

(*Spotlight slowly fades to black out*)

Sixth Station

Outdoors, at sunrise.

(BEST, LITTLE JOE, and RUPP approach from upstage, strap on their whetstones, pick up their scythes. BEST tests the blade of his scythe, pulls out the whetstone, hones the blade of his scythe.)

BEST: That's the first time Mady hasn't made it out of the sack.

RUPP: Probably thinks she's too good for work! (*sings:*)
    One night I dreamed I had
    A real good looking young feller,
    He stayed right in my bed
    Till the sun she shone bright yeller.

(BEST gives RUPP a dirty look.)

LITTLE JOE: But Mady doesn't sleep in a sack.

RUPP (*laughing*): How do you know that, heh?

(LITTLE JOE strains, trying to remember how he knew that, looks around and around.)

BEST: You're right, Little Joe, the only people who got a sack are the landowners. Us hired hands only get a stinkin' horse blanket.

RUPP: D'ja ever wonder why that horse blanket stinks?

(BEST takes LITTLE JOE'S scythe out of his hand, tests the blade, hones it, without dignifying RUPP'S question with an answer.)

RUPP: Little Joe!

LITTLE JOE: Huh?

RUPP: How d'ya say your prayers at night?

(LITTLE JOE kneels down, folds his hands.)

LITTLE JOE (*praying*):
    Holy Saint Vitus, I pray,

Don't let me sleep all day.
Wake up this sleepy head.
So I don't pee in bed.

(LITTLE JOE gets back up.)

RUPP *(laughing)*: Ya see, Best, now ya know why your blankets stink so bad!

(MADY approaches. Her poor health is obvious.)

BEST: Hey, Mady, don't ya feel well?

MADY *(softly)*: I'll be all right. I'll be all right.

(MADY picks up a scythe, a rake, and a pitchfork. BEST and LITTLE JOE watch her with obvious concern. The FARMER enters, picks up a whetstone, scythe, and a coil of twine. BEST and RUPP also take a coil of twine.)

FARMER: Let's go to work—in God's name! *(The FARMER starts out first followed by RUPP, BEST, LITTLE JOE, then MADY. When the FARMER reaches the roadside cross, he crosses himself, notices the blood-stained cloth. He stops, stares in astonishment, picks up the cloth.)* Huh. . . ? What the hell is this?

(RUPP, BEST, and LITTLE JOE all look at the cloth too, MADY looks at the cloth, then up at Jesus on the cross.)

RUPP: A bloody rag!

(The FARMER shakes his head in amazement, throws away the cloth, walks away. RUPP and BEST follow him, LITTLE JOE looks at the cloth, picks it up, thinks for a moment, then places it back on Jesus' feet, crosses himself, walks away. MADY crosses herself, too.)

MADY: Lord Jesus Christ, Thy will be done . . .

(MADY walks on, then sinks to her knees, overcome by weakness. LITTLE JOE comes back and helps her up, tries to take her tools from her, but MADY smiles and shakes her head. LITTLE JOE takes them anyway, almost by force, then walks away quickly, MADY following behind.)

(Lights slowly dim)

Seventh Station

Outdoors, a moonlit night.

(The FARMER'S WIFE and the PRIEST approach the farm, each holding a lantern. BOTH cross themselves as they pass the wayside cross.)

PRIEST: You say, on her hands and her feet?

FARMER'S WIFE: Yes, Father, on her hands and her feet!

PRIEST: You say, like the wounds of our Lord?

FARMER'S WIFE: Like the wounds of our Lord!

PRIEST: And you say, she doesn't eat or drink anything at all?

FARMER'S WIFE: No, nothing at all! She says everything tastes like vinegar and gall! The only thing she wants is the body of the Lord—holy communion!

(The FARMER comes out of the farmhouse, sits down on the bench stage left, fills his pipe, smokes.)

PRIEST: That doesn't sound good to me! Not good at all! That's gonna upset some folks, I'm telling you, that's gonna upset a lot of folks!

(The FARMER'S WIFE and the PRIEST approach the FARMER, who doffs his hat in greeting to the PRIEST.)

FARMER: Praise the Lord.

PRIEST: Forever and ever, Amen. Let me just catch my breath a bit, before we go in.

(The PRIEST sits down, the FARMER'S WIFE sits down beside him. The PRIEST pulls out a hipflask, takes a drink. ALL THREE sit for a while in silence.)

FARMER'S WIFE *(shaking her head)*: What's it all s'posed

to mean? How can something like this happen?

(The FARMER jabs his right index finger against the palm of his left hand.)

FARMER: That's how it happens. With a knife!

FARMER'S WIFE: But the hot flashes! And she hasn't eaten a thing for over a week now!

(The PRIEST takes another swig from his hipflask.)

FARMER: I'll boot her out!

FARMER'S WIFE: You'll do no such thing, farmer! You'll do no such thing!

FARMER: According to the law, I don't have to keep sick farmhands for more than seven days.

(The PRIEST takes another swig from his hipflask.)

PRIEST: Now let's go take a look.

(The PRIEST puts the hipflask back in his pocket, gets up. The FARMER and the FARMER'S WIFE also get up. ALL exit upstage.)

(Lights slowly dim.)

EIGHTH STATION

Split scene—indoors / outdoors, at night.

(MADY, half sitting up in bed, feverish, her eyes closed, arms under the blanket, a damp cloth over her forehead. LITTLE JOE is sitting beside her on the nightstool, fanning her with his cap. The tallow candle is standing on the floor, burning. The FARMER, the FARMER'S WIFE, and the PRIEST enter.)

FARMER *(to LITTLE JOE)*: Hey, what're you doin' in the maid's room? Better make sure I don't catch you in here again!

MADY *(opening her eyes)*: Praise the Lord, Jesus Christ! *(She takes the damp cloth from her forehead.)*

PRIEST: Forever and ever, Amen.

(LITTLE JOE has gotten up, puts on his cap.)

PRIEST: Stay where you are, Little Joe. *(to the FARMER)* Call all your hired help. We need witnesses for something like this. *(He sets down his lantern, sits down on the stool, looks at MADY.)*

FARMER *(calling offstage)*: Hey! Rupp! Best!

(RUPP and BEST enter.)

PRIEST: I've called you all here to act as my witnesses. Pay attention and remember everything you see. *(to MADY)* Well, then, Mady my child, let's take a look!

(MADY pulls her hands out from under the blanket, shows them to the PRIEST. He takes them in his hands, carefully examines them. Her hands have open wounds, both on the palms and on the backs of her hands. The PRIEST gently presses the wound on one hand, MADY shudders with a sigh of pain. The PRIEST looks at his own finger, it is bloody. He wipes off the blood with his handkerchief. He then gets up, walks to the foot of the bed, folds back the

blanket, looks at her feet and their wounds, then covers her feet back up.)

PRIEST: On your side, too? *(MADY nods.) I can't examine you there . . .*

(MADY reaches under her nightshirt, beneath her left breast, pulls out a folded piece of cloth, shows it to the PRIEST. There is a spot of blood on it. He takes the piece of cloth, looks at it with astonishment, the OTHERS look at it too. The PRIEST touches the spot of blood with his finger, wipes his finger off on the cloth, carefully folds it, puts it in his pocket, and sits down again on the stool.)

PRIEST: Now, tell me, Mady my child, how did all this happen?

MADY: A week ago, in the middle of the night, a bright light led me to the wayside cross. And the Savior started to talk and He said: Mady, if you want to help ease my pain, then climb up here and put your hands on my hands, and your face against mine, and your feet on my feet, and your breast on mine. And I climbed up and did it, and the Savior started to talk again and He said: Now I am promised to you and you have been promised to me, for ever and ever. Our faith and love will never end, you are completely mine, and I am completely yours. I am your groom and you are my bride. And then . . . then I felt a sharp pain in my heart, and it was bliss and agony. I just can't describe how I felt.

(The PRIEST pulls out his hipflask, takes a drink, puts the flask away.)

PRIEST: And that's the whole truth, Mady my child? You didn't make up any of this?

MADY: That's the whole truth, Father! I swear on a stack of Bibles and by the Lord Jesus Christ!

(The PRIEST nods several times.)

FARMER: Who's gonna believe that! But whether it's true

or not, she's gotta get out of my house! I need a maid out in the fields and not a maid in bed!

FARMER'S WIFE: Oh, come on! We could keep her on a little while longer. It doesn't cost us anything. Since she doesn't eat anything.

PRIEST: Honest-to-God, you don't eat anything at all?

(MADY shakes her head.)

FARMER: There's gotta be room for her in the parsonage. If the good Father would just—

FARMER'S WIFE: Now, there's a great idea! A sweet young thing staying in the parsonage! You can just imagine what kind of gossip that'd make!

(ALL fall silent for a while.)

MADY: Our Savior wants me to suffer with Him.

(The PRIEST nods, scratches his head in contemplation.)

MADY: Tomorrow I'll go back to work in the fields.

FARMER: In your condition?

MADY: The Lord's body will give me strength. If I could just ask you, Father, for your blessing . . .

PRIEST: What? Oh, I see. Yes, of course! *(He pulls out a gilded snuffbox, opens it, takes out a communion wafer, holds it high. ALL kneel down, MADY folds her hands in prayer.)*

PRIEST: And Jesus said: For my flesh is food indeed, and my blood is drink indeed.

MADY: Lord, I am not worthy to receive you, but only say the word, and I shall be healed. *(MADY repeats this prayer three times.)*

(The PRIEST places the wafer on her tongue, MADY swallows it, her head falls back, she closes her eyes, her expression is that of ultimate bliss. ALL rise.)

MADY *(whispers, more and more softly)*: My Savior. My Savior. Thou in me, Thou in me. What bliss. What bliss. Beloved above all.

(MADY'S breathing grows calmer, until she doesn't seem to be breathing at all. BEST approaches, looks at her.)

BEST: Mady! *(shakes MADY by the shoulders)* Mady! *(He places his ear on MADY'S breast, listens, suddenly becomes frightened.)* Nothin'! I don't hear nothin'! *(shakes MADY)* Mady! Come on, breathe! *(to the PRIEST)* She's dead! Dead!

PRIEST: She's not dead. Just far away. Far, far away. *(He blesses MADY, picks up his lantern and walks downstage. The FARMER follows him. Upstage lights go out.)*

FARMER: Well, Father, what do you think? Is it real or just religious mumbo jumbo?

PRIEST: I've known little Mady since she was a baby. She's not capable of lying or deception.

FARMER: Then I guess she can stay. But she's got to work. Otherwise she ought to be in a convent.

(The PRIEST nods slowly.)

PRIEST: We just can't let this get out. Otherwise we'll have all Hell to pay up here on your farm. People are curious about things like this.

FARMER: I'll tell my farmhands.

PRIEST: Well, then, good night!

FARMER: Good night, praised be the Lord.

PRIEST: For ever and ever, Amen.

(The PRIEST walks off in the direction of the wayside cross, the FARMER exits upstage. The PRIEST stops before the cross, removes his hat, crosses himself, sits down on the bench beside the cross, pulls out his hipflask, takes a drink. From time to time throughout the following monologue, he takes a little swig.)

PRIEST: Oh, Lord Jesus! Now she's married to You, on top of everything else. A husband . . . At least she has that consolation. I'm in the same boat as the hired hands. I've got to stay single, too. No wife, no chil-

dren. That wasn't my choice, You've known that from the beginning. I was the second son of poor farmers, we had two choices: I could work for a farmer or for the Lord. I preferred working for the Lord. I starved all through school. Year in, year out, I ate nettle soup and potatoes. Slept in a corner of the cellar, and on the side I worked as a mason's apprentice at the age of fifteen. Was the weakest student in seminary, never really did learn Latin. Afterwards served as assistant priest, was transferred from one filthy little village to the next . . . Everyday early Mass, no matter how cold it was, my fingers were numb and the wine was frozen solid in the cup. And for a bed I had a sleeping bag with hot plum pits to warm me up a little bit. I know, I know, of course—everybody respects me. The old wives kiss my hand, and the farmers beg me to bless their crops, and I've got enough to eat and wood for heating . . . But other than that . . . *(stands up, looks up at Christ)* They sit around in the confessional and blabber about carrying on with the opposite sex, and as for me, I do this . . . *(makes the sign of the cross for absolution)* . . . and they're free from sin once again, and can go back to living like pigs until their next confession! And what about me, eh? What've I got? *(lifts his flask)* This is it. *(He takes a drink, suddenly realizes where he is, and kneels down.)* Oh, Lord, forgive me! Forgive me! I don't know what's gotten into me! Guess I've got a bit of the devil in my soul! Forgive me, Lord! *(He crosses himself, rises, hurries away.)*
(Stagelights slowly dim)

Ninth Station

Outdoors, sunrise.

(MADY appears, now wearing half-gloves; no longer bare-foot, she's wearing shoes. She looks radiantly beautiful. She sits down on the bench stage right, looks at her hands, then looks around, takes several deep breaths, since it is truly a beautiful morning. BEST approaches from upstage, stops when he notices MADY, watches her, then BEST crosses to stage left, to the tools; he shoulders the whetstone, picks up a scythe, tests the blade, looks over at MADY, who hasn't noticed him yet. BEST puts the scythe back down, squats down, stares off into space, looks over at MADY, stares back off into space.)

BEST: But Jesus can't give ya any land. Can't give ya a farmhouse. Can't give ya any children. *(MADY doesn't answer, just looks at BEST with a fixed stare.)* And I really wanted to marry you. You were the one thing in the whole world I loved most. But I'm not going to give ya up. Just remember the old saying: the woman is the man's field. And just remember one more thing: people are meant to marry people, and not some god! *(BEST gets up, takes his scythe and a coil of twine, walks past MADY. She watches him go. She feels sorry for him. As he passes the cross, BEST crosses himself, then stops, looks back up at Christ.)* Give her to me! I'm beggin' ya! What do ya want with her, anyway? *(Since BEST naturally doesn't get an answer, he looks up in anger, turns away, and exits.)*

(RUPP and LITTLE JOE approach from upstage. LITTLE JOE shoulders his whetstone, takes a scythe. MADY stands up, walks over toward the tools. RUPP steps in her path.)

RUPP: So, you really think you've gotten rid of me, eh? You really think I'm afraid of your Lord Jesus? *(MADY looks at him with a blank look in her eyes.)* My God, girl, don't be so stupid! You really think the Lord Jesus is a better lover than me? And what've you got to show for it, huh? Wounds! Bleeding wounds! Don't you think that I'd've treated you better than that? I'd never crucify you, I'd do other kinds of things with you! (*He comes closer.*) As young and pretty as you are! (*He now stands directly in front of her.*) So clean all over, you look good enough to eat! (*He touches MADY gently on the shoulder, walks around behind her till he is standing right behind her. With his left hand he suddenly reaches up between her legs, with his right hand he grabs her breast. LITTLE JOE watches, astonished.*) Does the Lord Jesus do it this way too? Does He do it like this?

MADY (*resisting*): No! Let go! Let go, I tell you!

(*LITTLE JOE pulls out his pocketknife, leaps into the fray and slashes RUPP'S left hand with the knife. RUPP lets MADY go, as he cries out in pain, grabbing his injured hand.*)

RUPP: Are you crazy, you stupid ass?

(*RUPP goes after LITTLE JOE, who protects himself by waving the knife around. The FARMER enters from upstage.*)

FARMER: Hey, what's going on?

RUPP: He cut my hand, that asshole!

FARMER: Put the knife away, Little Joe.

(*LITTLE JOE obeys, folds up the knife and puts it away. The FARMER slaps him across the face so hard that LITTLE JOE staggers to the side.*)

LITTLE JOE: He grabbed Mady! (*gestures between his legs*) Right there, there's where he grabbed her!

FARMER (*to RUPP*): *Is he telling the truth?*

RUPP: A joke, that's all it was!

(The FARMER grabs RUPP by the hair, pulls his head down.)

FARMER: You, bum! When're you gonna cut that out? When're you gonna cut that out!

RUPP: It was just a joke, honest!

FARMER: That's not a joking matter! If I ever catch you doin' that again, you're really gonna get it! *(He lets RUPP go.)* Now, get to work!

(The FARMER picks up a whetstone, scythe, and coil of twine. LITTLE JOE, RUPP, and MADY do the same.)

FARMER: Where's the foreman?

MADY: Already gone on ahead.

(ALL walk in the direction of the road. The FARMER and LITTLE JOE cross themselves, RUPP doesn't. MADY smiles up at Jesus, and she too crosses herself.)

LITTLE JOE *(to MADY)*: You still haven't eaten a single bite.

MADY: I don't need anything, Little Joe.

LITTLE JOE: I just don't understand. I'm always so hungry. What can I do so I don't always get so hungry?

MADY: All you need to do is pray.

LITTLE JOE: I pray all the time—
Come, Holy Ghost,
With a platter full of roast
And dumplings galore,
Let me eat till I'm sore.

(ALL exit.)

(Stagelights slowly dim)

Tenth Station

Indoors / daytime, but with muted light.

(MADY is sitting up in bed, resting on two large, white-covered pillows. Even the blanket is now enclosed in a white coverlet. She is wearing her nightshirt. A large group of VISITORS, kneeling, surround her bed. Two-thirds are women, and of them two-thirds are farm girls. Three-fourths of the men are farmhands. We can recognize the farmhands by their miserable clothing, perhaps also by their faces. Among the visitors are two city folk, a LADY and a GENTLEMAN, both middle-aged, easily distinguishable by their totally different dress. They aren't kneeling. The FARMER is standing a bit to one side, obviously sullen; he's not about to kneel down before Mady. Kneeling directly in front of Mady's bed is the PRIEST with his rosary beads, saying Hail Marys which the crowd repeats after him. The FARMER'S WIFE is kneeling next to the PRIEST, LITTLE JOE is kneeling somewhat to the side and is crying out of sympathy with MADY'S suffering. RUPP is sitting on the handle of a scythe downstage left, BEST is sitting on the bench downstage right. Neither one wants to participate in this strange event which is clearly unpleasant for them. MADY is just experiencing the scourging of Christ. Her eyes are closed, her hands are clenched into fists, crossed in front of her body as if tied. Her wounds have not yet begun to bleed. MADY'S body arches forward, doubles over in pain, she hunches her shoulders. We can begin to see bloody streaks on the back of her nightshirt, and gradually the shoulders and upperarms of the nightshirt also become wet with blood.)

(MADY is moaning with pain. After a while the scourging is over, and MADY collapses in bed. The VISITORS continue praying throughout. After a short time, MADY opens her eyes, slowly regains consciousness, feels the pain and *emits a muffled moan, looks around and is frightened to discover all the people, looks at the PRIEST.)*

MADY *(pleading)*: Make them go away! Please, Father, make them go away!

(ALL stop praying. The PRIEST rises.)

PRIEST: Mady my child! You know I didn't want this to happen! I didn't want to make a fuss! But word just spread. It must be God's will that you not hide your light under a bushel.

MADY *(sobbing)*: I don't want any gawkers, Father! I'm ashamed! I'm so ashamed!

PRIEST: But, Mady my child, you shouldn't be ashamed! You're suffering the passion of Christ! You are one of the chosen few! God has chosen you to uplift the people, to strengthen their faith! *(makes an expansive gesture around the room)* Just look around, surely there are doubters and unbelievers among them. You've been chosen to show them the right path! You've been chosen . . .

(Without warning, MADY lapses back into the trance)

MADY: Oh, Lord Jesus! No! Don't hurt him! Take me instead! Take me!

(The PRIEST kneels down again, notices at the same time that the LADY and GENTLEMAN are still standing.)

PRIEST: Either kneel down or get out! This isn't some carnival sideshow! Do you hear me?

(The LADY and the GENTLEMAN kneel down, the FARMER exits upstage, the PRIEST continues to lead the visitors in prayer. In her trance, MADY now has the crown of thorns placed upon her head and nailed in place. With a cry of pain she grabs her head at the hairline, immediately pulls her hands away in pain, since she has "stuck" herself with the thorns. By now a large amount of blood is streaming down her face. MADY strikes her forehead time and

again with her crossed fists.)

MADY *(sobbing): Oh! Oh! Oh! Oh!*

(LITTLE JOE is completely beside himself, his prayers sound more like screams, he rises, wants to go to Mady, sobs, sinks back down on his knees. MADY'S fists fall to her side, her whole body is wracked with pain, she trembles, then collapses on the bed, breathing heavily.)

LITTLE JOE *(rising):* No! No! You shouldn't do that to any human being! *(The OTHERS stop praying.)* You just can't do that! *(goes over to MADY and kneels down before her)* Mady, don't suffer anymore! Please, don't suffer anymore!

(MADY opens her eyes, smiles at LITTLE JOE through her pain.)

MADY *(though it is extremely difficult for her to speak):* It's almost over, Little Joe. It's almost over.

(LITTLE JOE rises, pulls out his handkerchief, wipes her forehead with it.)

LITTLE JOE: I'll wipe away the blood . . .

MADY: No, Little Joe! Don't touch me! It hurts so much!

(LITTLE JOE shrinks back, kneels down. Without further warning MADY lapses back into her trance. Suddenly her hands are pulled apart, her arms are distorted in the shape of a crucifixion, her body convulses, her legs are extended, her arms seem to be pulled almost from their sockets. She unclenches her fists, blood streams from her hands, her mouth opens and she emits a silent scream.)

(Black-out)

(NOTE ON THE ROSARY: For every station of the cross, ten Hail Marys are said, always with the additional sentence: "Who was . . . for our sins." In this instance the VISITORS should pray the station which MADY is experienc-

ing at the moment. In other words, the VISITORS say the Hail Mary once, twice, or three times, depending on how long MADY suffers that particular station. At the scourging:

PRIEST (leading the prayer): Hail, Mary, full of grace, the Lord is with you, you are blessed among women and blessed is the fruit of thy womb, Jesus. Who was scourged for our sins.

ALL: Hail, Mary, Mother of God, pray for us sinners now and in the hour of our death. Amen.

When the crown of thorns is placed on Mady's head, ALL repeat: "Who was crowned with thorns for our sins." However, when Mady is crucified, ALL stop praying, since they are all so shocked by this unexpected, horrible event.)

Eleventh Station

Outdoors, daytime.

(Several simple tables and benches, made out of planks. Gradually, in pairs or in groups, a large number of VISITORS approach along the road. They can be the same people who appeared in the "Tenth Station," but there are also three people who haven't yet appeared on stage: a fragile OLD MAID, as well as a FAT GENTLEMAN from the city and his well-dressed WIFE. The first to arrive sit down on the benches or just stand around, etc. The FARMER'S WIFE enters from upstage.)

FARMER'S WIFE: God bless! God bless! Just have a seat, she'll be right out! Anybody like a beer or a little glass of wine? We also have some elderberry juice or a good home-made schnaps!

FIRST FARMER: A schnaps.

FIRST FARMER'S WIFE: Bring me some juice.

(The FARMHANDS don't order.)

RICH FARMER: Bring me a bottle of wine!

FARMER'S WIFE: You bet, it's on the way! *(calls upstage)* Little Joe! Little Joe!

VOICE OF LITTLE JOE *(from offstage)*: Yeah?

FARMER'S WIFE: A schnaps, a juice, and a bottle of wine!

VOICE OF LITTLE JOE *(from offstage)*: Comin' right up!!

FARMER'S WIFE *(to the NEW ARRIVALS)*: Just have a seat, she'll be right out!

(LITTLE JOE brings the drink orders, the THREE call him over and each takes the drink he or she has ordered.)

FARMER'S WIFE: Mind if I collect right away? . . . a bottle of wine is six farthings . . .

(BEST enters from upstage, sits down with the other FARMHANDS, greets them.)

RICH FARMER: Damn, that's awful expensive!

FARMER'S WIFE: Yes, well, it's the delivery costs . . .

(The RICH FARMER sighs and pays.)

RICH FARMER: Do you think Mady can help my wife?

FARMER'S WIFE: Certainly! Definitely! Mady has already cured lots of people who had given up hope!

(More VISITORS arrive, including the PRIEST.)

FARMER'S WIFE: Just have a seat, she'll be right out! Oh, Father! Praise the Lord! *(to the FAT GENTLEMAN from the city and his WIFE)* You folks like to order something?

FAT GENTLEMAN: A bottle of wine!

(The PRIEST sits down, wipes the sweat from his forehead and the back of his neck with his handkerchief.)

FARMER'S WIFE: You bet, folks, it's on the way!

SECOND FARMER: Two bottles of beer!

FARMER'S WIFE: Little Joe, hop to it! A bottle of wine, two bottles of beer! Something for you, Father?

(The PRIEST shakes his head, pats his back pocket where his hipflask is hidden, then pulls it out and takes a drink. LITTLE JOE exits upstage, the FARMER'S WIFE collects from the FIRST FARMER'S WIFE.)

FARMER'S WIFE: There you are, that's three farthings! Did you see that gal from the city? *(points to the FAT GENTLEMAN'S WIFE)* Her neck's bare and she's wearing that thin blouse so everybody can get a good look at her wares! Enough to make you throw up!

(New VISITORS arrive)

FARMER'S WIFE: Just have a seat, she'll be right out! She's still in that thingamajig, in that ecstasy, the Priest calls it!

(The FARMER and RUPP enter from upstage. The FARMER sits down with the other FARMERS, RUPP squats on the handle of his scythe.)

FARMER'S WIFE *(to some FARMHANDS)*: Well—what about you folks, don't you want something? *(A FARMHAND shakes his head. The FARMER'S WIFE turns to SECOND FARMER'S WIFE:)* Just like farmhands! How's a person s'posed to make a living? If I had my way, they wouldn't be allowed in here at all, but the Priest . . . *(LITTLE JOE enters, stumbles, almost falls over with the drinks.)* Hey, watch out, you clumsy rube!

(LITTLE JOE serves the drinks, then sits down on the ground. MADY enters from upstage. She is wearing her Sunday best, is calm and majestic. She is not wearing the gloves, so her wounds are plainly visible. Several of the FARMHANDS get up as she enters, a middle-aged TEN-ANT FARMER'S WIFE falls to her knees and kisses MADY's hand.)

MADY (*gently*): Don't do that, ma'am. Get up. (*MADY helps the TENANT FARMER'S WIFE up.*)

TENANT FARMER'S WIFE (*rises*): Ah got a sick boy ta home. Oh, please, help!

MADY: Why don't you take him to the barber?

TENANT FARMER'S WIFE: Ah'm just the wife of a poor tenant farmer. Ah ain't got no money.

MADY: I'll pray for your child.

TENANT FARMER (*rises*): Ma sheep're all dyin', one right after th' other. Please, help!

MADY: Why don't you take them to the barber?

TENANT FARMER: Ah'm just a tenant farmer. Ah ain't got no money.

MADY: I'll pray for you.

FOREMAN (*rises*): Ah got boils in m' armpits. Please, help!

MADY: Why don't you go to the barber?

FOREMAN: Ah'm just a hired hand. Ah ain't got no money.

MADY: I'll pray for you.

RICH FARMER: My wife's got woman troubles. Please, help!

MADY: Why don't you take her to the barber?

RICH FARMER: It didn't do any good.

MADY: I'll pray for her.

FAT GENTLEMAN (*stands up, under his breath*) I . . . I'm a bit constipated, problems with my stool, you know what I mean . . .

MADY (*glances at his potbelly*): Fast for fourteen days!

(*MADY turns away from him. The FAT GENTLEMAN sits back down, somewhat nonplussed. A frail, terribly OLD MAID slowly gets up.*)

OLD MAID: I can't die. Please, help!

(*MADY goes over to her, looks at her compassionately. *)

MADY: Why do you want to die?

OLD MAID: Ah been a maid m' whole life long, they threw

me out when m' strength gave out, for seven years now ah bin beggin' from farm to farm, beggin' for a piece a' bread and a drink a' milk, ah gotta sleep in the barn with the pigs, ah got lice and scabs, ah got water on m' feet, ah cain't hardly see nomore—but, no matter what, life won't leave me, life won't leave me, and ah'd give anythin' for some peace, some peace at last. Ah want t' die. Please, help.

(MADY embraces the OLD MAID.)

RUPP: Hey, why don't ya' just hang yourself, if ya' really wanna die!

(MADY turns around to face RUPP, her eyes are flashing, she's trembling with rage.)

MADY *(to RUPP, then in the direction of the RICH FARM- ERS)*: Woe unto you, you wealthy of the earth, you'll have no consolation! Woe unto you, you glut- tons, you'll starve! Woe unto you, you who are now laughing. You'll regret it, regret it for all eternity!

(The RICH FARMERS listen, annoyed, but also somewhat afraid. The OLD MAID sits down. MADY is in despair about her inability to really help. Her eyes fill with tears. She falls on her knees and sobs.)

MADY: Oh, God! Oh, God! What shall I do? What shall I do? You said, blessed are the poor for they shall in- herit Heaven! Heaven! *(She rises, screams toward Heaven, crying and angry, her arms raised.)* I want justice to reign here and now, on earth, and not just afterward in Heaven!

(MADY collapses on the ground, beats her forehead with her fists, is overpowered by sobs. LITTLE JOE, also strug- gling with his tears, gets up. The PRIEST appears some- what exhausted, takes a drink of schnaps. The OLD MAID gets up, goes over to MADY, kneels down to her, embraces her, gently strokes her cheek. MADY calms down, looks at the OLD MAID, kisses her on the cheek, gets up and helps

the OLD MAID up, leads her over to her seat. The OLD MAID sits down. MADY wipes the tears from her own eyes, looks at the VISITORS, looks over toward her FARMER. LITTLE JOE sits down again.)

MADY (*calmly*): Best, how much do you think our farmer took in last year?

BEST: Our farmer? Well, I'd say about fifteen hundred guilders.

FARMER (*to BEST*): Where'd you get a number like that, eh?

BEST: Well, I just figured it out. I'm right, ain't I?

FARMER: Well—so what if you are? That any of your business?

MADY: One thousand five hundred guilders. Best, how much do you get paid in a year?

BEST: Well . . . a total of thirteen guilders, and on top of that two guilders and twenty-four farthings for leather, a pair of boots and a pair of shoes, two pair of overalls and a coat.

MADY: Little Joe, how much do you get paid in a year?

LITTLE JOE (*jumps to his feet*): Six guilders and a pair of overalls and a pair of shoes and a coat! (*He sits back down, listens attentively.*)

MADY: And I get five guilders, a smock, three yards of rough cloth, one skirt and a pound of wool. So, we hired hands earn roughly thirty guilders in a year.

FARMER: And what about your meals, heh?

MADY: Your hired hand can tell you more about the food.

LITTLE JOE (*stands up, to the FARMER*):
Chicken guts and goat's leather!
Just you wait till I tell my mother!

FARMER (*threatening*): Why, you . . . ! (*He starts after LITTLE JOE, LITTLE JOE eludes him.*)

LITTLE JOE (*continues*):
Mom'll tell my dad,
Dad'll tell the smith,

(LITTLE JOE hides behind MADY, then continues.)
The smith'll tell his hammer,
The hammer'll strike you dead!

(The FARMER stands in front of LITTLE JOE and MADY with his fist raised, then lets his fist fall to his side)

FARMER *(to LITTLE JOE)*: Get out of here, you're such a stupid ass! *(The FARMER walks away from them. LITTLE JOE then sits back down on the ground near MADY.)*

MADY: So much for the food. If one of us wanted to buy something for ourselves, if we wanted to buy an ox, for example, then the foreman would have to save for ten years, the hired hand and me over twenty years. And so I ask you: Is that right? Can that be God's will?

(MADY looks around. The PRIEST has become increasingly uneasy and reaches for his hipflask more and more often. The FARMHANDS have been listening attentively and obviously agree with MADY, but are thinking: "That's just the way things are, always have been, and always will be." The FARMERS have been listening and grow increasingly sullen. The FARMER looks at MADY with rage, nods several times, looks toward the other FARMERS, finally at the PRIEST.)

FARMER: What've you got to say about her sermon, Father?

PRIEST *(squirming)*: Well . . . er . . . that's a difficult question, scripturally speaking. *(stands up)* Justice, of course, of course, there should be justice in this life. But what is it, this justice? There are people, and then there are other people, we just aren't all equal. It'd be nice, it sure would be nice. And, you know, Mady my child, there are higher powers, worldly powers, I mean. And this power regulates life, life here on earth. Not so long ago, for example, the higher powers were for indentured servitude. Then

that's no good. And they did away with it. For example, every one of you farmhands, when the year's
up, can say to your farmer: "So long, I don't like
working for you," and can walk away and take a job
on another farm. That's enormous progress,
wouldn't you say?

*(A few FARMHANDS nod and mumble their agreement.
The PRIEST takes a drink from his hipflask, lapses into
contellation. MADY sits down, stares off into space.)*

PRIEST: Don't forget what Saint Paul said in his Letter to
the Romans, that is, the following: Every man
should subordinate himself to the local authorities,
because there is no authority that doesn't come
from God. That's the word according to Paul. And
the local authority that is most directly over you, is
your employer, the farmer.

FARMER *(smugly)*: So, there you have it!

PRIEST: Ergo! Those of you who are hired hands or maids,
now head on home and get a good night's rest,
'cause tomorrow is another workday!

FARMER: So, there you have it!

*(The FARMHANDS get up and exit. The OLD MAID places
her hand on MADY'S head to console her, then exits too.
The CITY FOLK exit as well, only a few FARMHANDS stay
behind, along with BEST and LITTLE JOE. The PRIEST
sits back down, takes a swig, glances sheepishly over to
MADY, who is sitting there, staring at the ground.)*

FARMER *(to MADY)*: And as for you . . . ! Go pack your
stuff, right now, and get out of here!

PRIEST: But, farmer! Where's she supposed to go? She
doesn't have any living relatives!

FARMER: She's leaving, and that's that!

*(MADY gets up, starts upstage, but the FARMER'S WIFE
holds her back.)*

FARMER'S WIFE: Wait, Mady, wait! *(She goes over to the*

FARMER, *pulls him aside, whispers:*) Don't send
  her away, dear, please, don't send her away!

(The FARMER doesn't want to listen, tries to walk away.)

FARMER'S WIFE: Now, you listen to me! It'll bring us bad
  luck if you chase her away!

FARMER: Naw!

FARMER'S WIFE: That's right, just listen to me! Mady appeared to me in a dream, and the Lord Jesus was
  with her! And He said to her: Don't be afraid and
  don't be ashamed, I shall always be beside you. And
  whosoever tries to harm you, him I shall punish, in
  this world and in the next!

FARMER: Really?

FARMER'S WIFE: Really!—And besides, we're making a
  lot of money, too, selling food and drink! More and
  more people come every day!

*(The FARMER looks at his WIFE, thinks about it for a
while, looks at MADY, looks back at his WIFE, finally
makes up his mind and turns to MADY.)*

FARMER: All right, fine! You can stay! But no more of
  those sermons! (*more to himself than to the others*)
  Or else I'll settle your hash for good!

(Black out)

Twelfth Station

Split scene—indoors / outdoors, a moonlit night.

*(MADY, asleep in her bed. BEST, his face smeared with
charcoal, enters from upstage with a hunting rifle in his
hand, a backpack slung over his shoulder. He stops downstage, with his back turned to MADY.)*

BEST: Mady!

(MADY wakes up.)

BEST: Mady!

MADY: Best?

BEST: Ya know what ya said today, about just rewards and stuff—that wasn't right.

MADY: It was right.

BEST: Just imagine for a minute that you'd'a married me instead of our Savior, and we wanted to buy a farm and hire some hands. We'd do the same thing. I would, anyways. When you're an owner, ya got to figure things out. When you're an owner, ya got to multiply your wealth. That's what I came to tell ya.

(MADY nods, BEST waits for her answer. Since she doesn't answer, BEST turns to leave.)

MADY: Do you still go out poaching?

BEST: Yeah, I still go out. If I can't marry you, I'll find somebody else. (*He walks on down the road, MADY is left in thought, staring. When BEST reaches the wayside cross, he stops, looks up, and says with pent-up rage:*) You bloody bastard, you nailed-up bloody bastard!

(BEST exits. MADY, in bed, closes her eyes. After a while LITTLE JOE passes by with a bowl full of blood, stops for a moment, looks over in MADY'S direction, exits upstage.)

LITTLE JOE (*in leaving*): Mady doesn't eat anything anymore, or else I'd have given her some. I guess I'll just have to eat it all myself.

(After a while RUPP approaches, stops at the same spot where BEST and LITTLE JOE had stopped. RUPP puts on a devil's mask complete with horns, strides over to MADY, rips her covers off, leaps on the bed so that he lands astride MADY on all fours. MADY opens her eyes, sits up in fright, sees the devil's mask. RUPP hits her in the face several times with his fist, until her head falls limply to the

side. With both hands RUPP rips the top of MADY'S night-shirt open.)

(Black out)

Thirteenth Station

Split scene—indoors / outdoors, in the evening. It is still light. Later the darkness grows.

(MADY'S bed is in its normal place, though she is nowhere to be seen. A stool next to it. Approaching along the road: a big, strong BEARER carrying a wood-frame riding chair on his back, sitting on the chair is the MONSIGNOR. A second strong BEARER carrying a riding chair; sitting on it is the PROFESSOR OF MEDICINE. Both have leather satchels on their laps. Walking behind them: the PRIEST and the SCRIBE; the latter is also carrying a leather satchel; he has a scowl on his face, because he is not used to the climb. The PRIEST is agitated. As they pass the wayside cross, only the MONSIGNOR and the PRIEST cross themselves. The sound of bells, playing the "Ave Maria," can be heard in the distance.
When they arrive at the farm, the two BEARERS kneel down, the MONSIGNOR and the PROFESSOR dismount, stretch their arms and legs, walk around to get the cramps out of their legs. The BEARERS carry the riding chairs off to one side, put them down, and then sit down themselves on the bench stage right, wiping the sweat from their faces. The SCRIBE also sits down. The PROFESSOR takes a pinch of snuff.)

PROFESSOR *(gazing around)*: Lovely view!
MONSIGNOR: It is, isn't it! I come from this region myself!
PROFESSOR: You don't say!

MONSIGNOR (*pointing*): Over there, on the other side of the valley—do you see that opening in the forest?

PROFESSOR (*holds his hand over his eyes to shade the sun*): Where? Oh, I see! There's a farmhouse.

MONSIGNOR: That's where I was born!

(The PRIEST hands his hipflask to the two BEARERS, though he tries to conceal the flask from the two dignitaries. The two BEARERS gratefully accept, take a drink, return the hipflask. The PRIEST secretly takes a swig too, puts the flask back in his pocket.)

PROFESSOR (*during the above*): Yes, yes, it just proves once again that the Church's hope for the future comes from the peasant class! Wouldn't you say?

(The PRIEST, in the background, shakes his head in doubt, but the MONSIGNOR smiles, flattered.)

MONSIGNOR: And what about you, Professor?

PROFESSOR: I grew up in the capital. Come from a long line of doctors. Four generations.

MONSIGNOR: Excellent! Excellent!

FIRST BEARER (*to the SECOND BEARER*): Well, ready to go?

(The SECOND BEARER nods. They get up, shoulder their riding chairs. The MONSIGNOR notices them, reaches into a pocket of his habit, pulls out a pouch, hands each of the BEARERS a coin, then reaches into the pouch again, and, smiling, hands each of the BEARERS some small change as a tip. The BEARERS both kneel down and kiss his hand.)

FIRST BEARER: God bless, your Excellency!

SECOND BEARER: God bless!

(The MONSIGNOR nods in a friendly manner, the two BEARERS exit.)

PRIEST (*calling upstage*): Anybody home?—Must still be out in the fields, but they'll be here soon. They've already rung the bell for vespers.

PROFESSOR (*sits down*): I hope we can resolve the whole matter quickly. I have an important faculty meeting day after tomorrow.

PRIEST: Your Excellencies really should have come earlier, if I may say so! There have been major changes! She doesn't suffer the passion anymore, and now she's eating again.

(*Approaching along the road are the FARMER, the FARMER'S WIFE, RUPP, BEST, LITTLE JOE, and MADY. ALL are carrying sickles. MADY is wearing half-gloves.*)

MONSIGNOR: But she still has the wounds, doesn't she?

PRIEST: Yes, she still does. (*notices the group approaching*) Here they are now.

(*The PROFESSOR and the MONSIGNOR rise, as the group reaches centerstage.*)

FARMER: Well, God bless!

PRIEST: Praise the Lord! These two gentlemen here come from his Excellency, the Prince Bishop. This is the Reverend Father Monsignor Pfetscher, and this gentleman here is the famous professor of medicine from the state university, Dr. Rudolf von Achammer!

(*The FARMER'S WIFE drops to one knee, kisses the MONSIGNOR'S hand, the FARMER does likewise. RUPP, who ignores the whole procedure, is encouraged to kiss the MONSIGNOR'S hand by the emphatic hand motions of the FARMER'S WIFE. BEST also kisses his hand. LITTLE JOE watches with great interest and willingly imitates the others. MADY is the last one to kiss the MONSIGNOR'S hand.*)

MONSIGNOR (*to the kneeling MADY*): So, you're the one? Take off your gloves.

(MADY rises, removes her gloves. The MONSIGNOR takes her hands in his, looks at her hands, while the PRO-FESSOR joins them, observes the wounds, touches a wound with his finger. MADY recoils. The PROFESSOR lays his right hand on MADY'S forehead, with his thumb he raises her eyelid, briefly peers into MADY'S eye.)

PRIEST *(during the above)*: You know, Mady my child, these two gentlemen are a committee of inquiry, so to speak. On instructions from the Bishop, they are supposed to make sure that everything's legiti-mate, as far as you're concerned.

PROFESSOR: If we may proceed . . . We need a room.

PRIEST: It'd be best if we went to her room. *(to the FARMER'S WIFE:)* Chairs for the gentlemen!

FARMER'S WIFE: Right away!

PROFESSOR: Also a bowl of water and a towel.

FARMER'S WIFE: Yes, sir, whatever you need!

(The FARMER'S WIFE, the FARMER, BEST, RUPP, and LITTLE JOE all put down their tools and exit upstage. The PRIEST leads the way to MADY'S bed. The MONSIGNOR smiles and takes MADY by the arm, escorts her. The PRO-FESSOR and the SCRIBE follow. The SCRIBE takes along his leather satchel, as well as the leather stachels of the other two gentlemen.)

FARMER *(as he exits)*: Now we'll get to the bottom of this!

FARMER'S WIFE: What are you talking about? We've al-ready seen for ourselves that everything's on the up-and-up!

(The PROFESSOR indicates to MADY that she should sit down on the bed. MADY does. LITTLE JOE enters from upstage with stools for the men, the FARMER'S WIFE brings a bowl of water and a towel, and then they both exit. The PRIEST, the MONSIGNOR, and the SCRIBE sit down. From his leather satchel the SCRIBE pulls out a quill, bottle of ink, a notebook, and a tablet to write on, and

readies himself to take dictation. He writes down every-thing the PROFESSOR dictates, but also everything that MADY says or what the others say about her. The PROFES-SOR opens his medical bag and takes out a magnifying glass, sits down opposite MADY, takes one of her hands and examines the wound, both in the palm and on the back of the hand; then he takes MADY'S other hand and repeats the procedure.)

PROFESSOR (*dictates*): The wound on the back of the hand runs lengthwise, is approximately a finger's width long and almost a finger's width wide. The wound in the palm appears more rounded, but irregular. The radius is equal to a finger's width. No trace of abscess or infection.

(The PROFESSOR pulls a probe out of his bag, takes MADY'S hand and inserts the probe into the wound in her palm. The audience should have the impression that the probe easily passes through her hand and emerges from the back of her hand. MADY groans in pain. The PROFES-SOR repeats the procedure with MADY'S other hand. MADY groans again. The PRIEST secretly takes a drink from his hipflask.)

PROFESSOR (*dictating*): The wounds on both hands pass entirely through the hand. (*to MADY*) Remove your shoes.

(MADY takes off her shoes, removes the rags covering her feet, holds up one foot. The PROFESSOR holds the foot, ob-serves both feet without the magnifying glass, inserts the probe through both wounds. MADY moans in pain.)

PROFESSOR (*dictating*): The wounds on the feet are larger, whereby the wound on the instep is itself larger than that on the sole. Now, what else do we have here?

PRIEST: Before, she had some little wounds around her

hairline, from the crown of thorns, but I don't know . . .

(The PROFESSOR gets up, examines her hairline, looks through the magnifying glass.)

PROFESSOR: Yes, little dots . . . *(dictating:)* Along the hairline, a row of dark points that circle the entire forehead.

PRIEST: And then there was also the wound in her side—

PROFESSOR: Oh, yes. Remove your upper garments.

MADY: But I can't . . . Nobody has ever . . . *(looks to the PRIEST, imploringly).*

PRIEST: Mady my child, you must be humble and allow them to complete the examination. There's nothing we can do!

(MADY begins to remove her upper garment, the PRIEST and the MONSIGNOR turn their stools so that their backs are to her. MADY covers her breasts with her hands while the PROFESSOR examines the wound in her side, located beneath her left breast.)

PROFESSOR *(dictating)*: The wound in her side is two finger widths long and one finger width wide. *(He inserts the probe into the wound, MADY groans in pain, and the PROFESSOR resumes his dictation.)* The wound is approximately two finger widths deep. No trace of abscess or infection. *(to MADY)* Good—now remove all your clothes.

MADY: No! No! That's not proper!

PRIEST *(without turning around)*: Mady my child, do just what he says, or I'll never give you communion again. You hear me?!

(Tears come to MADY'S eyes, she stands up, slowly undresses, covering her breasts with her hands. The PROFESSOR takes a step back, examines her from head to toe.)

PROFESSOR: Put your arms out to your side. *(MADY obliges, but unwillingly. The PROFESSOR observes her.)* Turn around. *(MADY turns around, the*

PROFESSOR *observes her.*) That's fine. You can
put on your nightshirt now. (*MADY pulls her nightshirt out from under the pillow and puts it on.*) Were
there or are there any incidents in your family of
mental illness, venereal diseases, alcoholism?
(*MADY shakes her head.*) Which childhood
illnesses have you had?

MADY: I can't remember anymore. I just don't know.

PROFESSOR: Any illnesses since then? (*MADY shakes
her head.*) You gentlemen can turn around now.
(*The PRIEST and the MONSIGNOR turn their
stools to face MADY.*) No rashes, worms, fever attacks, spasms?

MADY: Yes, I did have a fever. That was when I received
the Lord's wounds. And spasms — er . . . ah . . . I had
those before, but I—I wasn't sick, I was just protecting myself.

PROFESSOR: Protecting yourself from what?

MADY: From the boogeymen.

MONSIGNOR (*suspiciously*): What was that? Did I hear
right?

PRIEST: She was actually exposed to the temptations of
the devil. But she resisted courageously!

MONSIGNOR: You don't say. I want to hear the whole
story, right now!

PROFESSOR (*smiling, to the MONSIGNOR*): Just a moment, my dear colleague, science comes first!

PRIEST: Huh?

MONSIGNOR (*to the PRIEST*): What?

PRIEST: I really didn't understand what you meant, Professor . . .

PROFESSOR: I was just asking the Monsignor to be patient. It would not be productive, it seems to me, to
confuse one examination with the other. (*to MADY*)
Lay down.

(*MADY lays down on the bed in a half-sitting position. The*

PROFESSOR sits down on the stool by the bed.)

PROFESSOR: Spasms and fever, you said? *(MADY nods, he turns to the SCRIBE* :) Did you write that down? *(The SCRIBE nods. The PROFESSOR looks at MADY, then says suddenly :) These wounds are self-inflicted, aren't they?*

PRIEST: Of course not, Professor, what are you trying to say? God is my witness, and hundreds of visitors who come every Friday saw the blood streaming out all by itself. Mady's not a liar, I swear to you by all that is holy! *(In his excitement, the PRIEST pulls out his hipflask and takes a swig. The MON-SIGNOR looks at him somewhat indignantly. The PRIEST, embarrassed, quickly puts the flask away.)*

PROFESSOR *(to MADY)*: When did you have your first period? Menstruation?

MADY: Oh, around sixteen.

PROFESSOR: Any irregularities? Excessive bleeding? Any missed periods?

MADY *(hesitates)*: Well, when I . . . when I accompanied our Lord during his sufferings, well, then . . . then blood not only came out of the five wounds, but also from . . . from down there.

PROFESSOR: What did you say? From where?

MADY: From down there.

PROFESSOR: Ah, I understand! *(to the SCRIBE:)* Menstrual bleeding during the so-called passion.

MADY: And now . . . now it's been almost ten weeks since my last period.

PROFESSOR: Your last period was ten weeks ago?

MADY: Yes, about that.

PROFESSOR: Have you ever had times in the past when your period was so late?

MADY: No.

PROFESSOR: Are you still a virgin?

PRIEST: Well, of course she is! Do you think our Lord Jesus would go out of His way to choose a sinner for His bride?

(The MONSIGNOR makes a gesture to the PRIEST that he should be quiet.)

PROFESSOR *(to MADY)*: So, you have never really had intercourse with a man?

MADY: Course not! I'm not married!

PROFESSOR: When did you last experience your so-called sufferings of the passion?

MADY: Oh, about ten weeks ago.

(The light gradually dims, as sunset nears.)

PROFESSOR *(thinking out loud)*: That would mean that the passion ceased with the cessation of her menstrual periods . . . *(The PROFESSOR is deep in thought.)*

PRIEST: Now tell us, Mady my child, about how the Virgin Mary appeared to you. As a matter of fact, that happened at exactly the same time, ten weeks ago!

MONSIGNOR: The Virgin Mary?

MADY: Oh, goodness, that was so beautiful! I saw the Mother of God, with the baby Jesus in her arms, and she looked at me so sweetly and held out the baby Jesus to me, and I took Him, and the baby Jesus kissed me and stroked my cheeks with His tiny little hands. I was so happy I could have cried.

MONSIGNOR: Very interesting!

(Naturally, the PROFESSOR considers all this to be nothing more than a figment of her imagination.)

PROFESSOR: I have to determine for myself that she is still a virgin! *(He removes his coat, rolls up his sleeves, pulls a container with soap powder out of his medical bag, washes his hands in the bowl of water, dries his hands on the towel. During this procedure he speaks to the PRIEST and the MONSI-*

GNOR:) If you two gentlemen will just turn your
backs again . . .

*(The PRIEST and the MONSIGNOR turn their backs.
MADY now realizes what the PROFESSOR is about to do,
slips under the blanket, pulls the covers up under her chin,
glares at the PROFESSOR. The PROFESSOR takes a
small jar of lubricating jelly from his bag, lubricates the
index finger on his right hand, and turns to MADY.)*

PROFESSOR: Don't be childish!

PRIEST: Mady my child, don't make me mad! Do what the
Professor says!

(MADY doesn't budge from her fetal position.)

MONSIGNOR *(turning his head slightly toward MADY)*:
In the name of the Church, I command you to obey!
Otherwise, I will see to it that you are excommuni-
cated and banned from the Church!

(MADY desperately looks around for help.)

PROFESSOR: It's all right, you can stay under the covers.
This won't take long and won't hurt.

*(MADY slowly sinks back down into bed, closes her eyes in
surrender.)*

PROFESSOR *(stepping up to the bed)*: Pull up your nightshirt. *(MADY complies, her eyes still closed.)* Bend
your knees and spread your legs. *(MADY complies.
The PROFESSOR puts his right hand under the
blanket and examines her. MADY moans softly
when he penetrates her with his finger.)* She is not a
virgin.

*(The PRIEST and the MONSIGNOR turn around to face
the PROFESSOR.)*

MONSIGNOR: What?

PROFESSOR: She is not a virgin.

(The PRIEST looks shocked, incredulous.)

MADY (*completely confident*): That's not true!

(*The PROFESSOR still has his finger in MADY and now thinks he has found an enlargement of the uterus. He stops short, then reaches under the blanket with his left hand as well and lays it flat on MADY'S stomach, thereby pressing the uterus against his examining finger. He discovers that the uterus is, in fact, greatly enlarged. Then he takes both hands out from under the blanket.*)

PROFESSOR: She is pregnant.

(*The PRIEST and the MONSIGNOR get up from their stools, MADY is stunned. The PROFESSOR washes his hands in the bowl, dries them on the towel.*)

PRIEST: Impossible! Impossible! You must be mistaken, Professor!

PROFESSOR (*slightly irritated*): As a priest, you are probably not as familiar with these things as I, wouldn't you say? She is pregnant! That is a fact!

(*The PRIEST collapses on his stool, drained, takes a swig from his hipflask, shakes his head repeatedly. He just can't believe it.*)

MONSIGNOR: Oh, I see! I see! So that's it! Naturally, that puts things in a different light! Not a virgin, and pregnant to boot! (*to MADY:*) Who is the father of the child?

MADY (*convinced of her innocence, indignant*): I am not expecting! I've never slept with a man, never in my whole life! I swear, by the Virgin Mary!

MONSIGNOR: Let's leave the Virgin Mary out of this, if you don't mind! You aren't worthy of mentioning her name with your wicked tongue! (*The MONSIGNOR, enraged, paces back and forth. The PROFESSOR glances at his pocketwatch.*)

PROFESSOR: I must be going. If you please, I will give you gentlemen a brief summary of the results of my examination.

(The MONSIGNOR sits back down.)

PROFESSOR: I must qualifiy my remarks with the fact that a truly thorough examination could only be carried out in a hospital and only under constant observation over an extended period of time. The wounds would have to be treated, bandaged, and then observed to see whether or not the healing process would occur.

PRIEST: We've already done that!

PROFESSOR: You have!? How? When?

PRIEST: She went through a period when she didn't think she was worthy of bearing the Lord's wounds, so we put salve on the wounds and bandaged them up.

PROFESSOR: And?

PRIEST: It didn't do any good. It just caused her a lot of pain.

PROFESSOR: My dear Father, these things are all unconfirmed! I am of the opinion that her wounds were self-inflicted and that she kept the wounds from healing by artificial means, either by reinflicting the wounds or by the application of an irritant, which one I cannot be certain! *(The PRIEST shakes his head in despair.)* Regardless, the periodic occurrance of convulsive spasms and of fever, as well as the accompanying symptoms, lead me to conclude that we are dealing with an hysterical epileptic. Along with her actual illness—epilepsy—her hysterical condition is compounded by an abnormal craving for recognition, by religious fanaticism, and an over-active imagination. That is my diagnosis! *(He rolls his sleeves down, buttons the cuffs, pulls on his coat.)*

PRIEST *(now completely crushed)*: But she didn't eat a bite for three whole months, aside from daily communion! And she didn't drink anything either! Not even water!

PROFESSOR *(not forcefully, trying to be considerate)*:

Nonsense. According to the laws of nature, that is completely impossible. (*He picks up his medical bag.*) Well, that's that, but now I really must leave, or else I will have to travel after dark. (*shakes hands with the MONSIGNOR*) Monsignor! (*shakes hands with the PRIEST, though somewhat condescendingly*) Perhaps one day I shall come back, on vacation. A lovely area! (*He walks away, without even casting so much as a glance at MADY, but then turns one last time.*) Perhaps you could donate her body to the University Medical School, when she— An interesting case, nonetheless . . . And she certainly won't live long. (*raises his hand in farewell*) I'll be on my way! (*to the MONSIGNOR*) And don't let them change your mind, Monsignor!

MONSIGNOR (*grimly*): You don't have to worry about that!

(*The PROFESSOR exits along the country road. MADY is devastated and at her wits' end. The PRIEST just shakes his head repeatedly. The MONSIGNOR paces back and forth, his hands folded over his stomach, stops in front of MADY, folds his arms, looks at MADY grimly, nods several times, reaches into a pocket of his garment, pulls out a pocketwatch and glances at it.*)

MONSIGNOR: First, we need to fortify outselves. We've got a lot of hard work ahead of us. (*to the PRIEST*) Could we get something to eat here? (*The PRIEST doesn't hear him, since he's lost in thought.*) Father!

PRIEST (*startled*): Yes?

MONSIGNOR: I'd like to have a warm meal!

PRIEST: Go right on in the house. It's dinnertime now.

MONSIGNOR: And what about you?

(*The PRIEST shakes his head. The MONSIGNOR gives a sign to the SCRIBE that the two of them should go eat, and THEY exit upstage. The PRIEST goes over to MADY, looks at her, sits down on the stool next to her, and gazes at her sadly.)*

MADY (*sobbing*): I'm innocent, Father!

PRIEST: I believe you, Mady my child, I believe you.

(The PRIEST takes her hand and strokes it, being careful not to touch the wound.)

(Lights slowly dim)

Fourteenth Station

Split scene—indoors/outdoors, night.

(It is almost dark. MADY is lying in bed with her eyes open. The PRIEST is sitting beside her, his lips moving in silent prayer. From upstage enter: the MONSIGNOR, the SCRIBE, the FARMER, the FARMER'S WIFE, RUPP, BEST, and LITTLE JOE. The FARMER'S WIFE is carrying a lantern that lights the set. BEST and LITTLE JOE bring additional stools, RUPP is carrying two ropes and a chair with a back. The FARMER'S WIFE hangs the lantern up on a hook, the chair and stools are set down. No one knows what will happen next—they are all bewildered and apprehensive. The SCRIBE takes his writing utensils and a stool, sits down under the lantern, and readies himself for dictation.)

MONSIGNOR: Everyone sit down.

(RUPP starts to sit down on the chair with the back.)

MONSIGNOR: That chair is for the maid!

(RUPP sits down on a stool. ALL look at the MONSIGNOR.)

MONSIGNOR: Friends! (*The SCRIBE begins to write*)Professor von Achammer has examined this subject

and arrived at the opinion that, first, she has epilepsy, and, second, that she is a fraud. *(The
FARMER nods with satisfaction, the FARMER'S
WIFE looks increduluous, LITTLE JOE is enraged,
RUPP and BEST really don't know what to think of
the whole affair.)* I, on the other hand, as an experienced representative of the Church and an expert
on miracles, have arrived at a different conclusion.
This subject is no common fraud, nor does she suffer from epilepsy. Instead, she is the pitiable victim
of one or more demons! In short, this subject is obviously suffering from demonic possession!

(The PRIEST leaps to his feet.)

PRIEST *(indignant)*: What drivel! Why, I've never . . . I've
never heard anything so ridiculous!

MONSIGNOR: Friend, watch your tongue! *(He goes over to
the SCRIBE, takes the notebook from his hands,
leafs backwards, then reads aloud the following
passage:)* Professor—"Are you still a virgin?"
Priest—"Well, of course she is! Do you think our
Lord Jesus would go out of His way to choose a sinner for His bride?" *(He looks at the PRIEST, who
stares straight ahead in desperation.)* You antici-
pated the evidence, my dear Father! Since she is no
longer a virgin—and especially since she is pregnant—she cannot be the bride of Christ! You were
completely right, my friend! *(The MONSIGNOR
returns the notebook to the SCRIBE. ALL are
stunned by the news that MADY is pregnant. RUPP
begins to squirm.)*

FARMER: She's pregnant?

MONSIGNOR: Yes, indeed! And that makes her a concu-
bine of the Devil!

FARMER'S WIFE: And what about the stigmata?

MONSIGNOR: Demonic trickery!

(BEST goes over to MADY.)

BEST (*calmly*): Who got ya pregnant?

MADY (*shaking her head in desperation*): I'm not pregnant! I'm a virgin!

BEST (*grabs her by the shoulders and shakes her*): Who did it? Who was the dirty bastard? Talk! Come on, talk, or I'll kill ya, I swear! (*BEST raises his fist, LITTLE JOE starts to come to MADY'S defense, but the MONSIGNOR intervenes.*)

MONSIGNOR (*to BEST*): Get away, boy! This is a matter for the Church! I'll find out what's behind all this!

(*BEST turns away from MADY with disgust. From this point on, the MONSIGNOR lapses more and more into his local dialect.*)

MONSIGNOR (*to MADY*): Now, tell me what happened with the boogeymen!

MADY (*softly*): They never let me alone.

MONSIGNOR: What? What do you mean?

MADY: They said I should deny my faith. And I should blaspheme against God. And ridicule the Virgin Mary.

MONSIGNOR: And? What else?

MADY: I should go with them, that's what they said. Then I'd have it real good.

MONSIGNOR: What? Real good?

MADY: That they'd show me a real good time.

MONSIGNOR: Fornication, that what you mean? (*MADY doesn't understand what he means.*) Obscenity! They wanted to seduce you into committing sexual obscenities! Right? (*MADY nods.*) And then what?

MADY: I resisted. And with the help of Jesus and the Sacred Virgin I defeated them, those black boogeymen. And then Jesus chose me for His bride, and from then on they left me alone.

MONSIGNOR: Lies! All lies! Who was it that later pumped up your belly, eh? The Lord Jesus? Was it Him? Talk! Confess!

MADY (*calmly*): I know I'm not guilty. But one time . . . one time I dreamed that the devil jumped up on me and forced himself on me.

(*RUPP starts to squirm again.*)

MONSIGNOR: Aha! Aha! So that's the way it was! Now we're getting to the truth!

MADY: I had a guilty conscience too, about that. But then . . . then the Virgin Mary appeared to me, with the Christ child, and I didn't think anything more about it. Because I knew that the Christ child would never stroke the cheek of someone who had anything to do with the devil.

MONSIGNOR: It's all trickery! Trickery! But I'll help the devil inside you! Sit down in the chair there! Come on, get going! (*MADY stands up, sits down in the chair. The MONSIGNOR says to RUPP:*) Tie her hands and feet to the chair!

RUPP: What?

MONSIGNOR: I'm now going to carry out the ecclesiastical rite of exorcism! The casting out of devils! And as we know from experience, the devil resists!

(*RUPP carries the ropes over to MADY'S chair, starts to tie her hands and feet to the chair.*)

LITTLE JOE: No, don't tie her up! Don't tie her up!

PRIEST: But, your Excellency, is that really necessary?

MONSIGNOR: You're not to interfere from this point on, my friend! How could you let yourself be deceived like this? I guess that alcohol clouded your vision somewhat, eh?

(*The PRIEST stares at the floor, aware of his guilt. LITTLE JOE starts after RUPP.*)

LITTLE JOE: No, don't tie her up!

(*BEST grabs LITTLE JOE by the throat, yanks him back, then looks at him with a threatening glance. LITTLE JOE stays right where he landed on the floor and looks sympa-*

thetically at MADY. MADY, in despair, can only sit there and allow herself to be tied up. The MONSIGNOR then takes from his leather pouch a violet stole, kisses it, and places it over his shoulders; then he pulls out a small red book—the Rituale Romanum, containing the rite of exorcism.)

MONSIGNOR *(to RUPP and BEST)*: Now, you two sit down on either side of her! When she starts to go crazy, you two hold on tight to the chair so she doesn't tip over!

(RUPP and BEST take their stools and sit down right next to MADY, one on either side of her. The MONSIGNOR plants himself squarely in front of MADY, crosses himself, and blesses MADY.)

MONSIGNOR: In nomine Patris, et Filii, et Spiritus sancti. Amen. *(opens the little red book and begins to read aloud)* I command thee, whoever thou might be, impure spirit, and all of thy accomplices who control this servant of God: by virtue of the mysteries of the incarnation, of the crucifixion, of the resurrection and the ascension of our Lord Jesus Christ, by virtue of the emanation of the Holy Spirit and of the return of our Lord Jesus at Judgment Day—speak thy name, the day, and the hour of thy going out, by some sign: And thou, God's unworthy servant, shalt obey me completely in all things; furthermore, thou shalt not harm this creature, or those present, or their messenger in any ways.

(The MONSIGNOR looks at MADY, who shows no reaction. He strikes MADY forcefully on the forehead.)

MONSIGNOR: You're in there, demon! I know it! You're afraid of me, eh? You don't dare do battle with me, eh? God's servant's too powerful for you, eh? But you gotta show yourself, you gotta show yourself, you got no choice! *(He stealthily circles MADY,*

speaking insistently to her:) Come on, come on,
show yourself! I know what kind of demon you are.
Lust! Fornication! Debauchery! Lust! Fornication!
Debauchery!

MADY (*whispers*): Lord Jesus, help!

MONSIGNOR: Lust! Fornication! Debauchery! Come on,
show yourself! Come on! I know you! You won't get
away from me! I'll catch you!

MADY: Oh, Virgin Mary, help!

MONSIGNOR: You got her hot, eh? You tickled her twat,
eh? You screwed her till she passed out, eh?

MADY (*screams in despair*): Jesus, help! Help! Please,
help!

MONSIGNOR: Show yourself, Satan, show yourself! I
know you're in there! (*MADY slips into a trance,
her eyes glaze over.*) Aha! I see you in there! I can see
you in her eyes! Come on out! Come on! Come on
out!

MADY (*screams*): Jesus!

GRESSIL (*speaking through MADY*): Leave us alone, you
black bastard!

MADY (*screams*): Jesus! Jesus!

GRESSIL (*speaking through MADY*): That bastard'd bet-
ter leave us alone, that dirty bastard! (*The FARM-
ER, the FARMER'S WIFE, BEST, RUPP, and
LITTLE JOE are completely dumbfounded.*)

MONSIGNOR (*triumphantly*): Aha! Here he is! Here he is!
Now I've got him! (*He races to his pouch, pulls out a
crucifix, rushes back to MADY, holds the crucifix in
front of her face.*) Here, Satan! Take that! Take
that!

*(By now, MADY is completely possessed. To escape the cru-
cifix, she pulls her head back in terror, growls like a dog,
spits on the crucifix, writhes. The MONSIGNOR presses
the crucifix to her forehead, MADY recoils with her whole
body. BEST and RUPP are barely able to hold her steady.*

Speaking through MADY, all three DEMONS commence a horrible howling. The MONSIGNOR laughs triumphantly, steps back, but continues to hold the crucifix in front of MADY'S face.)

BALBERITH *(speaking through MADY)*: Get that Jew out of here! Get that Jew out of here! I can't stand it! Get that Jew out of here! Oh, I can't stand it!

MONSIGNOR: Aha! So, there's another one! There are two in there! There are two in there! *(Grinning, the MONSIGNOR places the crucifix back on MADY'S forehead, very slowly and with obvious pleasure.)*

BALBERITH *(speaking through MADY)*: Take it away! Take it away! No! No! Argh, that hurts! Oh, that hurts! Ow! Ow! Ow! *(BALBERITH erupts in terrible screams of pain. The MONSIGNOR takes a step back, and the screaming stops. The SCRIBE faithfully writes down every word as fast as he can, though he seems to take the actual events rather calmly.)*

MONSIGNOR: There! And now I'm going to ask you one more time! What are your names, and what kind of demons are you? *(No word out of MADY.)* In God's name! What are you called? *(No word out of MADY. The MONSIGNOR passes the crucifix over her forehead again.)*

BALBERITH *(speaking through MADY)*: No! Don't do that! Take it away! Take that crazy fool on the cross away! Please, take it away!

MONSIGNOR *(pulls the crucifix back)*: What's your name, and who are you?

BALBERITH *(speaking through MADY)*: My name is Balberith! And my specialty is blasphemy! I hate everything that is sacred! Damn everything that is sacred! Damn it! Damn it!

(The MONSIGNOR grins, puts the crucifix and little red book down on the bed, pulls a little bottle of holy water out of his pouch, opens the bottle.)

MONSIGNOR: Look here, Balberith, I've got something really special for you! (*The MONSIGNOR sprinkles some holy water onto the palm of his left hand, smears it on MADY'S forehead, she writhes in pain.*)

BALBERITH (*speaking through Mady, screams frightfully*): Oh, oh, that burns! Oh, it burns! It burns! You damned monk! You dirty bastard! Get away from me with that bottle of piss! Get away! Oh, that burns! Goddamned holy water! Oh, that burns!

GRESSIL (*speaking through MADY*): Shut your trap, Balberith! Can't you see that he's trying to trap us with all his blabbering?!

BALBERITH (*speaking through MADY*): You're the one who answered him first, you ass! You're the one who should've shut your trap!

GRESSIL (*speaking through MADY*): He wouldn't leave us alone, the stupid son-of-a-bitch, the miserable black son-of-a-bitch!

MONSIGNOR: This black son-of-a-bitch'll show you what's what! In God's name I command you to tell me: What's your name, and what kind of demon are you? (*Silence.*) In God's name, answer me!

GRESSIL (*speaking through MADY*): Kiss my ass, you old masturbator!

(*The MONSIGNOR steps up to MADY, puts his stole over her shoulders and holds it together under her chin. MADY writhes, as if she were suffocating.*)

GRESSIL (*speaking through MADY, groans as if he were being strangled*): Oh, don't! You're choking me! You're choking me!

BALBERITH (*speaking through MADY, choking*): Tell him what he wants to know! Tell him! I can't stand it, argh, I can't stand it!

GRESSIL (*speaking through MADY*): I'll tell, I'll tell!

(*The MONSIGNOR removes the stole, places it back over*

his own shoulders.)

MONSIGNOR: Well, then, talk!

GRESSIL *(speaking through MADY)*: My name is Gressil! And my specialty is lechery! I hate everything that is chaste! Damn everything that is chaste! Damn it! Damn it!

MONSIGNOR *(thinking)*: Balberith and Gressil . . . Blasphemy and lechery . . . Could there possibly be another demon in there with you? *(There is no answer.)* By God, I command you to answer me: Are there only two of you, or are there any more? *(No answer, so the MONSIGNOR prepares to take down his stole again.)*

BALBERITH *(speaking through MADY, quickly)* Say something, say something! I'm begging you, say something! Otherwise this damn monk won't leave us alone till he knows everything!

VERRIER *(calmly)*: That damn monk can't do anything to us anyway. His own soul is as black as coal!

MONSIGNOR *(taken aback)*: Huh? What? What'd you say? Who in hell are you?

VERRIER *(speaking through MADY, calmly)*: My name is Verrier. And my specialty is rebellion. I hate everything that is obedient! Damn everything that is obedient! Damn it! Damn it!

MONSIGNOR: Aha! So that's the way it is, eh? And there's nothing I can do to you, you say? And you say my soul is as black as coal?

VERRIER *(speaking through MADY)*: That's exactly right!

MONSIGNOR: Well, I'll show you a thing or two! *(The MONSIGNOR picks up the little red book, quickly makes the sign of the cross over himself, opens the book, holds it in his left hand. He steps up to MADY, places his right hand on her head. Because she immediately tries to pull away, he grabs her head with a claw-like grip and squeezes it brutally. As the MONSIGNOR now begins to read, the DEMONS*

speak to him and to each other. Time and again, the
MONSIGNOR tries to drown out their voices with
his own, but is unable to do it.)

MONSIGNOR (*reads loudly and imploringly*): Therefore
I adjure thee, most vile spirit, the entire specter,
the very embodiment of Satan, in the name of Jesus
Christ (*makes the sign of the cross over Mady*) of
Nazareth, who, after his baptism in Jordan, was
led into the wilderness, and overcame thee in thine
own habitations, that thou stop assaulting him
whom he hath formed from the dust of the earth to
the honor of his glory, and that thou tremble not at
the human weakness in miserable man but at the
image of Almighty God. Therefore, yield to God
(*makes the sign of the cross*), who by his servant
Moses drowned thee and thy malice in Pharoah
and in his army in the abyss. Yield to God (*makes
the sign of the cross*), who made thee flee when ex-
pelled from King Saul with spiritual songs through
his most faithful servant David. Yield to God
(*makes the sign of the cross*), who condemned thee
in Judas Iscariot the traitor. For he beats thee with
divine (*makes the sign of the cross*) scourges, in
whose sight, trembling and crying out with thy le-
gions, thou hast said: What art thou to us, O Jesus,
Son of the most high God? Art thou come hither to
torture us before our time? He presses on thee with
perpetual flames, who shall say at the end of time
to the wicked: Depart from me, ye cursed, into ever-
lasting fire, which is prepared for the devil and his
angels. For thee, impious one, and for thy angels
are prepared worms which never die. For thee and
thy angels is prepared the unquenchable fire; because thou art the chief of accursed murder, thou
art the author of incest, the head of sacrilege, the
master of the worst actions, the teacher of heretics,
the inventor of all obscenities. Therefore, O impious one, go out. Go out, thou scoundrel, go out with
all thy deceits, because God (*makes the sign of the*

cross) has willed that man be his temple. But why dost thou delay longer here? Give honor to God, the Father Almighty (*makes the sign of the cross*), to whom every knee is bent. Give place to the Lord Jesus Christ (*makes the sign of the cross*), who shed for man his most precious blood. Give place to the Holy Ghost (*makes the sign of the cross*), who through his blessed apostle Peter manifestly struck thee in Simon Magus, who condemned thy deceit in Ananias and Sapphira, who smote thee in Herod the King because he did not give God honor, who through his apostle Paul destroyed thee in the magician Elymas by the mist of blindness, and through the same apostle by his word of command bade thee come out of the pythoness. Now therefore depart. (*makes the sign of the cross*) Depart (*makes the sign of the cross*), thou seducer. Thy abode is the wilderness. . . .

(*There is probably more text here than the speeches of the DEMONS requires, which take place simultaneously with the MONSIGNOR'S reading of the rite of exorcism.*)

VERRIER (*speaking through MADY*): That's enough, stop, that won't help you at all! If you want to have power over us, you must live according to the commandments of old Mr. Soandso; if you want to have power over us, you've got to have one thing above all: humility! But are you humble, you old goat? Are you really, eh? Weren't you the one who slandered that candidate for Bishop in Rome, didn't you lie up one side and down the other, didn't you kiss the asses of those guys in the Curia? And wouldn't you rather bite the hand of the man who's taken your place as Bishop than kiss his ring?

BALBERITH (*speaking through MADY*): So, you're amazed at how much we know, eh? What a shame, the crazy Jew's got real problems with his successors!

GRESSIL (*speaking through MADY*): And you really know

how to live it up, eh? You stuff yourself and drink your fill, sleep late in the morning in a big soft bed ... And the temptation of the flesh, the temptation of the flesh bothers you too, doesn't it? Can you still remember, two months ago? When you were in that place ... In that place overrun with tits and ass and cunts! Man, you fucked your brains out, wallowed in it, groveled in it, you horny bastard, you whore-monger, you ...

(By the end of GRESSIL'S speech, the MONSIGNOR has stopped reading, angrily picks up the bottle of holy water, opens it, and empties the contents over MADY'S head. ALL THREE DEMONS, speaking through MADY, emit a long, horrible howl. MADY writhes in pain, throws herself back in the chair, BEST and RUPP can't hold the chair, it falls over with MADY tied to it. BEST and RUPP strain to right the chair with MADY in it, hold on tight in shock. The MONSIGNOR observes MADY'S agony with grim satisfaction, then picks up the little red book again and continues with the incantation of the exorcism ritual.)

BALBERITH *(speaking through MADY, groaning)*: What a bastard, a miserable bastard! Goddamned asshole of a priest! Oh, it's too hot! I can't stand it much longer!

GRESSIL *(speaking through MADY)*: This son-of-a-bitch is the world's biggest sinner and thinks he's got power over us!

BALBERITH *(speaking through MADY)*: That's the power of that crazy Jew!

GRESSIL *(speaking through MADY)*: Oh, damn, I can't breathe in here! Verrier, what'll we do?

VERRIER *(speaking through MADY, calmly)*: Leave.

BALBERITH *(speaking through MADY)*: What! Just like that? Didn't you say that it wouldn't do him any good, that penguin?!

VERRIER *(speaking through MADY)*: Yes, that's just what

I said. And that's the way it's going to be, too! Listen here! I'll tell you what we're going to do!

(A few seconds after VERRIER'S last speech, the MONSIGNOR suddenly interrupts his incantation, casts the book away, and pulls off his stole, growling. His face now reveals an expression of demonic possession; simultaneously, MADY comes to her senses and watches the following events in astonishment and fear.)

VERRIER (*speaking through the MONSIGNOR*): Well, how do you like it in here?

GRESSIL (*speaking through the MONSIGNOR*): Ahhh, it's great in here, inside this fat, warm belly! Just like home!

BALBERITH (*speaking through the MONSIGNOR*): Oh, yeah, much better than being inside that bitch. *(The MONSIGNOR points to MADY.)* She's not our type! Always whining to that same old mother who has the little bastard on her lap!

GRESSIL (*speaking through the MONSIGNOR*): How 'bout showing us a dance, preacher!

(The MONSIGNOR begins to dance madly around MADY, making obscene movements.)

GRESSIL (*speaking through the MONSIGNOR, sings*):
Now the farmer likes to hammer,
And the blacksmith likes to hammer,
And the girl in the barn hammers too
Too bad my honey won't hammer.

(The MONSIGNOR stops, looks around wildly with bulging eyes.)

VERRIER (*speaking through the MONSIGNOR*):
I'll poison the Bishop.
I'll kill the dirty dog.
I was supposed to get the appointment,
And not that filthy hog!

(The MONSIGNOR resumes his wild dance ᵎ

GRESSIL (*speaking through the MONSIGNOR, sings*):
    Now a real sharp blade
    Needs oiling every day
    Needs lots of attention
    For work or for play.

(The MONSIGNOR stops dancing, looks at his habit.)

BALBERITH (*speaking through the MONSIGNOR*): I
    hate this stupid habit! I hate it! I hate it!

*(The MONSIGNOR shreds his upper garment, then
stretches his arms toward Heaven.)*

VERRIER (*speaking through the MONSIGNOR*): Down
    with the Almighty! Down with the Almighty!
    Down with Him!

*(The MONSIGNOR collapses, looks about fearfully,
gnashing his teeth, sits down tottering, stares straight
ahead with bulging eyes, making growling noises. LITTLE
JOE bursts out laughing, runs over to the MONSIGNOR
and makes the sign of "Shame on you" with the index fingers of both hands.)*

LITTLE JOE: Phooey! Phooey! Phooey! Got you this time,
    huh? Got you this time!

*(With a look of despair on his face, the MONSIGNOR bares
his teeth and growls at LITTLE JOE. LITTLE JOE goes
over to MADY and unties her bonds; no one stops him. The
PRIEST goes over to the MONSIGNOR, takes him by the
shoulders and shakes him.)*

PRIEST: Your Excellency! Your Excellency! Oh, Holy Vir-
    gin, help! Monsignor!

*(The MONSIGNOR looks up at the PRIEST. For a moment
the demonic possession passes, and he stares at the
PRIEST in despair.)*

MONSIGNOR (*tormented*): Ubique daemon! Ubique dae-
    mon! The Demon is everywhere! (*The MONSI-
    GNOR looks over at the others, his eyes focus on*

*BEST, and the expression of demonic possession re-
turns.*)

BALBERITH (*speaking through the MONSIGNOR*):
Best!

BEST (*frightened*): Huh?

BALBERITH (*speaking through the MONSIGNOR*): You
know, I really like you a lot, I like you a whole lot!

BEST: Whadd'ya mean?

BALBERITH (*speaking through the MONSIGNOR*):
Come on, Best! You know what I mean, don't you?

BEST: Don't know what you're talking about.

BALBERITH (*speaking through the MONSIGNOR*): So,
you don't know what I'm talking about, eh? Tell me
about your hand—about your hand that never
shakes! (*BEST becomes nervous. BALBERITH
mimics BEST'S voice:*) Every shot's right on the
mark. And if somebody tries to kill me, he can't do
it. A thousand bullets'd bounce off me, like bouncing off a stone. I'm invulnerable. (*BALBERITH giggles.*)

(*BEST is terrified. The FARMER glances back and forth,
from BEST to the MONSIGNOR*)

FARMER: What?

BALBERITH (*speaking through the MONSIGNOR*): Your
foreman, he's defiled the host. But, let's not talk
about it anymore! It's all right with me! (*He giggles*).

FARMER: But I want to know exactly what's going on!

VERRIER (*speaking through the MONSIGNOR*): Shut
your trap, farmer! You've done a thing or two in
your day!

(*The MONSIGNOR leaps up.*)

GRESSIL (*speaking through the MONSIGNOR*): I know
something else! I know something else!

PRIEST (*hesitantly*): What's that?

GRESSIL (*speaking through the MONSIGNOR*): I know

who jumped Mady!

(ALL leap to their feet, except MADY and RUPP. RUPP stares straight ahead, panic-stricken.)

BEST: Who? Who jumped her?

BALBERITH *(speaking through the MONSIGNOR, mocks)*: The mother always knows, the father never knows for sure!

(The MONSIGNOR points to RUPP.)

GRESSIL *(speaking through the MONSIGNOR)*: He's the one who humped her! Rupp!

(ALL are astonished.)

BALBERITH *(speaking through the MONSIGNOR, mockingly to RUPP)*: Cherry-popper! Cherry-popper!

(RUPP stands up.)

FARMER *(incredulously)*: My son? You think it was my son who did it?

GRESSIL *(speaking through the MONSIGNOR)*: Surprised, eh? He put on a devil's mask, the horny bastard, and pounced on her in the middle of the night! And the stupid bitch . . . *(The MONSIGNOR points to MADY.)* . . . she thought the whole thing was just a dream!

(MADY is stunned.)

VERRIER *(speaking through the MONSIGNOR, calmly)*: I wouldn't put up with that if I were you, Best.

GRESSIL *(speaking through the MONSIGNOR)*: And you didn't mind it a bit, now, did you, Mady?! *(mimics passionate moaning sounds)* Oh! Oh! Oh! Ah! Ah! Ah! Lord, that was great, wasn't it?

MADY: Not true! That's a lie! I swear by the Virgin Mary!

BALBERITH *(speaking through the MONSIGNOR, growling)*: Oh, come on, don't mention that old bitch again! I can't stand to hear that name!

VERRIER *(speaking through the MONSIGNOR, calmly)* : I wouldn't put up with that if I were you, Best.

(BEST slowly walks over to RUPP, grabs RUPP by the throat with both hands and squeezes, RUPP falls to his knees, gasping for breath, BEST continues to choke him. The FARMER and the FARMER'S WIFE rush over and try to tear BEST away, but BEST can't be stopped. The PRIEST tries to help, too, attempting to pry BEST'S fingers loose. The SCRIBE watches the action somewhat frightened, but remains seated. LITTLE JOE watches the murder with interest and not without a certain amount of satisfaction.)

FARMER'S WIFE: Let him go! Please, let him go! I'm begging you, Best, let go!

(MADY comes over.)

MADY: Best! Don't ruin your life! I'm begging you! Best!

PRIEST: For God's sake, Best, stop! For God's sake!

(The MONSIGNOR has watched the preceding events closely, gnashing his teeth and grinning. RUPP is dead, BEST lets him go, RUPP sinks to the floor. The FARMER'S WIFE kneels down over RUPP, shakes him.)

FARMER'S WIFE: Rupp! My baby! My baby! My baby!

BALBERITH *(speaking through the MONSIGNOR, giggles)*: Ha-ha! He's dead! He's dead! Now he's all ours! Now he's all ours!

(BEST now looks at MADY with profound disgust and bitterness, and exits upstage)

MADY *(calls after him)*: Best!

(Sobbing, the FARMER'S WIFE cradles RUPP's head in her lap. Stunned, the FARMER stands over them, looking down at his son. The PRIEST kneels down beside RUPP, murmurs a prayer, gives him the Last Rites and gets back up.)

FARMER *(in a monotone)*: My own flesh and blood. My

own flesh and blood. My only boy. My only boy. The last of my line.

(From offstage, the sound of a rifleshot. ALL turn their heads upstage.)

BALBERITH *(speaking through the MONSIGNOR, giggles)*: Ha-ha! Another one bites the dust! Now he's all ours! Ha-ha! Now he's all ours!

(MADY and LITTLE JOE run upstage and exit. The FARMER snorts in rage, looks around, completely beside himself, picks up one of the ropes lying on the floor, and also exits upstage. The MONSIGNOR emerges from his demonic possession, his devlish grin disappears, he looks at RUPP in confusion and torment. The FARMER'S WIFE runs after her husband.)

FARMER'S WIFE *(calls after him)*: Oh, dear! Dear!

PRIEST: Oh, my God! My God! Why do You let all this happen? Why?

MONSIGNOR *(softly)*: Help me, Father, I beg you, help me!

PRIEST: Of course, what can I do, your Excellency?

VOICE OF MADY *(from offstage)*: No, don't! Don't! What are you doing? Farmer! Farmer!!

(The PRIEST and the MONSIGNOR turn, look upstage. MADY comes running.)

MADY: Father! Please, help! The farmer's hanging Best!

PRIEST: What?

(The PRIEST runs upstage with MADY and exits. The MONSIGNOR is left sitting there in despair, suddenly feels himself sinking under the DEMONS' spell, leaps up and waives his arms to fend off the devils.)

MONSIGNOR *(screaming)*: Apage Satana! Apage Satana! Depart Satan! *(He kneels, makes the sign of the cross, begins to pray the 30th Psalm in a loud voice. The SCRIBE takes a pinch of snuff, watches the*

MONSIGNOR.)

MONSIGNOR *(praying)*: Ad te, Dómine, confúgio. In Thee, O Lord, have I hoped, let me never be confounded: deliver me in thy justice. Bow down thy ear to me: make haste to deliver me. Be thou unto me a God, a protector, and a house of refuge, to save me. For thou art my strength and my refuge; and for thy name's sake thou wilt lead me, and nourish me. Thou wilt bring me out of this snare, which they have hidden for me . . .

(From upstage enter: the PRIEST, the FARMER, the FARMER'S WIFE, MADY, and LITTLE JOE. The MONSIGNOR interrupts his prayer, gets up.)

PRIEST *(to the FARMER)*: To hang a dead man! To hang a corpse! What've we come to? I tell you, if I weren't God's servant, I'd curse you on the spot! Curse you! What a dreadful thing to do! What you've done is horrible! Just horrible!

(The FARMER doesn't answer, immobilized by his grief and anger; he sits down, stares at RUPP, buries his face in his hands. The FARMER'S WIFE kneels down before RUPP, looks at him in despair, gently brushes a strand of hair from his forehead.)

MONSIGNOR *(helplessly, to the PRIEST)*: I beg you, Father, help me! I can tell, they're coming back to get me!

PRIEST: Oh, leave me alone! Help yourself! After all, who was it who started all this devil crap? Eh? Who started it? Who was it who conjured up all this misery? You! It was you! You were the one who invited all this trouble, and then the devil came after all!

MONSIGNOR: What? What are you saying? I was the one who conjured up this mess? Well, I certainly won't take the blame for all this, most certainly not! I wasn't the one who caused this calamity, it was that damned woman over there! *(He points to MADY.*)

PRIEST: This damned woman, as you call her, your Excellency, is a pure white lily among stinking weeds! This damned woman, as you call her, your Excellency, is an innocent child of God! And if she were pregnant ten times over, she'd still be a saint, as far as I'm concerned!

MONSIGNOR (*with disdain*): A saint! Humph! That woman a saint! Never! And besides: Omnia mala ex mulieribus! All evil derives from woman! (*to the SCRIBE:*) Pack up, we're leaving!

(The SCRIBE sets about packing, when something occurs to the MONSIGNOR: he walks over to the SCRIBE, takes the notebook from his hands, thumbs through it, reads, looks at the SCRIBE in disgust, then tears out all the pages that have to do with him, puts them in a pocket of his cassock, and tosses the remains of the notebook back to the SCRIBE. While the SCRIBE is packing all his utensils together, the MONSIGNOR searches for his stole and for the little red exorcism book, puts them in his leather pouch, closes it, hands it to the SCRIBE, and exits, without so much as a word to the others. The SCRIBE follows,—also without a word to the others—carrying his satchel and that of the MONSIGNOR. It is almost completely dark outside, so the SCRIBE comes back in, silently picks up the lantern, exits after the MONSIGNOR. Neither the MONSIGNOR nor the SCRIBE cross themselves as they hurriedly pass by the wayside cross.)

Fifteenth Station

Outdoors, daytime.

(The FARMER is sitting on the bench, stage left, brooding. MADY enters from upstage, packed and ready to leave. She is carrying a bundle containing her few earthly possessions

*and wearing half-gloves. The FARMER'S WIFE, dressed
in black mourning clothes, comes running after her.)*

FARMER'S WIFE: Stay, Mady, oh, please, stay!

FARMER: She's leaving!

FARMER'S WIFE: Oh, husband, please reconsider!

FARMER: All because of her, my son had to die! (*He stands
up*) Either she goes, or I'll butcher her like a rabbit!

*(LITTLE JOE enters from upstage. He, too, is dressed and
ready to leave, carrying a tiny bundle and a wooden staff.)*

FARMER: And just where do you think you're going?

LITTLE JOE: If Mady goes, I do too!

FARMER: You're staying!

LITTLE JOE: I'm leaving!

FARMER: I say, you're staying put!

LITTLE JOE: If Mady goes, I do too!

*(The FARMER rips the bundle out of LITTLE JOE'S hand
and flings it upstage.)*

FARMER: Either you stay, or I'll get the police! There's no
such thing as quitting before the year's up!

FARMER'S WIFE: I've had just about enough out of you,
Mr. Know-it-all! Mady's carrying Rupp's baby! Our
grandchild, you hear? Don't you understand that?

FARMER: That's the devil's child!

FARMER'S WIFE: Oh, what're you talking about! The
devil's child! It's Rupp's child! It's your own flesh
and blood!

(The FARMER is confused.)

MADY: That's all right, Ma'am. It's probably better if I go.
Should've left a long time ago. Back when the
farmer first tried to kick me out. Then none of this
would've happened.

FARMER: That's right! That's exactly right! (*to the
FARMER'S WIFE:*) But you talked me out of it, you
and your stupid dream!

FARMER'S WIFE: Fine! Fine! Then that's it! Kick your own grandchild out of the house! (*She walks upstage, turns back.*) But you'd better get one thing straight: from now on there's a wall between us, and you'll never be able to break down that wall! (*The FARMER'S WIFE walks on.*)

FARMER: Wait! Wait! Aw, goddammit!

(*The FARMER'S WIFE stops, turns around. The FARMER can't seem to decide, then finally makes up his mind.*)

FARMER (*to MADY*): Okay! You can stay! But that child won't ever know that you're the mother! The child belongs to me, got it? I'm going to raise that baby! I want an heir for my farm!

MADY: No, farmer, that won't work.

(*MADY turns to leave. The FARMER'S WIFE runs after her.*)

FARMER'S WIFE (*aside, to MADY*): Mady! That's just a lot of hogwash! Don't believe a word he says! You'll always be the baby's mother! Always! Just leave it to me. That stubborn old goat . . . (*nods over toward the FARMER*) . . . well, I'll handle him!

(*MADY thinks it over, the FARMER'S WIFE looks at her, lovingly.*)

FARMER'S WIFE: Mady!

MADY: All right.

(*The FARMER'S WIFE hugs MADY, leads her back downstage.*)

LITTLE JOE (*to MADY*): You gonna stay after all?

MADY: Yes, I'm staying.

LITTLE JOE: Okay, then I'll stick around, too.

(*Black-out*)

Sixteenth Station

Inside, daytime.

(MADY is sitting on a chair next to her bed, spinning wool on a spinning wheel. She is very pregnant. She wears half-gloves. After a while she feels the child moving inside her, looks down at her stomach, stops spinning, removes the gloves, lays both hands on her stomach, feels the child and smiles, happily. Then her hands move slowly higher to her breasts, she gently fondles them. All the while she stares straight ahead with her hands on her breasts, then opens her blouse, exposing her left breast, gently touches the wound in her side, recoils slightly, then holds her left hand cupped under her breast, strokes her breast with her right hand and then expresses a few drops of milk, gently rubs it over the wound in her side, expresses a few more drops of milk and gently rubs it over the wound on her left palm, then expresses a few drops of milk with her left hand and gently rubs it over the wound on her right palm. Then she slips out of her wooden clogs, removes her wollen socks, expresses more milk from her left breast and gently rubs it over her footwounds. Then she buttons up her blouse, puts on her socks, her clogs, then her gloves, and resumes spinning. The PRIEST comes up the road and approaches MADY. He appears completely dejected.)

PRIEST: Blessed be the Lord, Mady my child!
(MADY stops spinning.)
MADY *(happily)*: For ever and ever, Amen, Father!
PRIEST: *(looking at her stomach)*: Anytime now, eh?

(Smiling, MADY nods. The PRIEST sits down on a stool, pulls out his hipflask, takes a swig, holds the flask in his hand, stares off into space, obviously depressed.)

MADY: Something wrong, Father?

(The PRIEST sighs, takes another swig, looks MADY in the eye.)

PRIEST: I got two letters. One is about you and the other one is about me.

MADY: Letters from who?

PRIEST: From the Archdiocese.

MADY: What do they say?

PRIEST: In mine they wrote that I'm being transferred, and in yours they wrote that you're ... excommunicated.

(They look at each other. The PRIEST takes a swig from his flask, gazes down at the floor. They are both silent for a while. MADY doesn't really comprehend the word "excommunicated.")

MADY *(softly)*: It's my fault that you're being transferred, isn't it?

PRIEST: Mady my child, that's not important at all! Whether I'm a priest in this town or in that one, what's the difference! But you've been excommunicated! That's the worst thing! Don't you know what that means?

MADY: Well, not exactly ...

PRIEST: Excommunication means exclusion from the community of the Church! You can't ever enter a church again, you can't ever take the sacraments again, no holy communion, nothing! And when you die, you won't be buried in consecrated ground — they'll throw you on the dung heap!

(MADY now understands the horror of his words, begins to cry, covers her face with her hands. Depressed, the PRIEST looks at her, takes another drink from his flask, puts it away, stands up and walks over to MADY, puts his hand on her shoulder.)

PRIEST: Now, listen here, Mady my child! God in Heaven, you, and I—the three of us know that you never sinned. And as far as those demons are concerned, well, that doesn't prove a thing. Every one of us, every single person has demons inside him. They're just waiting to be set free. And sometimes, I say to myself, a demon like that isn't necessarily satanic, isn't necessarily evil, it's just our desire for freedom. Monsignor Pfetscher ought to know that as well as anybody. But he doesn't want to hear about it, he doesn't want to admit it to himself! And so his guilty conscience caused your excommunication. That's the way it is, Mady my child. And that's why I'm going to ignore it. As far as I'm concerned, you're still a member of the Catholic Church. (*He reaches into his pocket, pulls out the snuffbox, opens it, offers it to MADY.*) Look, there are twenty consecrated hosts in here. Take one every Sunday. When they're gone, come see me in my new parish and I'll give you a refill.

(*MADY gladly takes the snuffbox, looks at the hosts, closes the snuffbox, kisses it, puts it in her pocket, falls on her knees, and kisses the PRIEST'S hand.*)

MADY: Praise the Lord! Praise the Lord!

PRIEST: That's all right, Mady my child, it's all right. Now let me give you my blessing, then I've got to go. The new priest'll be here tomorrow. (*He makes the sign of the cross over MADY.*) In nomine Patris, et Filii, et Spiritus Sancti. Amen. (*The PRIEST helps MADY up, smiles at her sadly.*) May the good Lord be with you.

MADY: And with your spirit.

(*The PRIEST exits.*)

(*Stagelights slowly dim*)

Seventeenth Station

Split scene—indoors / outdoors, daytime.

(MADY is sitting on a chair near her bed, in front of a cradle. She rocks the cradle with one foot, looks at the child lovingly. The wounds have disappeared, she is no longer wearing gloves. LITTLE JOE enters from upstage, running. He is all dressed and ready to leave, carrying a loaded backpack on his back and a milkcan in each hand.)

LITTLE JOE: Hurry, Mady, we gotta go!

MADY *(puts her finger in front of her mouth)*: Shhhh! Not so loud! He's sleeping.

LITTLE JOE: Come on, hurry up, we gotta go!

MADY: What for?

LITTLE JOE: I saw an angel!

MADY: An angel?

LITTLE JOE: Yeah, an angel! Little Joe, pack your stuff, he said, you and Mady've got to leave, as fast as your little feet'll carry you! Please, Mady, come on, come on!

(A SHERIFF in civilian clothes and two provincial DEPUTIES in uniform approach along the road. MADY hesitates, LITTLE JOE is beside himself.)

LITTLE JOE: Gotta go now, Mady! Get your baby stuff together! Bad people are coming, bad people! They want to take you away!

(MADY still hesitates, looks at LITTLE JOE, looks at her baby, then makes up her mind, reaches into the cradle, wraps the child in its blanket, takes it out of the cradle. LITTLE JOE leads the way, MADY follows him. Downstage they run into the SHERIFF. and his DEPUTIES. LITTLE JOE and MADY stop dead in their tracks, LITTLE JOE is so frightened that he drops both his milkcans. Milk spills out of the first can, blood spills out of the second.

The SHERIFF and DEPUTIES look down in amazement at the milk and the blood.)

SHERIFF: What's your hurry?

LITTLE JOE (*stammering*): We aren't the ones! We're migrant workers!

SHERIFF: That so? Migrant workers, eh? (*He looks at MADY'S hands, calls upstage:*) Hey, there, anybody in the house?

(LITTLE JOE motions to MADY, starts off in the direction of the road, but the SHERIFF gently puts his hand on LITTLE JOE'S chest to stop him. LITTLE JOE looks over at the two DEPUTIES and stops. The FARMER and the FARMER'S WIFE approach from upstage, are amazed when they see the SHERIFF and the TWO DEPUTIES, MADY and LITTLE JOE, the milk and the blood.)

FARMER (*to the SHERIFF*): What's going on?

SHERIFF: We're looking for a servant girl named Maria who goes by the name of Mady. She's supposed to have Christ's wounds.

FARMER (*pointing to MADY*): That's her. But she doesn't have the wounds anymore.

SHERIFF (*to LITTLE JOE*): Migrant workers, eh? (*He pulls out an official document, turns to MADY:*) The Office of Public Safety in the capital has received a report from the Archdiocese which says, among other things: (*unfolds the document and reads aloud:*) By the authority of his Excellency, Prince-Bishop so-and-so, etc., etc., the above-named individual was closely examined by Monsignor Pfetscher and Dr. von Achammer, Professor of Medicine, etc., etc., etc. . . . (*skipping over several sentences*) . . . and therefore the Monsignor has come to the conclusion that this individual was possessed by the devil; however, the Professor was of the opinion that the individual was a pathological liar. Regardless, both gentlemen agree that the

above-named individual represents a danger to society for numerous reasons, first and foremost because she incited the peasantry against the civilian authorities and against the Church. Etc., etc., etc. .
. . *(The SHERIFF folds up the document and puts it back in his pocket.)* On the basis of this report, the Director for Public Safety has issued a warrent for your arrest. Come along with me, please!

(The FARMER goes over to MADY, takes the baby away from her.)

FARMER: But the baby stays!

SHERIFF: I'm not interested in the baby.

(The FARMER places the baby in his WIFE'S arms. MADY lurches over to her, tries to take the baby back, but the FARMER flings her away, knocking her to the ground.)

SHERIFF *(to the DEPUTIES)*: Handcuffs!

(The FIRST DEPUTY pulls out handcuffs, the SECOND DEPUTY holds MADY, who has just gotten up and wants to get her baby. The FIRST DEPUTY tries to put the handcuffs on MADY, but meanwhile LITTLE JOE has pulled out his pocketknife and opened it, now leaps at the FIRST DEPUTY and slashes at him several times, wounding him on the arm. The SECOND DEPUTY lets go of MADY, tries to grab LITTLE JOE, as does the SHERIFF. The FIRST DEPUTY holds his bleeding arm. The FARMER doesn't interfere. LITTLE JOE retreats, holding the knife in front of him in a threatening gesture, then leaps at the SECOND DEPUTY, who retreats; LITTLE JOE then leaps at the SHERIFF, who also retreats.)

LITTLE JOE: Run, Mady! Run!

(MADY doesn't run. As the SECOND DEPUTY unshoulders his rifle, cocks it, and aims at LITTLE JOE, MADY throws herself with outstretched arms in front of LITTLE JOE. The SECOND DEPUTY fires, and MADY

falls to the ground, dead. Total silence for a moment. LIT-
TLE JOE stares incomprehendingly at MADY, then drops
his knife. After another pause, LITTLE JOE lets out an ag-
onized cry and falls to his knees, shakes MADY violently,
then takes her in his arms, pulls her up, cradles her in a
pieta. Then he starts to rock her in his arms, like a child.)

(A group of farmhands hurry down the road toward the
farmyard—the same ones as in the Tenth and Eleventh
Stations. Several of the FARMHANDS have long staffs
with iron tips, in fact three FARMHANDS are obviously
armed: one is carrying an axe, the second a sickle, the third
a manure fork. The SHERIFF and TWO DEPUTIES ap-
pear surprised and nervous. The FARMHANDS arrive,
discover MADY is dead, approach her, look at her, the men
take off their hats, a few look angrily at the SHERIFF and
the TWO DEPUTIES.)

SHERIFF: What's going on here? Huh? What do you want?
      All right, somebody'd better talk!

(Several of the FARMHANDS look at the SHERIFF threat-
eningly, the OTHERS pay no attention to him; they are
looking at MADY, stunned. The FARMHAND with the axe
starts to go after the SHERIFF, but another FARMHAND
holds him back—the SHERIFF doesn't notice. The SHE-
RIFF tugs at the FOREMAN'S shirtsleeve.)

SHERIFF: Hey, you, tell me what's going on here!

(The OLD MAID approaches, leaning on a stick for sup-
port, led by a YOUNG MAID.)

FOREMAN (*to the SHERIFF*): Two farmhands seen you
      guys coming up the hill. And they figured out right
      away that you was after our Mady. Didn't take long
      for the news t'spread like wildfire.
SHERIFF: Yeah—so what?
FOREMAN: We wanted to stand by our Mady.

(The FOREMAN looks at MADY, then suddenly grabs the SHERIFF by the throat. The SECOND DEPUTY pulls him off, aims his rifle at him. A couple of other FARM-HANDS slowly advance, place themselves in front of the FOREMAN as a shield, look calmly at the frightened TWO DEPUTIES who glance imploringly at the SHERIFF.)

SHERIFF *(screams)*: This is rebellion! Rebellion!

(The FARMHANDS just look at him calmly, and now the SHERIFF also becomes frightened. The OLD MAID arrives with the YOUNG MAID, she sees MADY, hobbles over to her, kneels down by her, looks at her. LITTLE JOE stops rocking MADY. The OLD MAID kisses MADY on the fore-head, looks up at the SHERIFF and the TWO DEPUTIES, slowly gets up, looks around at the assembled FARM-HANDS, then gazes up toward Heaven, remains in this po-sition a moment, then begins to speak, as if in a dream.)

OLD MAID: And there will appear in the heavens a great sign—a woman, cloaked with the sun, the moon be-neath her feet, and on her head a wreath of twelve stars. And the woman will commence to speak in a loud voice, saying: Gather unto me, you poor, gather unto me, you who have no voice, gather unto me, join in the great feast, to eat the flesh of kings, and the flesh of warriors, and the flesh of those who feast on our flesh and blood. Thus the woman will say, and we shall come, with hoes and sickles and scythes, and will harvest what is rightfully ours.

(The FARMHANDS have been listening attentively and with reverence to the OLD MAID. The SHERIFF and the TWO DEPUTIES are totally confused and frightened to death. A few of the FARMHANDS now look over at the three officers of the law, then very deliberately and threateningly approach them. The SHERIFF and the TWO DEPUTIES retreat, the SHERIFF suddenly turns and runs away in the direction of the road; the TWO DEPUTIES follow him, the SECOND DEPUTY running his first few steps backwards,

his rifle at the ready. The FARMHANDS watch them run off. When they've gone, the FARMHANDS return to MADY. The OLD MAID kneels down beside MADY and LITTLE JOE, ALL OTHERS follow her example. The FARMER remains standing. The FARMER'S WIFE, holding the baby in her arms, is the last one to kneel. After a while the FARMER slowly wanders upstage and exits. The stagelights gradually dim and go out; simultaneously, a spotlight , focusing on MADY and LITTLE JOE, grows ever brighter. Finally, we can see only MADY and LITTLE JOE in the radiant spotlight—which gradually grows weaker and weaker, until the entire stage is enveloped in total darkness.)

THE END

Visiting Hours

Four One-Act Plays

Translated by

Udo Borgert, Gertraud Ingeborg,
David Ritchie

Shunted into a Siding

Characters

An OLD MAN
His DAUGHTER-IN-LAW

Set

Visiting room in an old people's home

(A table and two chairs. The OLD MAN and his DAUGH-TER-IN-LAW come in, he has a walking stick and she supports him. she wears an overcoat, which she does not take off)

DAUGHTER-IN-LAW: Sorry, I'm a bit pushed for time.

(She helps him to sit down, then sits down herself, taking a bag of peanuts and a brightly painted hat out of a handbag) Here's your peanuts, and Anita wants you to have this. A paper hat. She made it at kindergarten.

OLD MAN: *(Taking the hat and looking at it)* Very nice. Glad to have it.

(He puts the hat on, the DAUGHTER-IN-LAW smiles, he reaches into his pocket, taking out some coins) Give her this. For an ice cream.

DAUGHTER- IN-LAW: Come on, there's no need for that. She gets too much ice cream as it is.

OLD MAN: Let her put it in her piggy bank instead, then.

DAUGHTER-IN-LAW: *(Looking at the schilling coins, she then takes them and puts them into her pocket)* We haven't been to see you for ages. Forgive us.

OLD MAN: Well, I understand that. After all, who wants to

come to an old people's home?

DAUGHTER- IN-LAW: Franz had to fix something on the car. Else he'd have come too. Sends his love.

OLD MAN: (*Nods. a few moments' silence*) How is my Haika?

DAUGHTER-IN-LAW: Well, you know. She's old.

OLD MAN: She doesn't like me not being there, does she?

DAUGHTER-IN-LAW: No, she doesn't like it.

OLD MAN: (*After a pause*) Much dearer is my dog to me. Than you, oh, man. Is that a sin? In howling storms my dog stays true, You pack and leave me in the wind. (*a few moments' silence*) How are you all?

DAUGHTER-IN-LAW: Oh, you know, we're all right. We'd like to get away for a holiday. But what with all the credit payments and everything . . . they've stopped Franz doing overtime.

OLD MAN: Holiday? . . . I've never been away. Except for the war. It's pretty enough around here.

DAUGHTER-IN-LAW: It would be good to see a few different faces.

OLD MAN: You think you'll see different faces in Jesolo?

DAUGHTER-IN-LAW: A few days without housework . . .

OLD MAN: You'll get nothing out of me, if that's what you mean. I'm leaving my savings to Albert.

DAUGHTER-IN-LAW: So. Did I say anything?

OLD MAN: Holidays are a new-fangled idea. Go for a good walk in the forest.

DAUGHTER-IN-LAW: I knew it. You are angry with us.

OLD MAN: No, I'm not. Not at all. I understand things well enough.

DAUGHTER-IN-LAW: I simply couldn't cope any more. And you're well looked after here.

OLD MAN: Everything is fine I've got what I need. Only the food's muck, that's got to be said : "Eat up nicely, Grandpa, or you won' t get any stewed fruit." What do I want with stewed fruit? I've complained to the director again and again, but it's useless. He grins at me and underneath he's thinking: " Why doesn't he bugger off, the old fool." (*Confidentially, in a low voice*) So, now, I've written to the President.

DAUGHTER-IN-LAW: What?

OLD MAN: "The food is terrible," I wrote. "The home takes nearly all my pension, and in return I expect nutritious and tasty meals," I wrote.

DAUGHTER-IN-LAW: Really! You mustn't do these things. I beg you ! What's the use of it. Fussy, that's what you are.

OLD MAN: What am I?

DAUGHTER-IN-LAW: You were always pestering me about my cooking.

OLD MAN: So that's it. Well then, goodbye. Thanks for the visit.

DAUGHTER-IN-LAW: Come on, Grandpa!

OLD MAN: I'm not your Grandpa. I'm your father-in-law. Now, please, you show me some respect.

(A moment's silence)

DAUGHTER-IN-LAW: I am fond of you, Helmut . Otherwise I wouldn't come and visit you.

OLD MAN: It's all right. I'm sorry.

DAUGHTER-IN-LAW: Don't you want to take that hat off?

OLD MAN: What for?

DAUGHTER-IN-LAW: Just because.

OLD MAN: It's something Anita made for me. She thinks of me.

(The OLD MAN opens the packet of peanuts, takes some nuts out, starts shelling them, eats)

DAUGHTER-IN-LAW: So, now you've run away. They phoned us.

OLD MAN: Just a little excursion.

DAUGHTER-IN-LAW: The police picked you up on a park bench in the middle of the night. You'd been sleeping on it.

OLD MAN: Because I was tired.

DAUCHTER-IN-LAW: You were "disoriented," the police said.

OLD MAN: "Disoriented"?

DAUGHTER-IN-LAW: Yes.

OLD MAN: You'd also be "disoriented" if the police woke you up from a deep sleep.

DAUGHTER-IN-LAW: Please don't ever do that again, Helmut. (*The OLD MAN silently eats the nuts, letting the shells drop onto the floor*) Where did you go, by the way?

OLD MAN: Around our neighborhood. Talking to people.

DAUGHTER-IN-LAW: You didn't come home and see us.

OLD MAN: Yes, I did. I stood outside the house. I thought I'd just see if Haika would pick up my scent. (*Sadly*) But she didn't notice anything. Maybe it's because I've got the smell of the old people's home on me now. It's quite a unique smell. All the inmates in an old people's home give off the same smell! A uniform smell! Actually, more of a stink. The stink of the grave.

DAUGHTER-IN-LAW: What?

OLD MAN: The stink of the grave! The smell of corpses.

DAUGHTER-IN-LAW: Stop it, Grandpa! Bathe more often! I was always telling you that at home!

OLD MAN: If you must know, daughter-in-law, it's got nothing to do with that. We do bathe. Twice a week! (*Laughs, whispering consplratorlally*) You know, when it's time for my bath I pretend to be all weak and frail.

DAUGHTER-IN-LAW: Why?

OLD MAN: Because then two of the slant-eyed lasses take me to the bathroom, undress me, lift me very carefully into the bathtub and wash me, all over! (*Laughing with satisfaction*) Then I feel as if I'm in a massage parlor in Thailand!

DAUGHTER-IN-LAW: How'd you know what goes on in a Thai massage parlor?

OLD MAN: One reads about it! In magazines! (*Laughing*) Ha, Ha! That's what I like! (*Raising his index finger, seriously*) And it's very good for the circulation! (*A few moments' silence*) But still. I'm surprised that Haika didn't pick up my scent. It grieves me. Is she ill?

DAUGHTER-IN-LAW: Well, she's just old. Why didn't you come in? When you were standing right in front of the house?

OLD MAN: You'd have transported me straight back here.

DAUGHTER-IN-LAW: Oh, come on!

OLD MAN: I sat down in my old pub. Had a glass of wine and found out about everyone who'd died. Then I went to the cemetery. To my Agnes.

DAUGHTER-IN-LAW: To the Western Cemetery? (*He nods*) But that would have taken you hours.

OLD MAN: Of course. That's why I was tired. First I got on the wrong bus. They have changed the routes. (*Eating peanuts, the shells dropping onto the floor*)

DAUGHTER-IN-LAW: Look, don't drop them all over the floor like that. Are you doing it on purpose?

OLD MAN: Oh, . . . good God . . .

DAUGHTER-IN-LAW: (*Standing up, goes over to him, kneels in front of him, carefully picks the shells off the floor, puts them on the table, sits down again. the old man splits open more nuts, dropping the shells onto the floor again, DAUGHTER-IN-LAW sighs. A few moments' silence.*) How is your health?

OLD MAN: Good. Very good. I'll live to be a hundred.

DAUGHTER-IN-LAW: Good.

OLD MAN: Only, the food's nothing but muck. Old people's diet. I need something good and fatty. All my life I've eaten fat. And I've never been ill. "Eat up nicely, Grandpa, or you won't get any stewed fruit!" What do I want with stewed fruit?!

DAUGHTER-IN-LAW: Yes, you've already told me!

OLD MAN: Oh, have I already told you that? (*A few moments' silence*) I share my room with an old Nazi. Now, suddenly, his conscience is starting to plague him. Because he's scared, maybe there really is a heaven and a hell. He goes to mass in the chapel here every day. (*Laughing out loud*) And do you know what he does there? He's an altar-boy! He's an altar-boy! In a sort of red and white dress! And he keeps spilling the communion wine, because he's shaking so much! (*He can hardly contain himself with laughter, then suddenly breaks off*) In the night he screams out loud! All day long he talks about "only obeying orders!" But I'll get him! "Only obeying orders." Don't make me laugh! I stood there, his blood-spattered brains on my left hand. A comrade. I had a comrade. Killed by the partisans. The others, yes, they were going to set fire to the next four houses and shoot the people inside—all civilians. But not me. What business did we have being there? In a foreign country. "Know something?" I said. "All I want is a decent coffin and a wreath." They ran. No, no, there isn't any "having to obey orders." I'm still alive. (*Pulling out a long piece of lavatory paper, he blows his nose noisily on it*) Now I tease him about euthanasia! I've convinced him they're bringing it back again. For the old, too. (*Laughing*) Now he doesn't dare to stay in bed, even when he's not well. He only has to see a syringe and he starts shaking, in terror.

DAUGHTER-IN-LAW: Come on, you mustn't do things like that!

OLD MAN: And why not? He was all for euthanasia himself! When he was young! "Anyone who doesn't work has no right to live!" You have to be consistent!

DAUGHTER-IN-LAW: But, you mustn't do such things,

Helmut. To terrify someone like that!

OLD MAN: The Nazis terrified us. And that's not all! "So, now you can divorce me," my Agnes said at the time. "No certificate of racial purity." "Nonsense woman," I said, "divorce you? Because of those swastika-maniacs!" (*Laughing out loud*) When Herr Hitler came to visit our beautiful city we went past the Rennweg. Heaps of people. Heaps of people. They screamed like idiots. "Heil, Heil Hitler, our Furhrer!" "We've got enough leaders of our own," I said to my friend—he was a mountain-tour leader, you understand. Did he laugh! Then we went to Mühlau, drank a glass of red wine, but not to Herr Hitler's health. But I can understand it. No work or anything. People will fall for such ranting and raving. "Herr Aigner," they said to me, "at midnight you'll be a soldier!" Good. Good. "And what about your wife? She still hasn't got a certificate of racial purity!" "Look, gentlemen," I said, "she's an illegitimate child from somewhere in Moravia and you won't get anything out of them anymore! And this is all I'm going to say: if you don't leave my wife in peace, then this thing, the Wehrmacht or whoever is responsible for the war, then you can fight the war yourselves, but without me. Do we understand each other? Take it or leave it."

DAUGHTER-IN-LAW: Look, I really must . . .

OLD MAN: Yes, I'm sorry. I'm talking about old times, yet again. I know you don't like that.

DAUGHTER-IN-LAW: We are living now. That doesn't interest me. (*The OLD MAN nods. A few moments' silence. The OLD MAN takes off his hat and looks at it*) And do you like it here? Apart from the food?

OLD MAN: Yes, well. . . . It's just that one has been shunted onto a siding. One day like another. Only old people. Terrible. They're often so stubborn. Afflicted with geriatric-stubbornness, so to peak. I like young people around me. In an old people's home like this you only see old people. Except the nurses Almost all nuns. Even three from the Philippines, such tiny things, slant-eyed. Very friendly, though, I must say. A friendly people, these Asians. But among the locals, there are a couple I can't stand at all. They talk in such a funny way. "So, Grandpa, we're going to eat nicely now, no spluttering, all right?" "So, Grandpa, now we are going to lie down" —but none of them will lie down with me. . . . I don't like it at all! I was a civil servant,had authority! And in here they treat me like a willful child! I won't put up with it any more! Who do they think they are? I wrote about that too, to the President. "You are also an old man," I wrote, "you are sure to understand!" More respect for the old, please! (*Eating a nut*) And my bed is far too high for me. It's like a hunter's blind! You'd almost need a ladder. They must think I'm a retired gamekeeper! And everything looks the same! The rooms, the doors, the corridors—I can never find the toilet door and I can never find my way back, because everything looks the same. In the corridor there's one of these potted plants, all wrinkled, I never liked the thing! (*A few moments' silence. the daughter-in-law looks at her watch*) I read quite a bit, though, but my eyes can never take it for long, I need new glasses. But is it still worth it, what do you think?

DAUGHTER-IN-LAW: Of course it's worth it! Why in the world not?

OLD MAN: Often I stare out of the window for hours. They're building a new highrise building over there, it's interesting. It grows higher from day to day. All of glass and steel and ready-mixed concrete. Sometimes the cranes sway in the wind. — (*The OLD MAN is lost in thought*)

DAUGHTER-IN-LAW: (*Looking at her watch again*) I must go now, Grandpa.

OLD MAN: I sleep quite a bit. They give us sleeping pills.

I don't mind. It won't be long now, then I'll find my
release. The old Nazi idiot is afraid of death! Not
me. They can give me an injection whenever they
like.

DAUGHTER-IN-LAW: Come on, Grandpa, don't talk like
that!

OLD MAN: Well, it's true. What have I got to live for now?
I wasn't even allowed to bring my dog with me.

DAUGHTER-IN-LAW: (*Standing up*) Grandpa, I must be
on my way. We've got people coming.

OLD MAN: Yes, it's all right. (*Reaching into his pocket, he
brings out a 500-Schilling note, which he hands to
her*) This is for my Haika. Buy her something tasty.

DAUGHTER-IN-LAW: (*Looking at him, she puts her hand
out hesitantly towards the note, then draws it back*)
Grandpa, I'm sorry, I really didn't want to have to
tell you, but . . . well, we had to have her put to
sleep.

OLD MAN: What? What have you done?

DAUGHTER-IN-LAW: She was old, Helmut. Half-blind.
She wouldn't eat any more. She just stayed put in
your old room and whimpered, all the time. And
hair all over everything! (*The OLD MAN stares
ahead of him*) Bye, then. Till next time. (*She extends her hand to him, which he takes after a while*)
Shall I see you back to your room?

OLD MAN: No, I'll just sit here for a bit. (*The DAUGH-
TER-IN-LAW goes out*)

THE END

Jailbird

Characters
HE and SHE, both middle-aged

Set
Visitors' room in a women's prison

(A table and two chairs. The table is divided into two halves by a partition. On the visitors' side, an ashtray. The shadow of an off-stage woman guard on the wall. She comes in, wearing prison uniform, sits down at the table. Her hairstyle is simple, without adornment. He comes in from the other side, wearing his Sunday best. He looks round uncertainly, glances at the guard, goes to the table, looks at her)

HE: Hi.

(Reaching out his hand to her. She looks at it, then at him, shaking her head)

SHE: Not allowed.

HE: Oh, right.

(Understanding, he looks at the guard, sits down, looks at her, feels uncomfortable, takes out his cigarettes, lights one, is about to put the packet away, but then holds the packet out to her)

SHE: (*Shaking her head*) Not allowed.

HE: Oh, right . . . (*About to put his cigarette out*)

SHE: No, go on, you're allowed to.

HE: Oh right . . . (*They look at each other. He glances at his watch, takes it off, and puts it down on the table*) No more than twenty-five minutes, they said. Because you've been bad.

SHE: (*Smiling bitterly. A few moments' silence. neither manages to say anything*) How are you all?

HE: Surviving. We've moved.

SHE: What for?

HE: Because of the talk. It's not easy, believe you me.

SHE: I believe you. And where've you moved to?

HE: Where to! To my mother, of course.

SHE: Of course.

HE: If I didn't have her. . . . I'd hang myself!

SHE: But that means the kids are a long way from school.

HE: That's all right. For the time being. In autumn I'll put them in another one.

SHE: What for?

HE: What for! What for! Again because of the talk, what else! What do you think they've got to put up with! All the kids are from the neighborhood. Everyone knows all about it. (*She stares ahead, dejectedly*)

(*After a pause*)

HE: Have you put on weight?

SHE: Yes, I look terrible

HE: Yes, yes, all the good food in here has fattened you up, eh?

SHE: (*After a pause*) What do the kids say about me?

HE: Nothing. It's not talked about. Better like that.

SHE: They hate me?

HE: I don't know.

SHE: They ask about me?

HE: No.

SHE: They send me their love?

HE: They don't know I'm here.

SHE: Why not?

HE: (*After a pause*) Because I said for me you're dead and buried. And that they are not allowed to talk about you any more. I got a divorce. You'll get the letter in a few days.

SHE: What're you visiting me for?

HE: Because I don't understand it. Why you did it. I can't grasp it. Can't get it into my head. Fifteen years of marriage.

SHE: (*After a pause*) I don't understand it myself. (*After another pause*) I tried to kill myself five weeks ago.

HE: So. And?

SHE: They caught me at it. They patched me up, then I had to wash the blood off the floor, then they handcuffed me and put me in solitary confinement.

HE: Most people who attempt suicide are only pretending. They don't really mean it.

SHE: You'll see.

HE: Am I supposed to feel sorry for you?

SHE: No, of course not.

HE: You've got everything. Television and table-tennis and running water. Sitting around doing nothing. Like a holiday camp. I know all about it.

SHE: If I'm on holiday, I'll visit you. In the dead of night.

HE: Don't talk such damn nonsense!

SHE: You're talking nonsense. Like a parrot. You really have no idea!

HE: No idea! Maybe you don't have television and all that?

SHE: Television once in ten days. From five to eight. If you're good. Sometimes on Sundays. Dallas.

HE: Dallas is Tuesday. Five past nine.

SHE: They use a video. They tape it.

HE: A video as well! There you are! What did 1 say? I haven't got a video!

SHE: (*Has not been listening*) Dallas. It's beautiful. Beautiful women and beautiful men. Beautiful hairstyles. A swimming-pool.

HE: You'll get one in here next.

SHE: Yes, if only. One bucket of hot water a day. That's our swimming-pool. And an open toilet in the cell. No curtain, nothing. Whenever I eat, one of the women goes to the toilet on purpose! Always! Not just for a pee! Everything! To get at me! I'll do her one of these days! (*A longish silence*) But this will make you laugh: there were a few weeks, after I'd got used to it here, when all of a sudden I felt free. Free, you understand? Free! Here in prison! I liked it better than at home. Can you believe that?

HE: You're crazy!

SHE: Oh yes? I get up at six—just like at home—at seven I get breakfast, served, not real coffee, of course, like at home, but still, they pour it out for me. Then I work my eight hours in the laundry. Then they leave me in peace. And at home? First I get breakfast for all of you, then get the kids off to school, then rush off to work, home again at midday, cook, see to the kids; clean, wash, shop; get dinner, wash up, wait on you hand and foot, darning; football on the television, then to bed, with you. Or you go to the pub and come home drunk at half past twelve and wake me up . . . And here—no chores. No responsibilities. Rules, of course. You have to follow the rules. But when there are a couple of women in the cell you can get along with. . . . The whole weekend free . . . a bit of gossip . . . play Ludo. . . . And not a man in sight!

HE: What did I say! Paradise! A health farm! And this is supposed to be a prison! This is supposed to be a punishment! God Almighty! It didn't use to be like that! The death sentence, you'd have gotten the death sentence then!

SHE: You'd've liked that!

HE: (*Yelling*) You wanted to kill me! Murder me!

SHE: Shh! Not so loud. Or they'll stop the visit!

HE: (*After lighting another cigarette, he puts his hand into his jacket pocket, takes out his wallet and extracts two folded newspaper articles, looks at them, puts one back, and smooths out the other)* There! A newspaper article about the case. The first report. *(Reading aloud)* At the hearing she said: *"He never stopped nagging!"* Tea time row: wife knifes husband. In an Eggenberg flat on Saturday night, a frenzied row about the quality of the food led to a brutal act of violence. Bettina Demel, a 42-year old clerk, plunged an eleven centimeter long kitchen knife into her husband's stomach. While the severely wounded man writhed about on the floor in his own blood begging for help, his wife calmly finished the washing the dishes. After about twenty minutes, the children of the couple came home from the movies to find their father unconscious on the kitchen floor. They called an ambulance and the man was rushed to hospital. After an emergency operation, he is now out of danger.

SHE: Why are you reading that out to me?

HE: *(Shoving the newspaper article at her)* There! There's the photo of the knife! *(She hides her face in her hands, beginning to weep)*

HE: *(Re-reading the same sentence)* "While the severely wounded man writhed about on the floor in his own blood begging for help, his wife calmly finished washing the dishes." *(He looks at her, carefully folds up the newspaper article again, replaces it in his wallet and puts it back in his pocket)* "Cold blooded attempted murder", the Public Prosecutor said! "No sign of psychiatric disturbance," the Court Psychiatrist said!

SHE: *(After a longish silence, wiping away her tears with both hands, she looks at him)* I don't know why I did it, Kurt! I don't know! I was asked so many questions at the time. By the police. By the examining magistrate. By the Public Prosecutor. By my lawyer. By the psychiatrist. I couldn't give anyone the right answer. And afterwards I pushed it out of my mind. Didn't want to know anything about it anymore. I went on as if it had never happened. (*After a pause*) Look, Kurt, I don't like you anymore. I haven't liked you for a long time. And you haven't liked me for a long time. Nothing but duty. Doing our duty. Marriage. Husband and wife. Children. Life's an extra. Lately I wondered what color your eyes were. I no longer knew. I no longer knew. When you came home, you said "hi," and you never looked at me and I never looked at you. . . . You got a beer out of the fridge, sat down in front of the television and waited for your dinner. And loaded everything onto me. And everything that aggravated you I did penance for. Out three times a week. Bowling, sauna, boozing. Never asked if I wanted to come. And slept with me only when you were drunk. I do understand. Some time or other it's finished. It'd be the same with lots of people.

HE: Yes! Yes! Sure! Sure it would be the same with lots of people! Dead right! But you wanted to kill me! That's not the same with other people! You criminal! (*She lowers her head. a short silence*) At work they laugh behind my back! "The sissy!" "The wimp!" "Lets his wife nearly butcher him."

SHE: Yes, I know. It's normal for a husband to kill his wife, not the other way round! (*After a silence, she suddenly starts sobbing*)

SHE: I'm so sorry, Kurt! What can I do? What's done can't be undone! (*She sobs. After a pause*) I take so many Valium these days and it still doesn't help. (*Silence*) Kurt, I must be sick. In my head. Quite certain. Although they couldn't find anything. See, over the last few years I've lived on pills. Everything seemed so meaningless to me. You didn't need me, except as a housekeeper, and the kids became strangers too. Live their own lives. Or I became a stranger to them. I don't know. But anyway: in the morning, when I had to get up, I found it so hard, so terribly hard. The day in front of me. . . . I was so scared of every day. I thought I won't make it, I won't make it any more. I took tablets. Stimulants, "for the increase of functional activity, for the treatment of mental depression," that's what it said on the packet . . . and then again tranquilizers. And at night sleeping-pills. More and more.

HE: But, I didn't know anything about it. How could I? Where did you get all that stuff?

SHE: Yes, well, I know a few doctors. Generous. Understanding.

HE: Come on, stop it! What are you talking about? We all have to work! It's not that terrible! I also have to put up with the boss and the customers at work. Do you think it's always enjoyable? And always doing overtime! Moonlighting on the weekends! So we could buy our own flat! So don't you talk! It drives me mad!

SHE: I knew you wouldn't understand. So I never said anything about it. It's my problem. It's probably all my fault. Labile, the psychiatrist said. Labile. Funny word.

HE: Of course it's all your fault! I didn't want to kill you! And I sure don't have an easy life either!

SHE: Let's just leave it. Thanks Kurt, thanks for coming. My first visit. (*Silence for a while. He lights another cigarette. She looks at it with longing*)

HE: The kids don't listen to me anymore. Nor to my mother. "The old hag! Silly old cow!" And so on! She's at the end of her tether. And music blasting away all the time!

SHE: But they've got earphones.

HE: They do it to get at her. Watching late movies whenever I'm out. Bad marks at school. Angelika's always hanging around discos. I think she's on drugs. And Markus is so rude! So rude! I'll kill him one of these days! (*Silence for a while*) Since you haven't been there. . . . she also gets on my nerves, my mother. To be honest. Talks like a book. Never lets up. Can't even watch TV in peace any more. And always about her illnesses. Every second day she's at the doctor's. Although there's nothing wrong with her. She'll outlive the lot of us. Can't stand going home any more, after work. Go to the pub nearly every day. (*Silence for a while*) One day Angelika said to me, it was my fault you wanted to kill me. I'm "primitive," she said; I don't understand a thing, she said. (*In desperation*) To have to listen to something like that from my own daughter! You've ruined all our lives. You succeeded in that. But I know who's responsible all right, who's to blame. In the final analysis.

SHE: Who?

HE: These feminists.

SHE: What?

HE: You heard! These feminists! They've finally succeeded! I'd never've believed it! But now they've finally succeeded! They're in all the newspapers! And the television! Everywhere! Stirring women up!

SHE: Come on, Kurt! I've never had anything to do with them!

HE: They spit their poison from every magazine. And you were always reading magazines. Soaking it all in! But now I've written one of these poisonous bitches a letter for her column. They even printed it. Couldn't believe it. (*Taking out his wallet again, he removes the other newspaper cutting, smooths it out, waving it at her*) There, read it!

SHE: (*Shaking her head*) You're not allowed to give me anything.

HE: Then I'll read it to you.

SHE: I don't want to hear it, Kurt!

HE: You're damn well going to! (*Reading quietly, with a*

sidelong glance at the warden) Frau Deissen! You've already been writing far too long in this poison-spreading paper! Unfortunately we couldn't find your address in the phone book, because we'd gladly pay you a visit to enlighten you about the physical strength of a real man, because it seems you haven't got a clue. But your day will come. If you continue to stupefy our wives and daughters with your feminist trash and try to persuade them that they could seriously stand up to the strength of a man (the weak will always stay weak and therefore intellectually inferior), then we will get rid off you, Madame, like a bothersome bedbug that sucks on the blood of a pure-minded people. (*Warming to it, he becomes increasingly hectoring and fanatic*) Or like a tick whose head you pull off! Woe to you, if you stir up our women any longer! We won't stand for it anymore! Do you actually know, you smart-arse, that according to the statistics, crimes committed by women are more and more on the increase and it is scientifically proved that this is linked to the so-called emancipation of women. But of course, you don't write that. You're a filthy, lying sow, and that would be enough by itself to gas you! Mauthausen can easily be made operational again. (*Putting the newspaper cutting back*)

SHE: Without a signature?

HE: What do you think! They'd smash all my windows in!

SHE: And you're proud of that letter?

HE: What do you mean: proud? It was something I had to say!

SHE: Terrible! I'm so ashamed for you! Such a terrible letter!

HE: (*Angrily*) You're ashamed for me? You're ashamed for me?

SHE: You're sick, Kurt! Anyone who writes a letter like that must be sick!

HE: Sick? Me sick? I've never done anything to anyone!

SHE: But you never stop threatening to! In that letter as well!

HE: My bark is worse than my bite! We've got proof of that, haven't we? You never barked. You were always silent. (*A few moments' silence*)

SHE: I think the time is up.

HE: (*Looking at his watch*) Yes, in three minutes.

SHE: Goodbye then.

HE: (*Not saying a word for a while, then looks at her*) It's not true that I don't like you anymore. Like you said. I do like you. In spite of everything.

SHE: Oh no, Kurt. That isn't true.

HE: It is. It is. I often hate you. Really hate you! And in spite of that I like you. And I miss you. But I don't understand you. I don't understand you. True, I've made mistakes. I admit that.

SHE: It's no use, Kurt. We'll never be together again. There will always be the knife between us. I must do penance for it. That's only just. I can't even ask your forgiveness. You don't forgive something like that. Impossible.

HE: (*Getting up*) The kids said, they wanted to visit you. I've forbidden it up till now. But if you want—

SHE: (*Getting up*) Yes please, please! That's what I want more than anything!

HE: But please, don't stir them up against me. It's difficult enough for me as it is.

SHE: No, of course not! Of course not, Kurt! I'm to blame! Only me!

HE: Do you need anything? Want them to bring you anything?

SHE: Yes, if possible. But—I can't pay for anything. I only get 100 Schillings a month spending money.

HE: It's alright, I'll pay for it. What do you need then?

SHE: Tampons. You only get pads in here. And some knickers. White. Plain. No patterns allowed. And deodorant. And skin cream. My skin's drying out.

HE: Right. See you.

SHE: See you, Kurt. . . . (*He starts going*) Kurt! (*He turns round*) I suppose you won't visit me again?

HE: No. Probably not. (*He goes out. She watches him go, then slowly sits down, staring ahead of her*)

THE END

Wheat on the Autobahn

Characters

An OLD MAN
His DAUGHTER

Set

Visiting room of a psychiatric hospital

(THE STAGE IN DARKNESS)
VOICE OF THE OLD MAN: (*Singing*)

> Small am I, small stay I,
>
> Mamma's raised me from a hazelnut!

(*Light on the stage. A table and two chairs. On one chair sits the OLD MAN in an institution dressing gown. On his head he wears an old dark hat. On the table in front of him lies a slab of wood—about 10 cm thick—from the trunk of a fir tree. The OLD MAN has an empty pipe in his mouth, his hands lie on the slab of wood, he stares at it. The DAUGHTER comes in, nouveau riche country clothes, in her hand a bunch of flowers*)

DAUGHTER: Hello, Papa (*She holds out a hand to him, he ignores her*)

OLD MAN: Oh. Hello! And who are you?

DAUGHTER: Oh please, don't start that again! It's me, Erika!

OLD MAN: Erika? Don't know her.

DAUGHTER: Now stop it, Papa. Or I won't come any more. I'm not going to go along with this play-acting any longer.

OLD MAN: (*He sounds sincere*) I really don't know you, Madam. Are you a relation, perhaps?

DAUGHTER: I am your daughter! For Heaven's sake!

OLD MAN: Can't be. My daughter looks quite different. (*The DAUGHTER looks at him resignedly, sits down, puts the flowers on the slab of wood*) Kindly take those weeds away.

DAUGHTER: What?

OLD MAN: Take those weeds away! I don't like them! Or are they for my funeral?

DAUGHTER: Funeral? I wanted to please you! 120 Schillings they cost me!

OLD MAN: What? 120 Schillings? Are you related to me then?

DAUGHTER: Papa, don't drive me insane! Please!

OLD MAN: Anyone who pays 120 Schillings for flowers must be a relation! (*He looks attentively at her*) But I can't remember you! With the best will in the world! You must forgive me! (*High German*) You should know that, in the opinion of my doctors, I suffer from a Michael Kohlhaas-Syndrome! Absolutely! Michael Kohlhaas-Syndrome! And yet I'm not called Michael Kohlhaas at all. Robert Moessmer is my name. And who are you?

DAUGHTER: (*With great self-control*) I am your daughter Erika, Papa.

OLD MAN: No, no, that can't be. You don't look like my daughter at all. (*Taking some battered old snapshots out of his own pocket, he selects one*) Here, here is the proof. A photo. A photo of my daughter. (*Holds it up in front of her*) That's what she looks like.

DAUGHTER: Yes, that is me! But as a child!

OLD MAN: (*Puts the photo away again*) You are a spy!

DAUGHTER: (*Looks sadly at him, then stares straight ahead*)

OLD MAN: And there is another bit of proof. My daughter, dear lady, wouldn't pay 120 Schillings for a bunch of flowers!

DAUGHTER: What?

OLD MAN: Not because she'd be too mean, but because she has her own garden! Because we have our own garden! At home! On the farm!

DAUGHTER: Please, Papa, we don't have a garden any more! You know that!

OLD MAN: Of course we've got a garden. And what a garden it is! Actually, it is a vegetable garden. But Erika keeps on planting more and more flowers in it. And such silly ornamental shrubs! Japanese. She'd rather buy her lettuce at the supermarket. Why, I don't understand. I must ask her sometime.

DAUGHTER: We haven't got a garden any more, Papa! It's a parking lot now!

OLD MAN: Lies. All lies.

DAUGHTER: You saw it yourself Papa, when they did it!

OLDMAN: Don't you call me Papa! I don't know you!

DAUGHTER: Papa! It doesn't make any sense to go on fooling yourself! You know well enough what the reality is! You don't fool me! You're pretending! Because you're in a fury!

OLD MAN: (*Stands up*) Take those weeds off my tree! (*The DAUGHTER picks up the flowers and places them on the table near the slab of wood which the OLD MAN picks up and clutches*) So, goodbye and God bless you! (*He turns to go, the DAUGHTER stands up and holds him back*)

DAUGHTER: Papa! Now come and sit down!

OLD MAN: Herr Moessmer is my name. Let go of me!

DAUGHTER: You're really driving me mad, Papa! I'm at the end of my tether!

OLD MAN: One doesn't address a total stranger as Papa!

DAUGHTER: All right then, have it your way! I am a friend of your daughter's, Herr Moessmer! I would just like to have a little chat with you!

OLD MAN: I see, yes, gladly! I hardly ever get any visits! Please, take a seat! (*The DAUGHTER sits down, the OLD MAN puts the slab of wood onto the table and sits down as well.*) So! Well then? What's new in the world?

DAUGHTER: Not much. Always the same. We all get by as best we can.

OLD MAN: Yes, yes. We all get by as best we can. (*They look at each other in silence for a while*) Actually, you're not all that disagreeable, when I really think about it.

DAUGHTER: Thanks.

OLD MAN: The harder the shell the sweeter the nut. (*The DAUGHTER gives him a sad look*) When people don't know each other, they have very little to say. (*Silence for a while*) I know a riddle. What is this: God sees it not, the king seldom, but the farmer every day.

DAUGHTER: What?

OLD MAN: God sees it not, the king seldom, but the farmer everyday. What is it?

DAUGHTER: (*Thinks for a while*) I give up.

OLD MAN: His equal.

DAUGHTER: What?

OLD MAN: His equal.

DAUGHTER: I don't understand.

OLD MAN: God never sees his equal, the king sees his equal seldom, but the farmer sees his equal everyday.

DAUGHTER: Aha. Now I understand.

OLD MAN: However, it's not true for me any more. I'm the only farmer in this place. (*They are silent for a while. The DAUGHTER looks at the slab of wood)*

DAUGHTER: What's this then?

OLD MAN: Just leave it there! That's mine!

DAUGHTER: I thought at first it was a table-top. A rustic table-top.

OLD MAN: It's not! This slab of wood belongs to me.

DAUGHTER: Who did you get it from then?

OLD MAN: Hansi brought it for me.

DAUGHTER: Has Hansi been here?

OLD MAN: Do you know him?

DAUGHTER: (*Infuriated*) Yes, I know him!

OLD MAN: He's the only one of my family who visits me. My daughter Erika and Mr Son-in-law, those two don't dare come here! Because they have guilty consciences! Only my grandson comes. . . . Hansi! Almost every day!

DAUGHTER: (*Shakes her head*) I had no idea! Why doesn't he tell us?

OLD MAN: Of course, he doesn't tell them ! They told him: "Hansi, your grandpa's off his head, he's crazy, he's round the bend, don't go near him!"

DAUGHTER: Next thing, you'll be claiming you're normal!

OLD MAN: How dare you talk to me like that—a total stranger?! I'll smack you in the face in a minute! What cheek! Why on earth are you pestering me like this? I didn't ask you to come here!

DAUGHTER: I can always go again!

OLD MAN: Yes, just go! I don't need you! I don't need anybody! Absolutely nobody! You're probably one of the gang too, I'm sure! That's right, one of the conspirators!

DAUGHTER: (*Stands up, about to go, looks at the OLD MAN who has collapsed in a heap, staring ahead of him. She changes her mind and sits down again*) Papa, please! What were we supposed to do? When you keep on behaving like this! (*The OLD MAN stares ahead of him*) If you hadn't been admitted to the madhouse, you'd be in jail by now!

OLD MAN: I'd be better off in jail. At least I'd get some peace there. No injections or pills or electric shocks. (*Quietly, despairingly to his DAUGHTER*) They're destroying my brain! It's true, they're destroying my brain!

DAUGHTER: Please, Papa!

OLD MAN: My head's like a wasp's nest. Or else it feels as if they've stuffed it with hay. (*Quietly*) Help me! Please, help me!

DAUGHTER: What can I do! They won't let you out! You're a danger to the community!

OLD MAN: What am I? A danger to the community? You, you better be careful making such statements!

DAUGHTER: The report states that you are a danger to yourself and to your surroundings!

OLD MAN: Ha, that makes me laugh! Me, a danger to my surroundings! (*Laughs*) There are quite a number of others who are a danger to their surroundings! (*Angrily*) They're the very ones who've sent me here! Can't you see that, you fool?

DAUGHTER: Let's leave it! There's no point to it!

OLD MAN: If you won't help me, Hansi certainly will!

DAUGHTER: Yes, and what else! He'll get a good slap across the face! He'd do better to pay more attention to his studies at the hotel management school! If he goes on like this, he'll fail!

OLD MAN: Hansi wants to be a farmer and not a cook in some hotel!

DAUGHTER: We, his parents, say what Hansi is going to be! Not you! Understand!?

OLD MAN: Erika has no say. Her husband says. Rudi says. Believe me! Erika didn't use to be like that. She didn't use to.

DAUGHTER: But, how can Hansi be a farmer? We haven't got any land any more!

OLD MAN: Lies. All lies.

DAUGHTER: (*Standing up, she goes over to him and shakes him by the shoulders*)I am your daughter and you are my father and you are in the madhouse and we don't have any land anymore!

OLD MAN: (*He looks calmly at her, she sits down again, buries her face in her hands*) And why don't we have any land anymore?

DAUGHTER: Because we've sold it.

OLD MAN: And why was it sold?

DAUGHTER: Because an Autobahn was being built! If we hadn't sold it willingly, we would have been given a compulsory purchase order! Can't you finally get that into your head!

OLD MAN: The best land far and wide! Smooth as a chessboard. We've farmed it for 400 years. And life was good to us. And we were happy. (*He looks at her for a while without a word, she hangs her head*) Daughter!

DAUGHTER: (*Looking up*) Yes?

OLD MAN: Can you still remember how the wind used to sweep across the wheat fields? How often have we sat in front of the house, you on my lap, with your dear little plaits, and we looked down at the wheat. It was like a golden sea in the wind. Like a golden sea. Can you remember?

DAUGHTER: Yes, I remember.

OLD MAN: And what can you see now?

DAUGHTER: (*Angrily*) Yes, I know ! I see an Autobahn intersection! I'm not blind!

OLD MAN: And all the exhaust fumes float up here! And night and day the noise!

DAUGHTER: Please, Papa! We're at least half a kilometer away!

OLD MAN: It's hardly 400 meters! I've measured it!

DAUGHTER: Stop moaning, Papa! It's no use. It is, as it is.

OLD MAN: If only I hadn't made over the farm to you! I never trusted him, that Rudi! But he gave me his word that he would go on farming! He gave me his solemn word, the mongrel! No, no, if only I hadn't done it! Then I'd still have a say in things!

DAUGHTER: The Autobahn would have been built in any case.

OLD MAN: But even so my farmhouse wouldn't be some hotel now!

DAUGHTER: What would you do with a farmhouse and no land?

OLD MAN: I would have bought some. Over three million Schillings compensation! Whatever you say, that's a lot of money!

DAUGHTER: Rudi would rather be a hotelier.

OLD MAN: Of course. Your husband would rather be a hotelier! The criminal. The criminal!

DAUGHTER: You stop that right now! Don't you talk about my Rudi like that! Don't! Or I'll go and I won't come back!

OLD MAN: (*Stands up*) Yes, go ! Go on! Stick up for him, your criminal husband! Perhaps you've already forgotten how you kicked me out? Have you already forgotten?

DAUGHTER: Come on, don't exaggerate.

OLD MAN: I sat out there on the bench in front of the house, I can still remember it well, your husband came up to me and said: "So, Papa, the land's been sold, now the rebuilding can begin. Our farm's going to be a hotel, farming doesn't pay any more!" "What's the matter" I asked, "What's the matter? Rebuilding? Hotel? Doesn't pay any more? What's the matter?" "Nothing is the matter", he said, your husband. "You'll soon see!" And afterwards I did see, I couldn't keep up with it! The remaining fields sold, cattle sold, stables pulled down, roof-trusses torn down, extensions built, two stories added, guest rooms built, with baths, running water, hot and cold! Then they said: "Papa, out of the living-room!" Hardly was I in the kitchen, when the wall to the stables was broken through and you'd built a dance floor, with all the trimmings. Then they said: "Papa, out of the kitchen!" I'd hardly sat down outside, on the bench in front of the house, when you were building a bar in the kitchen. And to give it a rustic appearance, you slapped tar all over the ceiling. To give the impression of old smoke stains. And so it went on! You pulled the bench out from under me and put up scaffolding and enlarged the windows and and repainted the outside and painted flowers around the windows and ornaments and all that rubbish. "Tourists like that," he said, your husband. Like a farmhouse in a musical comedy!

DAUGHTER: Papa!

OLD MAN: And on it went! Out of the vegetable garden, Papa, they said. And I'd hardly picked half of the red currants, when the bulldozers arrived, flattened everything, spread gravel over it and poured asphalt over that and the parking lot was ready.

DAUGHTER: Papa, can't you just. . . .

OLD MAN: And then we were standing in front of the new hotel. You and your husband, Hansi, Maria, the mayor and the representative of the Tourist Association and the band and heaps of people, and speeches were made and photographs were taken and free beer was given out and everyone had a hell of a time. I stood and looked. I don't see too well any more, but the neon sign on the wall was so big I could read everything. "Hotel Alpine View," it said. And "Country Cuisine." And "Dancing." And "Coca-Cola." And "Dortmund Union Beer."

DAUGHTER: Yes, I know all that! So why are you telling me . . .

OLD MAN: "You, Rudi," I said to my son-in-law, "you, Rudi, what has happened, huh? Where is my farm? What have you done with my farm, huh?"

DAUGHTER: Yes, and you hit my Rudi over the head with your stick, in front of all those people! To this day I'm still ashamed of it!

OLD MAN: So you should be! So you should be! You have every reason to be ashamed!

DAUGHTER: I was ashamed for you! For you! If the mayor hadn't taken your stick away you'd have beaten him to death, your own son-in-law!

OLD MAN: "The best thing is to put him into an old people's home," he said, the mayor. "He's not in his right mind!" "Yes, yes," he said, your Rudi, "you're right, you're quite right. He's no good for anything anymore. We haven't got any stables any more and he's already too weak to carry the suitcases for the tourists. I'll put him into an old people's home."

DAUGHTER: My God, because he was in a rage! You shouldn't have taken him so literally!

OLD MAN: So, I shouldn't have taken him literally, you say? Not literally? So, where have you brought me then? Just look around! Where am I now, then, huh? In the madhouse, that's where I am! In the madhouse!

DAUGHTER: That wasn't us! That wasn't us at all! The authorities did that! (*The OLD MAN sits down, bitter silence*) We have nothing to blame ourselves for, Papa. No, really not! Didn't Rudi pay the fine when you plowed up the newly graveled Autobahn in the middle of the night? And for the relaying, huh! They didn't make too much fuss about that. We sorted that out for you! But when you spread manure on the freshly concreted Autobahn, naturally they reported you to the police! All of 800 meters ruined!

OLD MAN: (*Laughs*) Ha, Ha! You should have seen their faces! When they couldn't get the manure out of the concrete! Ha, Ha! I almost died laughing!

DAUGHTER: You laugh about it? You can laugh about it? That's willful damage to public property! Who pays for the Autobahn then? Us taxpayers! Us taxpayers!

OLD MAN: Tell me more! What happened then? Now it's getting exciting, ha,ha!

DAUGHTER: Exciting! Exciting, he says! Such a disgrace! Such a disgrace! I could have put up with anything, but not that! No, not that! That was really too much!

OLD MAN: What then? Tell me! I can't remember any more!

DAUGHTER: Please Papa, stop acting! Of course you can remember it!

OLD MAN: (*Apparently serious*) No, seriously! I can't fit it together! Help me! (*THE DAUGHTER looks at him furiously*) Was it something to do with politicians?

DAUGHTER: Yes, it was something to do with politicians! At the official opening of the new section of the Autobahn you turned up with a seed-bag!

OLD MAN: With a seed-bag? That's impossible! We've got a seeding machine.

DAUGHTER: You turned up with a seed-bag! You marched up to the Local Government Official and the Minister who were about to cut the ribbon and started sowing wheat! On the Autobahn! Wheat on the Autobahn!

OLD MAN: Wheat on the Autobahn. . . .

DAUGHTER: Yes! But that wasn't enough for you! You also had to abuse the politicians! And brawled with the police, when they tried to remove you! And bel-

lowed and screamed and raved! Like an utter mad-
man!

OLD MAN: (*Standing up and screaming*) Down with the
machine people! Down with the machine people!
Rip open their chests and out with the wires! Break
open their skulls and smash their plastic brains!
(*He sits down, puts his hands on the slab of wood,
stares in front of him*)

DAUGHTER: You're really in the right place. You've certainly ended up in the right place. I have to say it,
as sad as it makes me.

OLD MAN: (*Softly*) Erika, you don't know it and you won't
believe me, like nobody believes me, but it is the ab-
solute truth, I'm quite sure: there is a conspiracy!

DAUGHTER: Yes, yes, of course.

OLD MAN: A conspiracy of a few thousand people, who
want to cover the whole world with concrete, to
drape it with electric cables, poison it with exhaust
fumes and sewage.

DAUGHTER: And why would they want to?

OLD MAN: Because they want all the people and all the
animals and all the plants to be killed off.

DAUGHTER: Yes, yes, of course.

OLD MAN: Because they, they who want this, they are not
people themselves. Do you know what they are?
(*THE DAUGHTER shakes her head*) I call them
the machine people. They have no heart in their
bodies and no brain in their heads. Nor do they
have to shit. They look like people, to be sure, but
they are not. They are machines.

DAUGHTER: They are machines.

OLD MAN: Yes, machines. And machines have no use for
nature. The machine people have only one idea in
their heads: Either to make us people into machines too or to exterminate all of us. That is the ab-
solute truth. Believe me, daughter! (*The
DAUGHTER looks at him depressed, looks sadly*

ahead of her) Didn't you bring me any tobacco? (*She looks up, reaches into her handbag, takes out packet of tobacco, gives it to the old man. He opens the packet, fills his pipe)* And a light? (*She gets out a matchbox, goes to give it to him, stops, takes out a match, lights it, is about to light the old man's pipe. He takes the match angrily from her hand, because he notices that she will not trust him with matches, lights his pipe. She looks at the slab of wood)*

DAUGHTER: What are you doing with that wood, then?

OLD MAN: I'm reading it.

DAUGHTER: What?

OLD MAN: I asked Hansi for it, so I'd have something worth reading.

DAUGHTER: Worth reading? You read that bit of wood?

OLD MAN: Yes, naturally! Shall I read you something?

DAUGHTER: Yes, please. I'd like to know what it says!

OLD MAN: (*Puts on his glasses, bends over the slab of wood, points with his finger, starting at the center and following the annual rings)* 1918: the tree is born, the seed sprouts. 1926: the tree grows beautifully. It gets enough rain and sun. The yearly rings are all even. 1932: the rings get out of true, because when the tree is nine years old, an avalanche shoves it to one side and it has to struggle to support itself. 1939: the tree grows quite straight again, but its neighbors, growing along with it, take some of the water and air and it grows more slowly.

DAUGHTER: You can read all that from the rings?

OLD MAN: This is like a book. 1942: On leave from the front I cut down its nearest neighbors. Now it grows faster again. 1945: During a fight with the Americans a forest fire starts. A brush fire runs through the forest. The tree is injured, but the bark protects it and the wound heals over later. 1957: the tree thirsts during a long draught and it stops growing. It needs a little time until it starts again. 1972: A plague of insects breaks out. The larvae eat needles and buds and nearly kill the tree. 1982: The tree is now sixty-five years old and healthy again. But now an Autobahn is being built and the tree stands in the way. It is chopped down. (*He leans back and lights his pipe again*)

DAUGHTER: Did you just make all that up?

OLD MAN: No, daughter, I didn't make it up.

DAUGHTER: (*After a while*) I miss you, Papa. Rudi has no time for me any more. And I have no time for the children.

OLD MAN: Is the business doing well at least?

DAUGHTER: No, it's not.

OLD MAN: Why not?

DAUGHTER: With all our debts we don't know left from right any more. The whole winter hardly any snow. After three days the guests leave. The interest rates go up and up and the number of guests down and down. It's a nightmare!

OLD MAN: Start rearing pigs. At least that'd put you back on your feet.

DAUGHTER: We can't do that. They'd drive the guests away. They stink.

OLD MAN: They stink. Naturally. They stink. (*He closes his eyes*) Sometimes, when I lie in bed, with my eyes closed, then I can see our fields. I drive over them with the mowing machine and I smell the fresh grass. And I bury my head in the pillow and feel the flank of a cow on my forehead. All warm and soft. (*The DAUGHTER begins to cry, the OLD MAN looks at her.*)

DAUGHTER: (*After a while*) I'll see that you get out.

OLD MAN: Leave it be, daughter. I don't want to come home anymore. I don't belong in a hotel. The living-room is gone, together with the stove . . . and everywhere the humming and thudding. . . .

DAUGHTER: What humming and thudding?

OLD MAN: All the machines. The stereo-whatsit and that thing there under the television and the dishwashing machine and the bread-toaster and the grill and all that stuff. And you can hear the pumping of the oil furnace in the cellar through the whole house. All the buzzing and thumping drives you mad.

DAUGHTER: (*After a while*) We've still got the log cabin, you know. The log cabin on the mountain. It's rented out to tourists, but we can get it back. You could live there.

OLD MAN: (*Hopefully*) Yes? Could I really?

DAUGHTER: You'd have to be good, though. You mustn't put on any more of these performances. Like with the Autobahn.

OLD MAN: No, I'd stay put in the cabin. No one would get me down into the valley again.

DAUGHTER: Then I'll see what I can do. They did say, that if we took the responsibility, they'd let you out soon.

OLD MAN: Then I'll sit in front of the cabin and look down at the valley. And I could also keep a few goats.

DAUGHTER: You'll have to give me a bit of time though. To talk Rudi over.

OLD MAN: Talk Rudi over?

DAUGHTER: Yes, of course! You know he doesn't want to have anything to do with you any more.

OLD MAN: Talk Rudi over?

DAUGHTER: We're legally responsible for you! He has to give his consent. I can't act against the wishes of my husband!

OLD MAN: (*Loud, angry*) Talk Rudi over?

DAUGHTER: Yes, Papa. But I'll bring him round all right! Believe me, please!

OLD MAN: (*Suddenly totally confused and horrified*) Rudi! Rudi! (*Stands up*) But don't you know who your Rudi is? Don't you know who that is?

DAUGHTER: Calm down, Papa! Please!

OLD MAN: Rudi ... Rudi ... I keep on forgetting ... I don't want to believe it. .... Or it's the injections, the tablets, that make me forget ... I don't know. .... Rudi, daughter, Rudi is the leader! Do you understand? The leader!

DAUGHTER: What sort of leader?

OLD MAN: (*Softly, anxiously*) Rudi is the leader of the conspirators! (*She looks baffled*) Yes! Yes! Really! Believe me! I know it!

DAUGHTER: I'll go and get the nurse.

OLD MAN: No, please don't! Just wait! Just wait! This is important! You must know this! Rudi is the leader! I've proof!

DAUGHTER: (*Angrily*) What sort of proof, Papa?

OLDMAN: (*Sits down, whispers*) It was three years ago, on a February night, I can still remember it well. I couldn't sleep and walked around the yard, as always, when I couldn't get to sleep. And in the toolshed, there I saw a figure. A figure that was doing something to another figure. I saw it quite clearly. It was your Rudi, with a soldering-iron in his hand. And on the chopping block was lying a body.

DAUGHTER: What? Come on, you're crazy!

OLD MAN: A body! A body with its chest opened!

DAUGHTER: Don't be silly!

OLD MAN: Rudi stood next to it and put the soldering-iron into its chest. And the chest, it was full of wires and made of concrete. That night Rudi built the first machine-man.

DAUGHTER: That night Rudi made a life-size puppet for the Carnival parade! And now I'm going! (*The DAUGHTER stands up, the OLD MAN also stands up and pulls her back)*

OLD MAN: Wait! Just wait! Please! It is true! It is really true, daughter! Rudi is the leader! And I am finished! I am finished!

DAUGHTER: Come on, stop it, I don't want to hear any more! I want . . .

OLD MAN: Because, you understand, if Rudi agrees, about the cabin, then, then he won't agree without good reason! He'll come, in the middle of the night, and he'll cut open my chest and he'll wire me up and he'll fill me up with concrete!

DAUGHTER: *(Screams)* That's enough! Stop it! *(The OLD MAN looks at her, something dawns on him)*

OLD MAN: *(Softly)* I understand. I understand. Why didn't I see it before? You are also one of them! You are a machine!

DAUGHTER: *(Shakes the old man)* Papa! I beg you! Come to your senses! Please!

OLD MAN: Now I want to know! Now I'll find out! *(He grabs her brutally in the chest)*

OLD MAN: Where are your wires, huh? Where are your wires? *(They fight with each other. The DAUGHTER pushes the OLD MAN back, he falls to the ground)*

OLD MAN: I knew it. The machine people are very strong. I knew it. *(The DAUGHTER goes to help him up, he pushes her back, stands up slowly alone)* Go! Clear off! You machine!

DAUGHTER: *(Desperate)* Papa!

OLD MAN: *(The OLD MAN sits down on the chair, puts his hands on the slab of wood)*

(Sings softly)

Small am I, small stay I,

Mamma's raised me from a hazelnut!

DAUGHTER: Papa!

OLD MAN: (*Sings louder*)
    Small am I, small stay I,
    Mamma's raised me from a hazelnut!
(*THE DAUGHTER looks at him in despair, goes out*)
OLD MAN: (*Sings softly*)
    Small am I, small stay I,
    Mamma's raised me from a hazelnut!

THE END

Beyond Our Understanding

Characters

HE and SHE, both mid-fifties

Set

Hospital ward

Scene 1

(The stage is in darkness)

HIS VOICE: A Merry Christmas and a Happy New Year and the best of health to you and your boys from your brother-in-law Sepp and his wife. I'm still healthy, thank God, only, my wife has been in the hospital for the last four weeks, we don't know what it is. Best wishes, bye for now.

(Lights come up. A hospital bed, a locker, a chair. SHE is lying in bed, attached to an intravenous tube. He is standing in front of her in his Sunday best, taking bananas, crossword puzzle, and a greasy paper bag out of a nylon shopping bag, and putting the things on the bedside locker)

HE: Look, here are the bananas. And a few crossword puzzles.

SHE: Thanks love. What's in there?

HE: Crackling. From Gerda. She said you really like it.

SHE: Oh God! I can't possibly eat that. I have to stick to my diet. That's far too fatty.

HE: *(Sitting down on the chair)* I didn't know that. I'll take it back then.

SHE: You forgot the magazines, mm ?

HE: Oh God, I thought I'd forgotten something!

SHE: Bring them next Sunday then. In the meantime I can borrow some from the others. (*HE nods*) And on my bedside table at home is a pile of romances. Bring the three on top. On the Track of the Poacher, The Secret of the Beautiful Doctor's Wife and I can't remember the third one right now. It's got a castle on the cover. The Romances of a Count or something like that.

HE: Good. Hope I remember.

SHE: It'd be wiser to knit you something. You've hardly got any winter socks anymore. But I just can't manage it. My hands are so stiff. And cold as ice. Just feel.

HE: (*Taking her hand, HE nods, and lets her hand go, looking at the intravenous tube*) What's that, then?

SHE: That's for the blood, I think. Because my blood's so terrible. They're putting something into me. Two bottles a day.

HE: And what does the doctor say? They still don't know what's wrong?

SHE: No, they don't know for sure. I'm being kept under observation, that's what he said, the doctor.

HE: I've never had a day's illness.

SHE: No, you were always fit as a fiddle.

HE: Except once after the war. But that was more because of the food shortages.

SHE: You were always strong.

HE: Suppose I must be. And I've always had my cigarettes. And my beer. And worked damn hard.

SHE: That's because you're a man. Because you've never had anything wrong with you down there, like me.

HE: Because that damn Seiwald threw you down the stairs.

SHE: Yes, that was the beginning. How I lost the first child.

HE: And because of that my child died afterwards, in your womb.

SHE: Well, it was an "ectopic" pregnancy. For a whole month I carried a dead child in my body. It just rotted away inside of me. If they hadn't operated on me in time, I would have died for sure.

HE: Seiwald did you in.

SHE: Well, I divorced him after that.

HE: Because he never worked.

SHE: And he had TB. God, he made my flesh crawl. He always wanted to sleep with me. He would drag me off to the bedroom in broad daylight. Never a moment's peace!

HE: You don't need to tell me that. I don't want to know about it. The consumptive bastard!

SHE: And he's still alive to this day. He's got his own house in Vorarlberg. I've told you before. Gerda found out. He married one of the Gsiberger girls.

HE: I could still kill him to this day.

SHE: He was good for nothing. Wanted to send me out stealing from the farmers. After the war. Then he beat me up, because I wouldn't do it. He was always stealing bicycles. And he was always after other women.

HE: My child didn't live because of him.

SHE: Now he's got a house. He's a somebody in a textile plant. Foreman or something. He was never stupid.

HE: We could have afforded a couple of kids. There's child benefits. And we've both always worked.

SHE: It wasn't to be. It was all just fate.

HE: Bastards like Seiwald should be lined up and shot.

SHE: He got me pregnant deliberately, just so I would have to marry him. He knew all right, that my mother would give me no choice.

HE: We could have had lots of kids.

SHE: You don't have to keep on blaming me.

HE: I'm not blaming you. It would've been nice, that's all.

SHE: I always told you we should adopt one. In '53, Inge Stettner put her twins up for adoption. We could've had them. But you wouldn't.

HE: It was just after my child had died. Thought we might have another go.

SHE: But the doctor had already told you there was no chance.

HE: You can always hope.

SHE: When they've taken everything out, there isn't any hope any more.

HE: An adopted child is not like your own.

SHE: A child is a child.

HE: But not my flesh and blood.

SHE: A child is a child.

(Black out. Music)

Scene 2

(The stage is in darkness)

HIS VOICE: A Merry Christmas and a Happy New Year, best of health and happiness to you and Lois from Sepp and the wife. I must tell you that my wife has been in hospital for four weeks, but so far they haven't found out what it is. Best wishes, bye for now.

(Lights come up. SHE in bed, HE on the chair)

HE: How're you doing?

SHE: A bit weak.

HE: You look a bit off-color.

SHE: I've got pain everywhere. In my stomach and in my kidneys and in my chest. My nails keep breaking and my hair's falling out.

HE: Are they doing anything for you?

SHE: Not up till now. They've examined me properly, though. Blood, urine, and they took something from the small of my back. The doctor said, I just need a proper rest. It's the fault of the Health Insurance doctor, that's what I say.

HE: Why?

SHE: Well, you know how awful I've felt the last few months. But the Health Insurance doctor never believes you. He always sends you back to work much too soon. He never even looks at you when you go for your appointment. He never even examines you. "You women never want to work, that's what's wrong with you," he said to me. As soon as you can stand up, he reckons you're well again.

HE: Yes, but what can you do?

SHE: As if it did him any good.

HE: It's probably because of the malingerers. You always get them. So, he never believes anyone.

SHE: If he had examined me, he'd've found out I wasn't malingering. When I could hardly stand up. And cold sweat on my face. Had a funny turn in the bus.

HE: Yes, well, what can you do? You can't win against these people. So, what do you do all day?

SHE: Lie here. Sometimes I read or do a puzzle. But I can't do it for long, because I get a headache. Sometimes I don't know what to do with myself, time goes so slowly. Then I lie here and everything goes through my mind.

HE: But you could always talk to the other women.

SHE: Oh, I do. That one over there in the corner, she's quite a character. She's got breast cancer, but she never stops laughing. I like chatting with her. But we always have to shout, because she's so far away and we're not allowed to get up. Also she's a Yugoslav, so it's hard to understand her. And now there are three over there who are not well at all. That's why we can't make much noise. That one next to me had a curette yesterday. Twenty-two years old. She sobbed half the night. Made me sob too. Then they gave her an injection. She's asleep now.

HE: You women don't have it easy.

SHE: No. Not at all. How are you doing, then?

HE: Oh, I'm all right.

SHE: Do you cook yourself anything?

HE: Yes, yes, I do a bit. At lunchtime I eat in the canteen. But at night I make myself something. And on weekends.

SHE: I can just imagine the mess you make.

HE: Cooking is no work for a man.

SHE: No, it's not. Have you figured out the washing-machine?

HE: Shrunk one of my pullovers.

SHE: Thought so. But I'll be home again soon.

HE: Hope so.

SHE: What do you do with all the time?

HE: In the evening I watch TV.

SHE: Don't you ever go to the pub?

HE: Yes, yes, I do.

SHE: Drink a few beers. . . .

HE: Yes, a few beers, then I leave again.

SHE: I'll be home again soon, though.

HE: Yes. It's nothing without you.

SHE: No, it isn't.

HE: The apartment's so empty.

SHE: Because you got used to having someone around.

HE: It doesn't feel right.

SHE: Well, it's already twenty-eight years since we got married.

HE: Yes.

SHE: I'll soon be back.

HE: Night before last I had seven beers.

SHE: Did you get drunk?

HE: Yes. I'm not used to it any more.

SHE: Go on, enjoy your beer.

HE: Made a damn fool of myself. I'm simply not used to it anymore.

SHE: Doesn't matter. It's no one else's business.

HE: I get drunk almost every day.

SHE: Makes no difference. It's no one else's business. It's your money after all.

HE: Once you're home again, I won't go to the pub any more.

SHE: Then I'll cook you something special. Then we'll have a bottle of wine and watch TV together.

HE: Hänsel and Gretel never stop shrieking.

SHE: What's wrong with them?

HE: Because you're not there. They're always shrieking and looking out for you.

SHE: They're not used to it, me not being there. You do always feed them regularly and clean out the cage?

HE: Of course. They don't do without a thing. They always get fresh water.

SHE: It's a pity you can't put them on the floor, where they get the lovely sun in the afternoon.

HE: But of course I do. In the morning, before I go, I put the cage in just the right spot.

SHE: Because they love it so much when it's warm. They're Japanese, you see, and they love the warmth.

HE: Yes, I know they love the warmth.

SHE: Is Gretel still pulling out Hänsel's feathers?

HE: Yes, I'll say! He's all bald again!

SHE: Then you'll have to separate them!

HE: I tried. I did put Hänsel in the second cage. But you know how it is. He gets really depressed. We've already tried it a couple of times.

SHE: But if she keeps on pulling out his feathers! That's
　　　not nice.
HE: Yes, I know. I know it's not nice. But when you put him
　　　in the second cage, then he just flops on the floor all
　　　depressed and doesn't sing and doesn't eat. He'd
　　　rather have his feathers pulled out than be on his
　　　own.
SHE: They're queer old birds. Maybe you should put the
　　　cages really close together, so they can see each
　　　other.
HE: Yes, they're funny birds, those two.
SHE: You must rub him with Nivea sometimes. That does
　　　him good. Especially under the wings. It itches him
　　　there. And then he pecks at it till he's all raw.
HE: Yes, he's already all raw again. But I don't trust myself
　　　to take him out. I'm always afraid I'll crush him.
　　　He's such a tiny little creature. Me with my huge
　　　hands. . . . It's much easier for you.
SHE: Yes, better leave it then. Before you squash him.
　　　He'll survive till I get home.
HE: When do you think they'll let you come home again?
SHE: I still don't know. The doctor tells me nothing. He al-
　　　ways just gives me a nice smile.
HE:　Is he nice, the doctor?
SHE:　Oh yes, very nice. Always joking.
HE: But he never tells you anything.
SHE: No, he never tells me anything.
(Black out. Music)

Scene 3
(The stage is in darkness)
HIS VOICE: A Merry Christmas and lots of happiness in
　　　the New Year and the best of health to all in your
　　　house from your nephew Sepp and wife. Anyway
　　　I'm well, only I've had my wife in hospital for four
　　　weeks, but I hope they'll soon find what's wrong

with her. Good wishes, and see you before long.

(Lights up on stage. SHE in bed, HE on the chair)

SHE: Do they want to throw you out?

HE: I don't really know what's going on. There's all kinds of rumors. But there must be some truth to it. The factory council rep. said another of the owner's factories has already been shut down.

SHE: Has he got more than one?

HE: Yes, of course. Three or four. The factory council rep. said, he doesn't really understand it because the orders aren't too bad. We've got that—hm—export contract with Italy, and it will be a long time before everything's delivered.

SHE: Well, what's it supposed to mean then?

HE: I don't know what's wrong. Anyway, the factory council rep. said that a lot of machines will have to be replaced, because they're obsolete and they no longer comply with the—hm—safety regulations.

SHE: Yes, well? So? They don't, do they? You told me yourself that three men got dragged into the machine and one man had his arm torn off.

HE: Yes, right. But that would cost heaps. And it looks like the owner doesn't want to invest any more. He owes taxes. A few million. But he said, in any case, that's what I heard, if he's forced to pay, then he'll close the plant straight away.

SHE: Is that right? What's his name?

HE: Gottlieb. He's a German, I think. At the factory we call him "The Good Lord." I've already told you that.

SHE: Ah yes. "The Good Lord." Because he always descends from the clouds!

HE: Yes, because he always lands in the factory grounds in his helicopter, when he comes to inspect the place. He turns up about four times a year. Like the dear Lord he descends from heaven. Then he storms through the factory, with two flunkeys with briefcases behind him, and after two hours he disappears into the clouds again.

SHE: Why doesn't he want to invest any more?

HE: I don't know. I don't understand any of it.

SHE: They won't sack you though, will they? You've always been a good worker. And you've been there so long.

HE: That's the reason. I'm already too old. The factory council rep. said, the first to go will be the ones over fifty. He also reckons it won't be so bad for me because I've only got a few years to go till early retirement anyway.

SHE: But you'll feel it in your pension, if you don't work till sixty-five.

HE: And how I'll feel it. I inquired about it. It will amount to quite a tidy sum.

SHE: And will you find anything else, if they lay you off?

HE: Not easily, no.

SHE: I'll just get another office then, to clean. I can manage that.

HE: Come on, when you can hardly bend down any more, with your back. Anyway, don't tempt fate, nothing is certain yet. We'll see soon enough how things are going to turn out. First you've got to get better, that's more important.

SHE: And if not, we'll find something or other. It's not as bad now as it used to be. Times are quite different now. You can't compare it with how things were.

HE: Yes, it was much worse then.

SHE: I can still remember it well. In '32, my mother went to the mayor and asked him if he didn't have a job for her. Dad had been in an accident, and there wasn't enough for us kids to eat anymore. My mother said, she would do anything, no matter what it was, even pick up the stones behind a plough, if she had to. And the mayor—he was a relation of hers, you have to imagine—do you know

what he said to her? "Go into the forest and collect
some pine-resin, it also fries beautifully in a pan,"
he said, his Worship the Mayor. I've never forgotten
it. Never!

HE: Yes, there's nothing you can do about it. You can't win
against these people.

SHE: But at least he came to a miserable end, the pig! Because my mother cursed him. The resin, that you
wish on my children, may it stick in your gullet"
She said to him. And three years later, he was dead.
Stomach-cancer. From then on, everyone went in
fear of my mother. The witch of Lana. Under the
Nazis she always said "Good Day !" never "Heil Hitler".

HE: No one was unemployed in Hitler's day.

SHE: No, that's true. We had a war instead. (*Nodding in
agreement, HE stares straight ahead, miserably*)
Come on, don't despair. It'll all turn out for the best.

HE: Yes, of course.

(*Blackout. Music*)

Scene 4

(*The stage is in darkness*)

HIS VOICE: A Merry Christmas and a Happy New Year,
and the best of health to you and your loved ones,
your brother Sepp and his wife. Thank God, I'm
healthy, apart from my stupid sciatica, only I've
had my wife in hospital for four weeks, I hope I soon
find out what's going on. So with good wishes, bye
for now.

(*Lights up on the stage. SHE in bed, HE on the chair. he is
not in his sunday best, but looking very unkempt, as he
reads out a letter to her.*)

HE: Recent fluctuations in market forces unfortunately
give us no alternative but to introduce long overdue

measures of rationalization and the gradual reduction of the over-capacity of our work force. We would like to thank you for your long years of loyal service.

SHE: And that means, that you're out?

HE: That means that I'm out!

SHE: They treat you like a dog.

HE: That's it, then.

SHE: Perhaps you'll find something else.

HE: (*Shaking his head*) I've already been to the local Employment Service several times. They look at me with pity , as if I've got one foot in the grave.

SHE: Why didn't you come straight away? I've been worried.

HE: I couldn't face you.

SHE: Come on, it's not your fault.

HE: Twenty-three years work and then you get a letter like this. (*Cries silently*)

SHE: Perhaps you'll find something. How many did they sack?

HE: They've laid off sixty-four so far. The older ones and the single men. The young ones will find something. But us old ones . . . Toni Klausner wanted to kill himself. Threw himself into the river. But they fished him out.

SHE: Did they? Well, he was always over-sensitive, poor Klausner.

HE: He's suffered a lot already. And how's he supposed to meet the mortgage payments on his house?

SHE: But that's no reason to go and kill yourself. He's no right to that. With a wife and kids. What a thing to do!

HE: Well, I can understand it. Suddenly, you're no use to anyone any more. Suddenly, you're redundant. Living on charity. (*Taking out a half-full bottle of beer, he has a swig*)

SHE: We'll find something. Just wait till I'm home.

HE: When'll that be?

SHE: Don't know yet. But I feel better already. It won't be long now.

HE: Sitting at home all day on my own, I can't stand it.

SHE: I understand.

HE: I'm not used to it. I've worked all my life. I don't know what to do with the time. How to get through the day.

SHE: Been playing cards again?

HE: Yes.

SHE: Won anything?

HE: No, lost.

SHE: When the doctor does his rounds today, I'll ask him. If he'll let me go home. I feel a lot better already.

HE: I lost 250 Schillings.

SHE: You've often lost more than that before.

HE: I haven't played for fifteen years. Now I'm drawn to it again.

SHE: Because you're bored.

HE: I don't really want to. But you've got to talk to someone. Have a few beers. Enjoy yourself. Slam cards down on the table. Then you don't have to think.

SHE: I'm not cross with you.

HE: I'd never have thought it, that I'd miss you so much.

SHE: Because we've got so used to each other.

HE: And I haven't always been good to you.

SHE: Me neither. That's life.

HE: Now I feel like crying, every day.

SHE: Because everything comes together.

HE: I won't be able to put up with it much longer.

SHE: You mustn't talk like that.

HE: The day after tomorrow's Christmas Eve.

SHE: Yes. Christmas.

HE: Will they let you out?
SHE: Of course. I already feel a lot better.
HE: Because it would be awful.
SHE: We've never been apart, at Christmas.
HE: But perhaps they'll let you out.
SHE: Of course.

(Blackout)

HIS VOICE: My dear sister Gerda, I have to tell you that
unfortunately my wife died yesterday and I don't
know what it was from. I don't know what's going
on any more. It's beyond our understanding. The
funeral will be on the 27th of December, if you could
please come. Good wishes, your brother Sepp.

THE END

Dragon Thirst
or
The Rusty Knight
or
Black and White, Money and Bread,
The Living and the Dead

An enchanted play

Translated by

Heidi L. Hutchinson

Characters
DRAGON (an enchanted prince)
DOE (a fairy queen)
NIKLAS (a knight)
JAKOB (a squire)
MARTHA (a lovely maiden)
NORG (a gremlin)
SCHNECK (a sorcerer)
YOKER (a man-eating beast)
NIX (a fresh-water mermaid)
MOTHER
FATHER
4 CHILDREN, 3 GUARDS, 1 BEAR

LOCATIONS:
A lake and its shore
A room in a miner's cabin
A mountain valley, with cave
A sleeping chamber in the Dragon's iron fortress
A clearing in the forest, with cave

Prelude

(By the light of the full moon; the black and yellow
DRAGON and the white DOE)

DRAGON: Many hundreds of years ago
　　　　I wanted to take you for my own
　　　　and when you said to me: Nevermore!
　　　　you opened up a wound so sore
　　　　that still today it burns inside
　　　　whenever I see you.

　　　　Ever since that time, you know
　　　　I've wanted to tear your heart out so.
　　　　I've wanted to throw you in the fire
　　　　so that nothing would remain on the pyre
　　　　but ashes and dust.

DOE: I know well your hatred of me
　　　　and well I know your anger
　　　　But should ever our blood mingled be,
　　　　I would be Doe no longer.

　　　　And even if I long for you
　　　　I dare not feel desire,
　　　　for then I must succumb to you
　　　　and forfeit all my power.

　　　　I am the people's comfort and shield,
　　　　you are envy, defiance and evil,
　　　　you are cold and I am warm,
　　　　I am love and you are scorn,
　　　　you are money and I am bread,
　　　　I am the living and you are the dead.
　　　　And so we shall remain at war
　　　　eternally and forevermore.

Scene 1

(A lake with its shore. On a large boulder in the lake sits the NIX. She is singing a song without words. After some time, the gremlin NORG sneaks up from the side. On all fours he crawls through the shallow water, attacks the NIX suddenly, pulls her from the rock, and, grunting, drags her toward the shore. The NIX struggles desperately, and tries to return to the water. NORG throws her down on her back, sits on her belly, and pins her hands to the ground. The NIX's fish tail thrashes in desperation; the thrashing motion slows, the tail is still)

NORG: Now I've got you, you cold fish!
      Heh, heh, you'll make a tasty dish
      for my Lord the Dragon!

NIX: Sisters, help me,
      I cannot defend myself!

NORG: Stop your wailing!
      Shut your mouth, they can't hear you!
      All they hear is the rush of the water!
      (he gets down off of her, shakes himself in
      disgust, and wipes his wet hands on himself.)
      Ugh, what a wet sack you are!

(the NIX immediately attempts to crawl back into the water, pulling herself along by her hands. NORG reaches for her long hair and pulls her back)

      Whoa, Fishy! Wrong way! We're going this way!
      (he tries to pull her along; she resists)

NIX: Oh, I'm so afraid!
      Gremlin, I beg you, let me go!
      I don't want to die, life is so lovely!

NORG: You're coming with me.
    There's no way out!
    If I don't bring home a fishwoman,
    I'll catch hell from the Dragon!
    (he drags her along a few feet)

NIX: Oh woe, oh woe, what shall I do?
    Gremlin, listen, I know how much you love
      to squeeze!
    You can have me anytime you want!

NORG: But I don't even want you!
    I only like to squeeze warm-blooded crea-
    tures!
    Your fishy body does nothing for me!
    So come, quit your fussing,
    I'm taking you with me.

(he tries to lift the NIX onto his shoulders; she resists; he drags her along the ground a little ways)

    Damn, this ornery cod is struggling so hard
    that I can't move her!

(he drops her)

    All right, then I'll just wait a while.
    Out of water I know you won't last long!

(he sits down between the water and the NIX. The NIX begins to weep and moan, rocking sorrowfully to and fro. After a while she grows weaker, sinks to the ground, opens her mouth wide, gasps for air, and looks silently but longingly toward the water. NORG whistles the tune that he will be singing in Scene 2, when sitting on top of the child. The NIX shows more and more signs of suffocating, clutches at her throat, her tail thrashes wildly to and fro. In desperation, she attempts to crawl back toward the water.

NORG *gets up and stands in her way. The NIX grabs onto his legs)*

NIX: Gremlin, I beg you! I must return to my watery home! *(gasping for air, she turns over on her back. Her tail moves more slowly. NORG begins to feel pity)*

NORG: Oh, what a scene! *(he can no longer stand to watch and turns away, but then looks again. The NYMPH wheezes)*
I can't stand to watch this any longer!
I'll bash her skull in and be done with it!

(he looks around, finds a large stone, picks it up, raises it over the NIX's head. At this moment MARTHA enters. On her back she is carrying a bundle of wood, in her hand a basket of mushrooms. She is briefly taken aback, drops both bundle and basket, runs to NORG and pushes him aside)

MARTHA: *(to NORG)* What in the world are you doing?
You toad, you!

(NORG growls angrily, lunges at MARTHA; she grabs a branch that is lying on the ground nearby and hits NORG over the head with it. NORG falls, screaming and clutching his head with both hands, and rolls on the ground in pain)

NORG: Ow, ow, ow! I'm dead! I'm dead!
My skull is broken! Ow, ow, my head!

MARTHA: *(runs to the NIX and kneels next to her)*
You poor thing! How can I help you?
What should I do?

NIX: *(whispers)* To the water! To the water!

(MARTHA pulls the NIX to the water. NORG sees this)

NORG: Stop! Stop!
(points two fingers at MARTHA)
Flesh, stand still,

as long as I will!

(MARTHA freezes in place, but the NIX is already in the water, swimming away. NORG runs over, wades into the water, searches here and there for her, but in vain)

NORG: Oh, I'm angry!
Ooo, I'm furious!

(to MARTHA)

What do you think you are doing,
you human bitch?
Wrecks my plans and throws me in a ditch!
And on top of that, my head she cracks!
Is this the proper way to act?

(he strikes at MARTHA a few times; she doesn't move. He clutches at his head again)

Ow, ow, ow, my head hurts so!
What'll I do now?
I'll have to catch a doe.
Or a pheasant. Or a hare.
My Lord will have my hide for sure!
Ow, ow, ow! He'll cover my body
with kicks and punches for punishment

(feels his head)

but I've already got a dent!

(to MARTHA)

And all because of you,
you scourge of the human race.
Just for that you'll stay there, frozen,
until your body rots in this place!

(he turns away, then turns back again, because he has just had an idea. He examines MARTHA from head to toe)

That is . . . *(to himself)*

> She might be just the thing for the Dragon!
> Not bad looking . . .
> Might even please him some,
> the cute little mouse! *(calls out)*
> Flesh, move!

(MARTHA finds she can move again, and looks astonished)

> Mark my words, maid!
> We'll see each other again soon.
> And then I'll throw you down
> and squeeze you as much as I please!

(he runs away. MARTHA watches him disappear. The NIX reappears in the water. She has regained her strength)

NIX: *(to MARTHA)*
> I thank you! You saved my life!
> I assure you it will not have been in vain.
> From now on, you will never be alone again.
> I will tell the Queen about you.

MARTHA: Fine, whatever you wish.
> But now I must go home
> and make supper for my mother.
> Must take her the mushrooms.
> Farewell, Nix!

NIX: Farewell, dear child!

MARTHA: *(walks over to the basket, picks up the mushrooms that have fallen out, hoists the bundle of wood onto her back)*
> Now, quickly home!

(she waves at the NIX, the NIX waves back; MARTHA hurries off. The NIX watches her leave and then disappears under the water)

Scene 2

(A shabby living room in a poor miner's cabin. Night. The dying FATHER is in bed in a half-sitting position. The MOTHER and five CHILDREN are standing beside the bed. The oldest of the children is MARTHA. The FATHER collapses and is dead. The MOTHER closes his eyes and straightens the bedclothes around him)

MOTHER: You fought hard, my dear husband. Hard.
    Not because you need to be afraid
    of what lies ahead for you.
    Certainly not, I know that's true.
    It was worry about us that
    kept you struggling so,
    worry about our daily bread.

(the other CHILDREN are quiet, MARTHA begins to sob)

    Five children and no one left to go
    down to the mine to keep us from the dread
    of hunger and poverty.

MARTHA: No, Mother, you needn't despair!
    I'll find work for myself somewhere.
    I'll go to a noble family and serve
    in the kitchen, the barn or in the fields.
    We'll see what it yields!
    MOTHER: Yes, go on, go, you're right.
    You'll make enough for yourself alone.
    You'll get along out on your own,
    I have no fear of that.

MARTHA: I'll make enough for all of us.
    You know how swift I am at work!

MOTHER: Oh, but Martha, my dear child!
    Do you believe that as barnyard help
    you could earn enough to feed us all?

Your meals and perhaps a place to sleep
is all they'll give you for your keep.
I know those people, those nobles!
No, I don't see a way out.
What ever will become of us?

(suddenly the DRAGON appears at the door, in the form of a handsome man, elegantly clothed in black and yellow, with a walking stick and hat)

DRAGON: *(tips his hat)* I wish you all a good evening!
I must have come at a bad time.
But . . . the road is long
and the days grow ever shorter.

(looks over at the dead man)

I see *(to MOTHER)*
your husband has passed away.
That is bitter, a source of great grief.
But where there is sorrow,
it's often not far to joy and relief.
And that is why I am here today,
because I would like to take away
yonder maiden *(points to MARTHA)*
to be my wife.

MOTHER: *(to MARTHA)* Do you know this man?

MARTHA: No, Mother! I've never seen him before in my life!

MOTHER: *(to the DRAGON)* My Lord, this is certainly not
the proper time to talk of marriage!
My husband's body is still warm,
and it is local custom here
that we should mourn him for a year.
We put on black clothes every day
and think of the one who has passed away.

For his road is long
and he is alone.
It is narrow and steep
and scattered with stones
that we must clear away for him.
And now don't stay a moment more:
there is the door!

(the DRAGON reaches into his satchel, brings out a large sack, walks over to the table, opens the sack and turns it over. A multitude of shiny gold coins fall jingling onto the table. The CHILDREN approach the table and stare with wide eyes. One of the CHILDREN reaches for the gold coins, MOTHER slaps his hand. The DRAGON brings forth a second sack and dumps more gold coins onto the table)

DRAGON: *(to MARTHA)*
You don't know me,
but I know you!

MARTHA: I can't imagine how you do!

DRAGON: I saw you in the forest.
You were gathering wood,
looking neither right nor left, full of arrogance.
On my white horse
I came riding by.
For an instant you glanced up—
with eyes like the sky
in the throes of spring.
That is when I knew one thing
for sure:
she must come with me,
she my wife shall be!

(MARTHA is intrigued by the DRAGON; MOTHER notices this)

MOTHER: *(softly)* Beware, Martha, he is nothing but a
　　　peacock!
　　　(to the DRAGON) What is your name and what
　　　your rank?

DRAGON: I have nothing to hide,
　　　I'll tell you with pride!
　　　My name is Wolf Hatzes,
　　　Hatzes of the Gorge!
　　　I have a castle,
　　　many acres of land, and
　　　seven thousand people
　　　at my command!

MARTHA: *(looks at MOTHER, who averts her eyes in re-
　　　sentment)*
　　　Mother! This way
　　　all our troubles would be over!

MOTHER: A nobleman! And you, a miner's child!
　　　That will never work out!

DRAGON: Blue blood means nothing to me,
　　　it doesn't make a difference.
　　　And I am wealthy myself;
　　　I need nothing further.

MOTHER: We need to think this over
　　　in peace—give us time!

DRAGON: No, I am sorry, it's late,
　　　there is no time to hesitate.
　　　On the table you see the dowry,
　　　it's more than enough!
　　　So *(to MOTHER)* consider this well
　　　before you say no!

MARTHA: Mother, I am going with him!
　　　I don't know him, but I like him!
　　　And the money, you know you can use that!

MOTHER: No, you mustn't sell yourself!

MARTHA: I am not selling myself,
      I am giving myself away!
      The dowry is for my parents to keep.

(walks over to the DRAGON)

      Stranger, I like you well.
      Your face so pale and that wonderful hat—
      And your whole manner—
      I've never seen anything quite like that!

(she takes his right hand and looks at it)

      Look, Mother, his hand, so soft and pale,
      not a scratch and not a callous . . . *(smiles)*
      it seems he doesn't do much work,
      more likely he plays at cards.
      I'll take him, Mother,
      please let me go!*(walks over to FATHER)*
      I know, Father, you have nothing against it
      and you'd certainly be glad to know
      that there is no more poverty and hunger in this
      house!

(smiles at FATHER, softly)

      And I am getting a noble husband!

MOTHER: Well, then . . . So be it! You have
      my blessing! Go, if you must!

(MARTHA hugs her MOTHER)

(to the DRAGON)

      But treat her with kindness,
      for she is like a doe!
      She knows nothing of men,
      nor of the wide world.
      She has never been out

beyond our forest and field.
Life could easily overwhelm such a young thing.
And give us at least three days time.
We need to lay our father to rest.
And I would like to have my daughter
for a little while longer.

DRAGON: *(shakes his head)*
I have no more time to waste.
How many times must you be told?
Come along, girl, let us go,
my coach is waiting down on the road!

(MOTHER and MARTHA look at each other, MOTHER sighs, MARTHA takes heart and begins to say good-bye to everyone.)

MARTHA: Heaven protect you, Father! And you, children!
Mother, farewell! Please don't grieve.

(she walks over to the DRAGON)

MOTHER: *(softly) I feel there is trouble ahead.*

(the DRAGON bows politely and turns toward the door with MARTHA)

MOTHER: *(to FATHER with despair)*
Father, have we done the right thing?

(The DRAGON lays his arm and his cloak around MARTHA so that she nearly disappears; they leave the room.)

But, Sir, please tell me, where are your lands?
Are they far away?
Will I be invited to your wedding day?
And will you ever come back this way?

(but MARTHA and the DRAGON have already left. Silence. MOTHER walks slowly over to the table, sits down, and stares sadly into space. Sudden darkness, thunder and lightning, smoke rises from the table, then the light re-

*turns. The gremlin NORG is now sitting on the table, and
the gold coins are gone. NORG is convulsed with laughter,
and rolls around on the table. The CHILDREN run to their
MOTHER, who rises, frightened. NORG begins to dance
around on the table)*

NORG: *(sings)*

> Now he has, he truly has
> fooled you,
> the Dragon, my great Lord!
> For he is one who always lies
> and never, ever keeps his word!
> Every four-and-twenty days
> he needs a fresh new woman;
> the old one would have died away!
> Her body grows as cold as clay,
> and Yoker dines on the remains.
>
> Now Martha, too, will meet this fate.
> To save her life it is too late.
> And you will starve in misery,
> for the gold was nothing but sorcery!

*(NORG giggles, looks around, hops with a gleeful shout
over to the dead FATHER, sits on his chest and begins to
press on him, grunting with pleasure)*

MOTHER: *(goes over to him)* Get away! Get away!

NORG: *(stops)* Aw, damnation! He's cold and stiff!
And I wanted so much to squeeze him!

MOTHER: *(tears him away)* Get away!

NORG: Whoa! Not so ferocious, woman!
I am Norg, I need to squeeze!

*(he throws himself at one of the children, pushes it over, sits
on its chest and presses. The other children stand by in terrified silence)*

MOTHER: Get away, you filthy swine!

(she tries to pull him off, but NORG holds on to the child; she goes and gets a kitchen knife and starts toward NORG with it. He sees this)

NORG: Knife, jump!

(the knife jumps out of MOTHER's hand; NORG points his finger at her)

NORG: Flesh, stand still,
        as long as I will!

(MOTHER freezes in place; NORG begins squeezing the child again, singing)

> Sleep, little one, sleep
> you're safe in Norg's keep.

(the child falls asleep)

> And if you dream of obscene things,
> these are the dreams that Norg brings.
> Sleep, little one, sleep.

(the DOE appears in the doorway, in the form of a beautiful woman in white)

DOE: *(to MOTHER)* Flesh, move!

(MOTHER can move again. NORG looks up in panic, sees the DOE, and is suddenly filled with dreadful fear)

NORG: It's the Doe! Ow, ow, ow!

DOE: Knife, jump!

(the knife flies up from the floor and toward NORG; NORG jumps up off the child in horror and runs away. The knife follows him around. NORG tries to climb the walls; the children laugh. NORG tries to crawl under the bed, but the knife blocks his way, and he can't escape. Finally it forces him into a corner and hovers in front of his nose)

DOE: Norg, lie down!

NORG: I don't want to lie down,
  I'm not tired!

(the knife closes in on one of NORG's eyes. He lies down immediately)

  I'm lying down! I'm lying down!
  Ow, ow, ow, this is what I get!

(the knife retreats and lands on the table)

DOE: *(to the CHILDREN)* Now you may squeeze him for a
  bit!

NORG: No, don't squeeze!
  Pretty please, don't squeeze!

(the CHILDREN sit down on NORG and begin to press)

  Ow, ow, ow, this is terrible!
  Ow, ow, ow, I feel horrible!
  No, I can't stand it any longer!
  I beg you, go away, it's over, your joke!
  Ugh, I feel like I'm going to choke!
  Children, I beg you, get off!

(the CHILDREN get up; NORG rises shakily)

  Oh, what a scandal,
  my, what a fright!
  I'll never be able to show my face
  among gremlins again; I've lost that right!
  (he limps to the door)
  So awful, so awful, what a torment, I could almost
  cry!

DOE: Norg!

(NORG turns to her)

  Tell the Dragon he had better beware!

NORG: I'll tell him, I'll tell him!

(he leaves, and as he goes, one can still hear him whimpering)

> Ow, ow, what a fright!
> I can't believe I'm still all right!
> Ow, ow, ow!

DOE: I am the Doe,
> the queen of the fairies.
> And the Dragon is an enchanted prince,
> the mightiest in all the land.
> He has tricked you,
> as you now know,
> and certain death awaits your daughter.
> I would like to help her now,
> But I can do nothing,
> for she went of her own free will.
> I am bringing you something to eat;
> more I cannot do.
> Here's bread . . .

(she hands MOTHER a small loaf of bread. The CHILDREN run over immediately, taking the loaf away from their MOTHER, they tear it apart and begin to eat. There is much more bread than it at first seemed)

> . . . and now bring me a pitcher,
> so that I may give you some milk.

(MOTHER brings a pitcher, the DOE holds a fir cone above it and milks the cone. Milk squirts out the bottom. The CHILDREN crowd around, one of them takes the pitcher, drinks from it. The DOE hands the fir cone to one CHILD and places the child's other hand on the cone. The CHILD tries to milk, and it works)

DOE: The bread will never run out
> and the milk will never run dry.

Until the children are grown,
you will always have food in supply.

MOTHER: I thank you, I thank you
from the bottom of my heart, White Lady!
But . . . my daughter, my Martha,
is there no hope and no help?

DOE: We shall soon see
if there might be
help for her.
There is *(she smiles)* a rusty knight,
who is traveling throughout the land,
and he is unmarried as yet,
and he has a fine strong hand.
Perhaps he can develop a plan
and coax the black and yellow dragon
out of his iron fortress,
which remains closed to me,
for I have no power over iron,
but only over wood and stone. Farewell!

(she exits)

Scene 3

(Mountain ravine. On the left is a cave, the interior of which is only partially visible to the audience. A gloomy day. Rain showers. Fog. Inside the cave a mighty battle is raging. NIKLAS is fighting a dragon. We can see nothing, only hear the sounds of battle, and the snorting and raging of the dragon. Every once in a while light flashes from the interior of the cave, when the dragon breathes fire. Smoke is pouring out of the cave)

VOICE OF NIKLAS: Jakob, the lance! Quick!
     Well, come on, darn it!

(a terrible cry of pain from JAKOB as he stumbles out of the cave, his hands pressed against his eyes. He falls to the ground, whimpering. His hair is burned, his head is smoking. JAKOB is the squire of NIKLAS. He is carrying, on various parts of his body, a number of weapons, namely different types of swords, lances and spears, spiked iron balls on chains, as well as two longbows and two quivers with many arrows. Most of the weapons are in leather scabbards attached to JAKOB's back. In addition, JAKOB is carrying two shoulder bags, two rolled blankets and a banner, whose pole is also affixed to a leather scabbard on his back. While JAKOB kneels on the ground, whimpering, the battle in the cave rages on)

VOICE OF NIKLAS: Jakob, a spear! Jakob! Where the
     heck are you?

(NIKLAS lunges out of the cave, looking for JAKOB. NIKLAS is wearing a rather rusty suit of armor, which is missing some pieces. The visor of his helmet is closed, on his left arm he is carrying a heavy shield. A bundle of dragon tongues dangles at his hip. NIKLAS sees JAKOB, runs over to him, in the heat of battle fails to notice his condition, grabs a spear from his back, throws it into the cave, the dragon roars, NIKLAS observes the dragon)

NIKLAS: Doesn't want to die, the son-of-a-gun!

(NIKLAS drops the shield, takes a bow from JAKOB's back and shoots a lightning-fast volley of arrows into the cave. With each shot the dragon roars in agony; the last time, he roars particularly horribly)

NIKLAS: Right in the eye! Now I've got you!

(NIKLAS pulls a large sword out of the scabbard on JAKOB's back, holds it with both hands, raises it high, and runs with a yell into the cave. Another battle. Suddenly

NIKLAS appears, stumbling backward out of the cave. Then the head of the dragon appears. NIKLAS is covered with dragon's blood, the dragon is bleeding from several head wounds, an arrow is embedded in one of its eyes. The dragon opens its mouth, roaring, and smoke pours out. NIKLAS plunges his sword deep into the throat of the dragon, who roars one last time and dies. His head crashes to the ground. For a moment there is complete silence. NIKLAS looks at the dragon and then suddenly lets out a shout of triumph. Then he lifts his visor, pulls the long sword out of the dragon's throat, and lays it aside. He grabs hold of the dragon's tongue with both hands and pulls it out, takes his shorter sword from the scabbard on his own hip, and cuts the tongue out. He puts his sword away, comes out of the cave carrying the bloody tongue, and looks around for JAKOB, who is no longer whimpering, but is still holding his hands in front of his face)

NIKLAS: Hey! You don't have to be afraid anymore, it's all over! Here is its tongue, look!

(JAKOB takes his hands away from his eyes and looks in the direction of NIKLAS. He is blind.)

JAKOB: Sire, I can't see anything anymore!

NIKLAS: What? *(he walks over to JAKOB, kneels down in front of him, looks into his eyes, holds a hand up in front of them, moves it back and forth)*
Can you see my hand at all?

JAKOB: I see nothing but a red wall.
A wall made of pure fire.
The monster blinded me.

(JAKOB bows his head, NIKLAS looks at the dragon tongue in his hand, then looks at JAKOB)

NIKLAS: What a way to end . . .
Poor Jakob, my faithful squire and friend!

JAKOB: It can't be helped.
> This life is tough.
> It's dangerous business,
> this dragon-hunting stuff.

NIKLAS: *(lifts JAKOB to his feet)*
> Jakob! We have to take just one more chance!
> I still must kill the bane of the land!
> The dragon Hatzes, the magic prince,
> the one who is both animal and man.
> I have to get him,
> then we'll go home,
> then the journey is over,
> the last battle won.
> Then I'll reward your hard work and courage.
> I promise you, your life will be good!
> The doctors from all the land will come
> and servants from everywhere will run
> to bring you what you desire.
> Everything will be done just as you say,
> and you'll have your very own tavern some day.
> You'll no longer be squire, no longer be small,
> but a lord, a free man;
> you have earned this all!
> Believe me, Jakob, no cost is too great.

JAKOB: Yes, yes, it's all right, Sire,
> don't take it so to heart!
> But just now be a friend,
> and help me to mend . . .
> In here *(reaches for a shoulder bag)*
> is a salve. Spread it on my eyelids,
> and I will be much better.

(NIKLAS reaches into the bag, rummages around, and fishes out a small wooden box)

And then let's be on our way
to the black and yellow dragon.
We'll conquer this last one as well!

Scene 4

(Sleeping chamber in the Iron Fortress of the DRAGON. Black iron walls, no windows. At rear a large double door. A collection of human hearts hangs above the door. The hearts glow red. The only piece of furniture is in the middle of the room: a black wrought-iron bed with black linens. MARTHA lies asleep in the bed, clothed in a yellow night-shirt. NORG is sitting on MARTHA's chest and squeezing lustily. MARTHA is having nightmares and groaning. All of this is not visible yet, as the room is pitch dark. Only the red human hearts glow through the darkness. The door opens, light enters the room. Two GUARDS, with faces like vultures, are visible outside. The DRAGON enters, this time in the form of a dragon. He is carrying a candelabra with burning candles. NORG is startled, jumps quickly off MARTHA, and looks terribly sheepish. The DRAGON closes the door and approaches him)

DRAGON: *(angrily)* Didn't I tell you
not to squeeze my women?
(raises his hand to strike NORG)

NORG: *(shrinks back)* Don't hit me! *(bows in deference and backs away)*
Please forgive me, Lord!
Forgive me! You know me, it's an irresistible urge!

DRAGON: But not for much longer!
If I catch you one more time,
I'll slaughter you like a sheep!
(walks over to the bed and looks at MARTHA)

> She has a good, sound sleep.
> Like all innocent young people.
> *I* won't, ever again. Ever again.
> *(shakes MARTHA by the shoulder)*
> You! You! Wake up!

(MARTHA opens her eyes, sees the DRAGON, screams and shrinks away from him. NORG giggles. Martha looks over at him. He waves at her, giggling)

MARTHA: *(to the DRAGON)* Who are you?

DRAGON: The handsome man from last evening!
> Don't you remember me? I bought you!

NORG: *(giggles)* I like that: Bought!

MARTHA: Handsome man? Ridiculous!
> You're nothing but an ugly old dragon!
> *(screams at the top of her lungs)* Mother! Mother!

DRAGON: Screaming won't help you.
> No one can hear.
> Not a sound can escape my iron fortress!

MARTHA: *(looks around in desperation)*
> It's hopeless!
> Not even a window to jump out of.

DRAGON: No, not a window in the whole place.
> You see, I can't stand the sun on my face.

MARTHA: Change yourself back into the handsome man,
> I ask you with all my heart!
> And then I'll obey you as best I can!

DRAGON: *(shakes his head)*
> It's not good for me,
> the strain makes me sore.
> I'm a thousand years old,
> not young any more!

MARTHA: A thousand years? Now you are lying!

That cannot be true.

DRAGON: I'm telling you:
a thousand years.
And I feel myself growing old,
which is why I need young blood,
for mine is already cold.
Your blood is now yours to give;
I need it to live!

MARTHA: *(jumps out of the bed on the opposite side)*
I will give you nothing, you despicable creature!
I want to go home! Let me go!

NORG: Shall I break her neck now?

DRAGON: *(sets down the candelabra, approaches MARTHA)*
You will stay here!
And I will have no more argument!
Or else much worse will be your plight.
Do you think you can put up a fight?

(he grabs her by the shoulders. MARTHA beats at him with her fists)

MARTHA: You swine, go away, I don't want you!

(she escapes the DRAGON's grasp, but then NORG jumps on her back. She falls down. NORG is sitting on her chest instantly. He giggles and squeezes her, MARTHA beats at him. The DRAGON goes to them, grabs NORG and throws him aside)

DRAGON: *(to MARTHA)* Get up!

MARTHA: *(gets up; to NORG)*
Just you wait, you hideous dwarf!
I'll repay you yet, somehow! *(NORG laughs)*

DRAGON: *(to MARTHA)*
The servants are at hand

to bring you food at my command.
And later we will here recline,
and let your blood mix with mine.

MARTHA: No, I want nothing to eat!
I want to go back to sleep!
It is still the middle of the night!

(she jumps into bed and pulls the covers up to her chin)

DRAGON: Outside the sun is shining,
it's the middle of the day!
You will get up now,
or there will be Hell to pay!

(MARTHA pulls the covers over her head; the DRAGON walks over and pulls them back off. MARTHA lies there, rolled into the fetal position. The DRAGON pulls her out of bed and throws her to the ground with a swipe of his paw)

DRAGON: *(roars)*I am so full of wrath,
my dragon blood is boiling within.
The spittle is running out of my maw,
and my tolerance is wearing thin!

(MARTHA gets up off the floor, cowering in fear)

NORG: Tear her in pieces, tear her up!
Go on, go on, tear her apart,
'til nothing is left of her, not one bit!

DRAGON: You won't do as I see fit?
What, do you think there is a choice here?
Maid, I am capable of every torture ...
I have the power!
I can have you bound and whipped and tied to the
bed . . .

NORG: She'll be grateful to lick your feet instead!
Every one of the women has given in!

MARTHA: *(in despair)*

Oh, Mother, why did I go with him?
Now I am caught in a trap!

DRAGON: *(to NORG)*
Call the guards!
I want them to lash her to the bed!
I have such a craving for her blood!

(NORG turns toward the door)

MARTHA: *(sinks to her knees)*
Oh dread, oh dread,
I wish I were dead!

(outside the door there is suddenly the sound of fighting, the rattle of weapons. The three in the room stop and stare at the door. The door suddenly bursts open and NIKLAS becomes visible outside, battling the three vulture-faced GUARDS. Several other GUARDS lie dead in the background. The blind JAKOB stands helplessly and fearfully nearby. His eyes are now covered by a filthy cloth bandage. NIKLAS enters through the door swordfighting, with the GUARDS right behind him. He is brandishing his sword, holding the large shield on his left arm for protection. It is a wild battle. NIKLAS is fighting fiercely. He kills the first of the three GUARDS. NORG hops over to the fighters and points his finger at NIKLAS)

NORG: Flesh, stand still! Flesh stand still!

(in his excitement, and because he is having no effect, he begins to babble)

Flesh, still stand! Flesh, stall stind!
Uhh, still stesh flesh! Uhh, flash slash stash!

(NIKLAS kills the second GUARD)

NORG: Ow, ow, ow, what is happening?
What is this? This can't be!

(NIKLAS kills the third GUARD, NORG hops to the door—

making a wide detour around NIKLAS—looks out and sees the dead guards)

NORG: *(shouts into the hallway)* Guard! Hey, guard!

NIKLAS: Shut up, you dog,
you are shouting in vain; they are all dead!
I've killed every last one!

(he walks to the door. NORG flees to the safety of the DRAGON. NIKLAS leads in the frightened JAKOB)

NORG: Ow, ow, ow, we're in for it now!

DRAGON: Tell me who you are, young man,
before I toss parts of you into the hall!

NIKLAS: *(laughs)* You are the one who had better take
care
that I don't dash you against a wall!
(sings) My name is Niklas von Laudegg,
they call me the Rusty Knight.
I am the greatest dragonslayer —
to this title I've earned the right!
Look here! *(shows them his dragon tongues)*
Eleven tongues I've collected till now;
with yours the dozen will be complete.
And even if you are as strong as a cow,
with my strength and wit you can't compete!

DRAGON: All right, then come,
let us fight, Rusty Knight!
But I'm sure I'll be
changing your mind tonight!

NIKLAS: Where is your sword?

DRAGON: I don't need a sword,
I pass out my blows like this!

(roaring and with raised sword, NIKLAS runs at the DRAGON. The DRAGON simply catches the sword in his

left paw and pulls it out of NIKLAS' grasp, tosses it away, looks at the baffled NIKLAS, grabs the shield from his left arm and tosses it away as well. NIKLAS leaps over to JAKOB, pulls a lance from his collection and runs toward the DRAGON with it. The DRAGON takes the lance away from NIKLAS and breaks it in two, then takes NIKLAS by the throat with one of his paws and begins to strangle him. NIKLAS falls to his knees, gasping for air. NORG hops over and watches the gasping NIKLAS with glee)

NORG: Yes! Yes! Do him in! Do him in!

MARTHA: *(runs over and tries to pull the DRAGON away.)* No! Please don't strangle him!

NIKLAS: *(gives up his resistance, drops his arms, sobbing)* Yes, do! Strangle me! Strangle me!

MARTHA: Mr. Dragon, please!
Let him live!
I'll do anything! You may have all I can give!
I'll give you my blood, to the very last drop!

JAKOB: Oh, my heart is about to stop!
I can't stand it!

(the DRAGON looks at MARTHA and lets go of NIKLAS, but NIKLAS presses the paw against his throat again)

NIKLAS: Strangle me! Kill me!
I couldn't bear the humiliation!

MARTHA: *(pulls NIKLAS away from the DRAGON)*
You mustn't say things like that!
What humiliation, you silly knight?

NIKLAS: Well, isn't it right?
I am conquered, I am vanquished!
Only death can save my honor!

(NIKLAS walks over to JAKOB and starts to pull a sword from its scabbard, JAKOB notices and tries to resist, moving away and fending off NIKLAS with his hands)

JAKOB: But, Sire, I beg you,
        you can't do that!

(NIKLAS attempts to pick up the sword that is lying on the floor, but MARTHA kicks it away and shakes NIKLAS)

MARTHA: Stop this now!
        Stop and think a moment!
        You have no reason to be ashamed at all!
        You've slain eleven dragons
        and all the guards in this hall!
        Others only dream of such deeds!

(she strokes the hair out of his eyes)

NORG: Let him go, you silly cow!
       If he wants to kill himself . . .

MARTHA: You, little demon, be silent now!
        This is no affair of yours!

DRAGON: Tell your noble knight, somehow,
        he needs to make up his mind!

NORG: Oh, but I would love, and how,
       to lop off his head myself!

NIKLAS: All right, then, I'll go.
        But, fair maid, what will become of you?

MARTHA: Well, you see, the dragon beast
        wants my blood. I will have to
        give him a little.

(NIKLAS looks horrified)

MARTHA: It's not so bad; I have enough!

NIKLAS: Now that makes me mighty angry!
        What do you care about my life?
        We are complete strangers, don't even know each
        other!

JAKOB: Sire, please, let's go!

MARTHA: I'm sorry, I just don't like to see
people getting killed. *(smiles)*
And besides, you are still young!
And a man, a handsome, strong man!
Someone who needs to live!

DRAGON: *(to NIKLAS)*
It's about time you left!
I've had enough of this chitchat!
Either you go or I'll finish you off!

NIKLAS:*(picks up his sword, puts it away, extends his
hand to MARTHA)*
Farewell! Perhaps we'll meet again . . . ?

MARTHA:Yes, perhaps. My name is Martha. Think of me
now and then.

NIKLAS: I'll surely not forget you!

*(he walks over to JAKOB, unrolls a length of rope that is
wrapped around his waist and pulls JAKOB by the rope toward the door. He turns around one last time, looking with
despair at MARTHA)*

MARTHA: Go! Go on! *(NIKLAS and JAKOB exit)*

DRAGON: So, now, maiden, come to me!

MARTHA: *(fearfully)*
What I have promised,
I know I must keep.
I am hoping the wounds
won't be very deep.

Scene 5

*(Clearing in the forest, near a hillside with a cave. Night.
The moon is shining, crickets are chirping. Several large*

boulders, suitable for sitting on, lie scattered around. The entrance to the cave is covered by a rock slab. At the side of the cave there is a pile of bones, human skeleton parts, and rotting scraps of clothing. Toward the front a small camp-fire, next to which are a rucksack, a shoulder bag, and a walking stick. In the middle of the clearing, a strange wooly ball with glowing eyes is rolling about, growling and curs-ing. It is the magician SCHNECK, who has changed him-self into this ball by mistake)

SCHNECK: Rats, what's going on here?
        I'm going to lose my temper!
        Bumbledeboom and rat-a-tat-tat,
        Sniffetysnuff and jiminy-cat!
        Oh—nonsense!
        Lizard tongue and mushroom spore,
        I wish to be the old Schneck once more!
        And now! Presto! I'm myself again!
        —But no, I'm not! What chagrin!
        I'm still the same thing as before!
        Lordy, I get dumber every day!
        What is this thing, anyway?
        Goodness me, I'm cross and sore
        I won't put up with this much more!
        Spirits, wherever you are, I pray
        help me with an inspiration!
        It would be a cruel fate
        if I had to stay the way
        you see me today!
        Rats, I'm about to go
        stark raving mad!
        This is the third time
        it's happened to me,
        I've given myself
        the wrong identity!

Oh, what a torture!—Hmmm . . .
Hunkadung, shivermoo,
Hoarfrost and whisker of cat,
I want to be Schneck, and that's that!

(nothing happens. SCHNECK roars angrily and rolls around furiously. NIKLAS and JAKOB enter. NIKLAS looks dejected and dishevelled. He notices the strange creature, lets go of the rope on which he is leading JAKOB and draws his sword)

NIKLAS: Who's there?

SCHNECK: What? What's the matter? Who is speaking?

NIKLAS: It's me, Niklas, the Dragonslayer!
        And I can tell you right now,
        one mangy varmint more or less
        won't make much difference to me!
        So, who are you?
        Go on, speak, or I'll cut you right open
        with my sword!

SCHNECK: Don't you dare!
        Can't you see, I am not armed!
        What cowardly dog would do me harm?

NIKLAS: Stop your tirade and litany
        long enough to answer me!

SCHNECK: Just a minute, I have to answer the call!

(he rolls off to the side and disappears)

JAKOB: Sire, who is it you are talking to?

NIKLAS: If only I knew!
        I've never seen anything like it before!

(one can hear a sound like a horse urinating)

JAKOB: I think I hear a horse urinating!

NIKLAS: No, it's that creature, taking a leak.

(the sound stops. There is a moment of silence)

SCHNECK: Ha, now I have it! *(he returns)*
Toecheese, calves' knees,
Buckets full of bumblebees,
Camelspit and whisker of cat
I want to be Schneck, and that's that!

(sudden darkness, lightning and thunder, smoke, light again. In the midst of the smoke, the magician SCHNECK appears, where the fur ball used to be. NIKLAS and JAKOB are frightened. NIKLAS raises his sword. SCHNECK looks disheveled, and his clothing is that of a wandering conjurer)

SCHNECK: I'm back!—
My, that took a bit of doing!
And now, honored, fair Knight,
let me tell you who I am!
(sings)
I am the sorcerer Schneck,
the greatest in the world!
From a bit of insect neck
I can make a string of pearls!

And if I wish to ruin someone
all I do is say the word,
instantly he will succumb,
in violence and pain absurd.
And if a man for love does pine,
but a woman won't glance his way,
I'll mix her up a special wine,
and she'll be his that day!

And should the rain not come one spring,
the crops die in the field,

then I can make the heavens sing
and streams of water yield.

So, now you know with whom you are dealing!
Take care not to vex me!

NIKLAS: *(is impressed and puts away his sword)*
    I wouldn't think of challenging you!
    My sword is useless against your sorcery!

SCHNECK: *(looks at JAKOB)* You're well equipped,
    I must say!

NIKLAS: *(nods)* If you want to slay dragons,
    you have to be well armed!

SCHNECK: I believe it! But tell me, could you spare a bite
    to eat, or a swallow of wine?

NIKLAS: We don't have much ourselves. A bunch of water-
    cress,
    a piece of bread, and some water is all I can offer.

SCHNECK: Anything will do right now.

NIKLAS: *(sits down on a rock, looks over at JAKOB, whose
    facial expression says that he doesn't want to share
    his food)*
    Well, what's the matter, Jakob? Open your pack!

*(JAKOB reluctantly reaches for the provisions bag and
pulls out a piece of bread and a bunch of watercress)*

SCHNECK: Why does he have a bandage around his head?

NIKLAS: Oh, the poor fellow ...
    It was a dragon. Scorched his eyes.
    Now he is blind.

SCHNECK: Oh, my! *(approaches JAKOB)*
    And his hair is missing around the wound!

*(he takes the bread from JAKOB, but pushes the watercress
away)*

You can keep the green stuff,
I don't like it! Have you no wine?

JAKOB: No! Only water!

(JAKOB reaches for a canteen, SCHNECK accepts it grouchily, walks over to a rock near the fire, sits down, eats the bread ravenously, drinks some of the water. NIKLAS gets up and walks over to JAKOB)

NIKLAS: Come, sit down!

(he leads JAKOB to a rock and seats him, then sits down himself)

JAKOB: I hope I will be able to see again soon!
Sire, I can't take this much longer!

NIKLAS: *(looks at SCHNECK)*
It is indeed a great honor
to meet up with you this way, today!

SCHNECK: I should hope so!

NIKLAS: I hadn't heard of you, to be sure
although I've traveled here and there,
but I have seen that you can conjure . . .
I have a request, if I may dare?

SCHNECK: You can say anything,
I won't bite you!
As long as you keep feeding me . . . !

NIKLAS: *(gets up)*
I have been wandering about the countryside
for twenty-four days and twenty-four nights.
My mind has gone dull from sorrow and cares!—
To the North, not very far from here,
there is an iron fortress.
An evil dragon resides within,
an enchanted prince.
He is invincible.

I fought bravely, but to no avail . . . !

SCHNECK: *(wishing to change the subject)*
 You should clean your armor once in a while!

NIKLAS: Yes, I know, it's pretty rusty!
 I've been on the road a long time.
 It wasn't Heaven, believe me!
 But I've been killing dragons
 with diligence and courage all along!

SCHNECK: Bravo! Damned dragons!
 Ah, but I can still hear
 my stomach begging to be fed.
 Is there no more bread?

NIKLAS: Jakob!

JAKOB: *(reaches, grumbling, into the pack, rummages
 around and brings out a piece of bread)*
 The very last piece!

SCHNECK: *(walks over to JAKOB and takes the bread)*
 Wouldn't happen to have some bacon?

JAKOB: No!

SCHNECK: Are you sure?

JAKOB: No! I swear by my life and limb!

(SCHNECK sits back down and eats)

JAKOB: *(grumbles)* He's eating our last bit of bread!

NIKLAS: Forgive me, Schneck, but I am quite poor!
 I can't afford more!

SCHNECK: Hah, now you must be pulling my leg!
 A knight with no money! Never heard of it!

NIKLAS: The slowest of his horses and just half a bag of
 gold
 was all my father gave me!
 Go forth and prove yourself in the world, he said,

return home in three years' time!—
The money is long since spent
and the horse is long since dead,
but as for me, I am doing just fine,
for I am the greatest dragonslayer of all time.

SCHNECK: But listen, I know a fellow
who only killed two of those beasties
and is now drawing an enormous pension
from his prince!

NIKLAS: I don't accept money, I fight for honor!

SCHNECK: Well, you could ask for a little more!
This isn't exactly a piece of cake!—
And what about women?
Plenty of them must have shown interest . . . ?

NIKLAS: I don't take those favors either!
And besides, I haven't found one I liked yet!

SCHNECK: You don't say? My blood begins to boil and fret
anytime I see a female!

NIKLAS: I am a bachelor and hope to remain one
until I've found the perfect mate.
And perhaps I have just found her,
(grief-stricken) and perhaps it's all too late!

SCHNECK: Now, now . . .

NIKLAS: My heart is so heavy, so full of pain!
She gave her life for me!
Eyes like a doe!—This is what I
meant a while ago, Sorcerer Schneck!
My favor, my request . . .

SCHNECK: *(is afraid of failing again)*
No, I can't help you,
I can't do a thing! *(gets up off his rock)*
I am tired, I have to lie down!

JAKOB: Scaredy-cat!

SCHNECK: What?

NIKLAS: Schneck, I beseech you, listen to me!

SCHNECK: *(to JAKOB)* You're asking for a punch in the
     nose!

NIKLAS: The enchanted prince is holding a maiden cap-
     tive!
     I don't know exactly what he is doing with her,
     but he wants her blood,
     that's what she said!
     He wants her young blood!
     And so I ask of you, can't you help her?

SCHNECK: You think I'm the King of the Elves?
     It's not so simple!

NIKLAS: *(kneels before SCHNECK)* I beg you! I am on my
     knees!

SCHNECK: Oh, stop, get up, I can't stand these pleas!
     I will try!

NIKLAS: *(gets up off his knees)* Oh, Schneck, I thank you!

JAKOB: *(mumbles)* He's going to make an ass of himself!

SCHNECK: What?

NIKLAS: *(to JAKOB)* Shut your mouth, you blind ape!
     (to SCHNECK) Don't listen to him! The dragon
     fried his brain!

SCHNECK: *(to JAKOB)*
     This is your last warning!
     I won't take one more impudence from you sitting
     down!
     Right! And now gather round!

*(he looks around, picks up a twig off the ground and draws
a circle around himself in the dirt)*

Where is this fortress?

NIKLAS: There! *(points)*

SCHNECK: *(turns in the direction NIKLAS is pointing, covers his face with his hands, mumbles a bit, curses a bit, then raises his arms in the direction of the fortress and shouts)*
Up above and all around,
heavenward and forward bound,
come to me, come to me,
neither door nor gate
shall hinder thee!

(darkness, lightning and thunder, a great deal of smoke, then light again. When the smoke clears, there is a rusty stand holding a rusty washbowl in front of SCHNECK. NIKLAS looks on in amazement, SCHNECK scratches his head)

SCHNECK: You know, Knight, I'm not in a very good state and magic just hasn't come easy of late.

JAKOB: What did he do?

NIKLAS: Well, it didn't quite . . .

SCHNECK: Next time it will work, just watch!

JAKOB: *(mumbles)* If anyone believes it . . .

(SCHNECK concentrates once again, mumbles, raises his arms in the direction of the fortress again)

SCHNECK: *(shouts)*
Up above and all around,
heavenward and forward bound,
come to me, come to me,
neither door nor gate
shall hinder thee!

(darkness, lightning and thunder, a great deal of smoke, then light again. In front of SCHNECK there is now a fes-

tively set table with wonderful things to eat, and one chair)

SCHNECK: Well, at last! I've been trying to do that all evening long!

JAKOB: Sire, what has he done now?

(SCHNECK immediately sits down at the table, tucks a napkin under his chin, and begins to eat.)

NIKLAS: *(astonished)* Now there is a table filled with wonderful things to eat!

JAKOB: *(gets up)* Oh! Finally something decent to sink our teeth into! *(He stumbles around, searching, with outstretched arms.)* Where is the table? I want something, too! *(he passes close to the table, SCHNECK catches him by the arm and presses a roasted chicken into his hand)*

SCHNECK: There, fill your stomach! Sir Knight, come here, there's enough for us all!

(NIKLAS walks over to the table, JAKOB bites into the chicken. Suddenly there is darkness, thunder and lightening, smoke, then light again. SCHNECK sits baffled on the ground, the table and chair have disappeared, the chicken in JAKOB's hand is also gone)

JAKOB: What happened? Where is my chicken? *(searches on the ground)* My chicken is gone! My chicken is gone! Hey, Schneck, what have you done? Are you trying to make fools of us, you squirrel, you?

SCHNECK: *(gets up)* Oh, just shut up, you idiot!
I did nothing! The meal disappeared on its own!

JAKOB: Magic just isn't your strong suit, is it?
Come on, Sire, let's move on!

NIKLAS: Just hold your tongue a minute, Squire, damn you!
He can do magic, I saw it with my own eyes!

Schneck, please try one more time, I beg you!
Look, I have no one else I can turn to!

SCHNECK: *(looks at NIKLAS, sighs, steps back into the circle, concentrates, covers his face with his hands, mumbles, curses, then stops. His arms sink to his sides)*
It's not working, Knight, I'm sorry!
I can't do it anymore! It's over!

JAKOB: I told you he's a fraud.

NIKLAS: *(rushes over to JAKOB and kicks him so that he falls down, goes back to SCHNECK and grabs him and shakes him)*
A thousand gold pieces! I'll give you a thousand gold pieces!
My father is rich! And I'll be going home soon!

SCHNECK: *(tears himself away and sits down dejectedly on a rock)*
Leave me alone!

JAKOB: Sire, let's go!

(NIKLAS doesn't listen to JAKOB, but looks pleadingly at SCHNECK, who sees the look in his eyes)

SCHNECK: Sire, you saw it! It's all over with me! I have no more strength, no more power! Let me be!

JAKOB: But he *was* boasting before!

SCHNECK: *(gets up)*
Yes, I admit it!
I lied to you, I was leading you on.
I am nothing but a circus charlatan,
look at me!
All I can do is rid people of their purses
and then run quickly away
so that they don't cut my hands off!
But this you must know:

In days gone by,
six, seven years ago,
I was still in good form.
Back then I was the best sorcerer in the land!
But then I became a court magician,
received many honors
and plenty of money,
traveled the world
with my great lord.
But when life is that good
it is easy to become arrogant.
And so I misused my powers at every event:
just for the amusement of the nobles
I did entertaining magic tricks.
Toward the end I was using
my magic powers for evil things.
My lord convinced me
to ruin his enemies!
And suddenly I felt
my strength abandoning me.
And my arrogance
was my undoing!

The powers that be
became angry with me
because I had betrayed wizardry
and succumbed to black magic.
My grave had been dug.
To be burned at the stake was my immediate fate,
for my lord believed
I had been bribed by his enemies.
One night I escaped through a secret door,
and since then I have wandered from hill to moor,

> hardly ever a crust of bread
> and no roof over my head,
> a poor wretch, in the world adrift,
> who had forfeited a great gift!

NIKLAS: *(sadly)* Too bad! You were my last hope!
Martha!—She is in grave danger,
I feel it!—And I cannot save her!

SCHNECK: *(looks at the desperate NIKLAS, suddenly moves back into the circle, covers his face with his hands, mumbles briefly, raises his arms once more in the direction of the fortress and shouts)*
Up above and all around,
heavenward and forward bound,
come to me, come to me,
neither door nor gate
shall hinder thee!

(darkness, lightning and thunder, then light again; then a yellow nightgown comes flying and lands on SCHNECK's head. He pulls it down and looks at it)

There, that was my final deed!

(throws the nightgown down)

JAKOB: The same old mess again?

(SCHNECK goes over to his pack, opens it, unrolls a blanket, wraps it around himself, and lies down. Meanwhile NIKLAS runs to the nightgown, picks it up and looks at it)

NIKLAS: *(excited)* This is her nightgown, I recognize it, I saw it on her!

JAKOB: What happened? Her nightgown came? Well, then . . .

NIKLAS: *(interrupts JAKOB)* Bravo, Schneck, you are quite close!

Now, back into the circle, quick!

(SCHNECK gives no answer, but pulls the blanket over his head. NIKLAS walks over to him)

Schneck! This is proof that your powers are returning! You mustn't give up now!

SCHNECK: This is not a good sign,
as you seem to believe!
If the nightgown comes,
then the contents of the nightgown
should come, too. If they are alive.

NIKLAS: *(looks at SCHNECK in horror, then looks at the nightgown)*
I feel the ground trembling beneath my feet . . .
Or is it fear shaking me?
Do you think . . .

(sits down on the ground; SCHNECK props himself up in his blanket and looks at NIKLAS)

SCHNECK: At the risk that you should weep
or should want to strike me down, I have to tell you:
I sense that she is no longer alive!

VOICE OF NORG: Ow, ow, ow, is this one heavy! Ugh, what a load!

(NORG appears, carrying on his shoulders the dead, pale, bloodless MARTHA. She is wearing her original clothes)

NIKLAS: *(with resignation)* I feel my heart breaking.

JAKOB: *(listens)* Who is coming? Is that the gremlin, the servant of the Dragon?

NIKLAS: *(runs to NORG)* Martha!
(pulls MARTHA from NORG'S shoulders, lays her on the ground, and shakes her) Martha! Give me a sign! Show me that you are still alive!

NORG: You can cling to her as much as you want,

she won't wake up ever again!
How could she live, without a drop of blood?
And can't you see the hole in her chest?

NIKLAS: Yes. I see it. *(touches the hole)*
He has torn her heart from her body.

NORG: Quite right!
You must know
my Lord, the Dragon
has a collection of them!

(NIKLAS breaks down, sobbing, over MARTHA'S body)

JAKOB: *(stands helplessly nearby)*
Sire, I am so sorry! Oh, what a shame!

NORG: *(to NIKLAS)* Come on, stop your blubbering,
You're a strapping young lad!
You'll find another woman in no time!

(NIKLAS lets go of MARTHA, gets up slowly, turns to NORG, runs at him and begins to choke him. NORG is able to free himself and jumps clear. NIKLAS draws his sword and swings at NORG. NORG ducks agilely. JAKOB listens carefully, his head raised)

NORG: *(points his finger at NIKLAS)*
Flesh, stand still! Flesh, stand still!
Good grief, I can do whatever I will,
the spell doesn't work on this knight!

JAKOB: Sire, kill him, hit him, finish him off!

NORG: *(hides from NIKLAS behind JAKOB)*
Shut your trap, Knave!

(NORG grabs JAKOB and uses him as a shield, pushing him to and fro, so that NIKLAS cannot strike at him. JAKOB begins to thrash about, NORG falls down, bounces back up, NIKLAS wounds him with his sword, NORG grabs at the wound, looks in horror at the blood, runs hys-

terically back and forth, all the time trying to avoid NIKLAS)

> Oh, oh, he got me!
> How he swings with all his might
> swings his sword,
> what a gruesome sight!

JAKOB: Sire, squash that lout!

NORG: Blood! Torrents of blood! I'm running out!
> I'm done for! Ow! Ow! Ow! *(kneels down)*
> I beg of you on bended knee,
> have mercy on me! *(jumps away again)*
> Stop it! Stop it, I tell you!
> Stop it, you silly knight!
> Have a heart for my plight,
> It's not my fault!
> The dragon beast killed her,
> not I!
> I have no power of my own,
> I am only a helpless pawn!
> Oh dear, he's not listening!
> Whatever shall I do?

JAKOB: Stop your moaning,
> it's not helping you!

NORG: *(flees in the direction of the cave, NIKLAS following close behind) (to NIKLAS)*
> Just you wait! Now you're in for it!
> *(calls in the direction of the cave)* Yoker! Hey, Yoker!
> Open your eyelids, your next meal is here! Hey, wake up, you lazy bag of bones! Can't you hear me? *(still dancing around to avoid NIKLAS)* Here's something to eat! Young tender meat! Veal!
> *(the boulder at the opening to the cave is pushed aside with a crunch. NIKLAS stops)*

JAKOB: *(listens)* What is happening now?

(the man-eating giant YOKER comes out of the cave, looks around sleepily, yawns. In his hand he carries a small tree complete with roots, on which the soil is still hanging)

YOKER: *(to NORG)* You woke me out of the soundest sleep!

JAKOB: Who is this now?

NORG: *(to YOKER)*
>Please don't be angry
>that I woke you!
>Look, I've brought a nice gift for you!
>Sweet, tender meat! You can eat your fill!

(hides behind YOKER)

>But first you need to kill
>the little tin man!
>He'll keep it from you, if he can!

YOKER: Where is the tin man?
>I can't see him!

NORG: Well, right here, you blind old mole!
>In front of your nose!

YOKER: It's taps for him, it is!
>I'll smash him to bits with my fist!

NIKLAS: Come here, if you dare!
>I'll slaughter you like an ox!

YOKER: You'll have to grow a bit first, or stand on a box!

(YOKER approaches NIKLAS slowly, lifts the tree, brings it down with a crash, NIKLAS dodges it, the tree hits the ground roots first, the dirt billows out. JAKOB readies the heavy shield that he is holding)

JAKOB: Sire, take your shield, protect yourself!

(NIKLAS stabs YOKER with his sword)

YOKER: No fair tickling.

JAKOB: Sire, your shield! And maybe you need a lance!

(NIKLAS is not listening to JAKOB. YOKER swings at him like a machine, NIKLAS hops to and fro, dodging him. NORG circles around the two fighters, giggling)

NORG: See, Knight, he'll make you dance!

(YOKER hits NIKLAS with the tree, dirt billows out of it, NIKLAS falls to the ground, NORG laughs and jumps for joy)

SCHNECK: Oh, my, this doesn't look good! I have to make one more attempt!

JAKOB: Sire, hold your ground!

(NIKLAS rises again and continues to fight. Meanwhile SCHNECK enters the circle and begins to concentrate. YOKER hits NIKLAS on the right arm. NIKLAS drops his sword. A further blow knocks NIKLAS to the ground. SCHNECK mumbles frantically. NORG immediately jumps onto NIKLAS' chest and presses on him with enthusiasm. YOKER approaches slowly, lifting the tree high)

YOKER: Stand aside, Norg, I'm going to pound his skull to pudding!

(sudden darkness, lightning and thunder, smoke, then light again. A wine barrel lies on the ground in front of YOKER, with NORG sitting on it. Baffled, YOKER stands with the tree poised in mid-air. SCHNECK and JAKOB have also been turned to barrels. YOKER lowers the tree and looks around)

Now where did the tin man go?

NORG: Ow, ow, ow, a cursed affair! *(jumps down from the barrel)*
There's sorcery in the air!

YOKER: No need to get excited!
At least they are out of the way

and I can dine at last!

NORG: I am so angry I could tear my own leg off!

YOKER: *(looks at the wine barrel)* A swallow of wine with dinner would be quite nice! *(removes the plug, looks into the barrel, knocks on the side; it sounds hollow)* There's nothing in it! Too bad!

Oh, well, no matter.

I'll have to eat the roast dry.

(he walks over to Martha. NORG kicks the NIKLAS-wine barrel)

NORG: A pox upon you,
you mangy cur!

YOKER: *(looking at MARTHA)*
She's so pale, was she not well?

NORG: As well as any of them! Do you think I would bring the Dragon a sickly maiden?

YOKER: *(picks up MARTHA)*
A beautiful body, I must say! *(carries her to the cave)*
Well, then, so long! Thanks very much for the meal!

NORG: No problem. I won't let you down!
I'll return in another twenty-four days!
Enjoy!

(YOKER disappears into the cave and pushes the boulder back into place. NORG looks at the NIKLAS-wine barrel, then at the JAKOB-barrel, then at the SCHNECK-barrel, and hops over to it)

Evil eye! You deserve to die!
It was you!
You did the magic!

(a stream of wine squirts out of the barrel into NORG's face, and he jumps back, startled)

SCHNECK: *(in a hollow-sounding voice)*

Beware, gremlin,
don't get too bold!
I'll change you into a lump of coal,
if you're not instantly gone from here!

NORG: *(backing away, frightened)*
Are you crazy? Leave me alone!
No, I think I'd better make tracks.

(he hops away. There is a moment of complete silence)

NIKLAS: *(in a hollow-sounding voice)*
Schneck! Schneck! Where are you?

SCHNECK: Where do you think I am? Right next to you!

NIKLAS: Well, say, what have you done now? I can't see a thing, I can't feel a thing, and my voice sounds hollow, as if it were coming from a barrel!

SCHNECK: You *are* a barrel!

NIKLAS: *(after a second of shock)*
You know, Schneck, I'm losing my patience! You're no help at all! I would have gotten him, the man-eater!

SCHNECK: Oh, of course! I just thought it would be better if I did something before he pounded your head to pudding! But I do admit, it didn't go exactly as I wanted! I wanted to give you more strength, make you a giant! But I heard your bones being crushed, and in my haste, I slipped up a bit! You mustn't hold it against me.

NIKLAS: All right, all right! Now do something to fix us!

JAKOB: *(in a whimpering, hollow voice)*
Hey, Sir Niklas, this is your squire speaking!

NIKLAS: Are you a barrel, too?

JAKOB: I think so!
At any rate, I'm wet through and through!

SCHNECK: All right, I'll try again. *(begins to mumble)*

JAKOB: I think I have wine inside me!
   My head is all dizzy and fuzzy!

NIKLAS: And now he's in there eating my Martha, every
   last bit!

(sudden darkness, lightning, and thunder, smoke, then light again. All three are changed back into themselves and standing in the same positions as before)

JAKOB: I sure am getting tired of this thunder business!

(NIKLAS looks around in confusion, gets up, grabs his sword, runs to the entrance of the cave, and tries to roll away the boulder. He can't)

NIKLAS: *(shouts)* Come out here, you!
   I'll cut off your head and knock out your teeth,
   so that you'll never chew again!
   Come out, I say, I want to tear you limb from limb!

(nothing happens. NIKLAS comes back from the cave looking despondent, suddenly kneels down, turns the sword around, holds the hilt against the ground with his one hand, directing the tip toward his throat with his other hand, and gets ready to throw himself on the sword. SCHNECK has approached him, pushes him backwards, tries to take the sword away. They fight over it. JAKOB listens, confused)

JAKOB: Sire, what is the matter?

NIKLAS: Give it to me! Give it to me! I must die!

JAKOB: He's trying to kill himself again! Schneck, don't
   let him!

SCHNECK: I'm too weak! Help me, Jakob!

(JAKOB feels his way toward the two of them, finds them and touches them, trying to figure out which one is NIKLAS. He is pulled down by the two of them, stands up

again, feels around for NIKLAS, and recognizes him by his breastplate, which he has laid his hands on. He grabs onto NIKLAS from behind and pulls him back. SCHNECK succeeds in getting the sword away from NIKLAS; he tosses it away. JAKOB is still holding on to NIKLAS. SCHNECK touches JAKOB's arm)

SCHNECK: It's all right, Jakob. His sword is gone.

(JAKOB lets go of NIKLAS, who sinks to the ground)

JAKOB: Forgive me, Sire, I am usually not so impudent, but I just couldn't . . .

SCHNECK: *(to NIKLAS)* Come on, lad, don't be so hard on yourself!

NIKLAS: Be still! *(looks at him)*
What do you know of my pain?
What do you know of my misery?
I let my love down,
my love who gave her life for me!
Shouldn't I hate myself?

JAKOB: Sire, get a grip on yourself! You didn't know that she was to die!

(NIKLAS doesn't reply, but looks straight ahead. Suddenly the boulder at the cave's opening is pushed aside, NIKLAS and SCHNECK look over at it, because there is a crunching sound. JAKOB lifts his head and listens. The skeleton of MARTHA lands on the pile of bones. It is complete, not a bone is missing. JAKOB stands up in consternation)

JAKOB: Is he coming out again?

(the boulder is rolled back into place in the opening. NIKLAS walks slowly over to the pile of bones, lifts the skeleton, brings it forward to the others, sits down on a rock, holds the skeleton in his arms, looks at it, presses it to his breast, and breaks down in grief)

JAKOB: What's happening? Schneck, tell me, be so kind!

SCHNECK: *(mumbles)* He's out of his mind!

JAKOB: What? What's the matter?

(the DOE, in the form of a beautiful woman in white, enters the clearing. Suddenly it is morning; the sun rises. The DOE walks over to NIKLAS and observes him and the skeleton. NIKLAS looks up slowly and sees her; SCHNECK is also looking at her in amazement. The DOE lays both of her hands on the skull. Sudden darkness, but this time without lightning and thunder. Instead there is a strange hissing and ringing sound. Light again. JAKOB listens, perplexed. A live MARTHA now lies in NIKLAS' arms, in the same position as the skeleton previously. The DOE steps back, MARTHA and NIKLAS look at each other. NIKLAS cannot believe what is happening; MARTHA just smiles absently)

NIKLAS: Martha! *(he hugs Martha, looks at her, stands up still holding her, hugs her again, looks at her, and is beside himself with joy. MARTHA just smiles)*

JAKOB: What? Can it be? Martha is alive?

SCHNECK: Yes, it looks that way!
    That woman gave her back her life!

JAKOB: Woman? What woman? There's a woman here, too?

SCHNECK: She came softly as morning dew!

(walks over to the DOE)

    May I introduce myself, honorable lady?
    I am, so to speak, a colleague of yours,
    the sorcerer Schneck!
    Unfortunately, my magic powers are something of
    a wreck. And who are you, if I may ask?

DOE: I am the Doe, the Mother of the Forests, the Queen of the Fairies!

(NIKLAS kneels down before the DOE and kisses the hem of her dress.)

NIKLAS: You heard my heartfelt plea,
you delivered me from my disgrace!
I've never seen anything so wonderful,
(kisses her hand)
Oh hand of mercy and grace!
Let me be your servant beginning today!
You may ask of me what you want;
I'll do whatever, whatever you say!

DOE: *(smiles)*
Arise, Dragonslayer! I don't need a servant. But I like you well, as a man . . .

(NIKLAS is charmed and dazzled by the DOE, and nearly forgets about MARTHA, who is staring into space, smiling quietly and a bit stupidly)

JAKOB: If only I could see!
Introduce me, too, please, Sire!

NIKLAS: *(doesn't hear JAKOB, stands up)*
That you find me pleasing is a great honor for me! And I would go with you on the spot! But that maiden . . .
SCHNECK: . . . saved you from the Dragon! You fickle knave!
NIKLAS: Yes, you are right.
But I still need to ask Martha herself if she really likes me!
(walks over to MARTHA)

SCHNECK: I can't believe what I am hearing!
She died for you!

JAKOB: Yes, but remember, she wooed him, and not he her!

NIKLAS: *(takes MARTHA's hand)*

Tell, me, Martha, does your heart beat for me
alone?

MARTHA: *(smiling)*
You are asking too much, I don't really know!

NIKLAS: But Martha, please, you must know these
things!

*(SCHNECK approaches MARTHA and looks at her
closely)*

SCHNECK: Strange! She looks so vacant!
Her eyes are quite blank! It appears to me
that the maiden is not quite herself yet!
(to MARTHA) Are you sure you have all of your wits
about you?

MARTHA: *(smiling)*
I don't know, I couldn't say!
I don't feel well and don't feel bad,
I can't complain, anyway.
I feel a little cold inside,
as if I weren't human, not really alive.
Feel like I might be a stone.

DOE: *(walks over to MARTHA and gently lays her hand on
MARTHA's left breast)*
No heart. No heart in her body.

*(she withdraws her hand, but MARTHA quickly presses it
to her breast again)*

MARTHA: Oh, please stay! Your hand is so wonderful!

DOE: *(to NIKLAS and SCHNECK)*
Her heart stayed behind in the Dragon's collection.
He'll have to give it back to us.

*(the DRAGON suddenly appears, in the form of a hand-
some man. As he approaches, the sun disappears; the atmo*

sphere is gloomy. MARTHA is not afraid; she continues to smile)

DRAGON: You'll never see that day, Doe!
I won't give it to you ever, no!
And I'm taking the maiden with me when I go!

JAKOB: Uh-oh, now he's going to get us,
we're in trouble now!

DOE: Are my eyes deceiving me?
The Dragon out in the light of day?

DRAGON: Even if I don't like the sun,
nonetheless, you see I've come!

(shows them MARTHA's glowing, pulsating red heart, which he holds in his hand)

I fastened it over my bedroom door,
like all of my other conquests before!
Suddenly I see it start beating again.
And I realized, there and then,
who puts flesh back on bones?
That can only be the Doe!
And so I have come to ask for
what is rightfully mine.

(NIKLAS picks up his sword from the ground, runs at the DRAGON with a roar. With a mere wave of his hand, the DRAGON throws NIKLAS back, so that he falls. Suddenly the heart flies from the DRAGON's hand to the DOE; she catches it. NIKLAS rises again, stunned)

DRAGON: Doe, beware!
If you thwart my designs
just one more time,
my wrath will know no bounds!

(the DOE goes over to MARTHA and lays the heart to her breast; it disappears. Now real life returns to MARTHA,

and she runs over to NIKLAS, hugs him and caresses him)

MARTHA: Niklas! Dearest Niklas! My beloved! Now we
    can stay together for the rest of our lives!

(NIKLAS is confused, but doesn't resist)

DRAGON: I'll show you yet!
    I'll change you all to worms and rats!
    I'll tear you in a thousand bits!

DOE: No, Dragon! You'll never harm anyone again!

DRAGON: Just wait, Doe, it's your turn next!
    I'll get you in a minute!
    I know your vulnerable spot.
    Dragonslayer, quick,
    come here to me!
    Come here, I command you!

*(NIKLAS looks at the DRAGON wide-eyed and falls under
his spell)*

DOE: Stay where you are, Niklas!
    Don't move, and don't look at him!

NIKLAS: *(helplessly)* I cannot resist!

DRAGON: Come here, Niklas, I am calling you,
    do you hear my voice?

*(NIKLAS looks at the DRAGON, MARTHA takes NIKLAS'
face in her hands and turns it toward her)*

MARTHA: Niklas, don't! You know he is evil!
    He wants to ruin us!

DRAGON: You are right! You all must die!
    Niklas! Come over here!
    I won't wait much longer!

(NIKLAS looks at the dragon again)

DRAGON: Come! Don't listen to those whining women!

(NIKLAS wrenches himself free of MARTHA and starts to go toward the DRAGON, but MARTHA holds him back)

MARTHA: Niklas, I beg you, please stay!

DRAGON: Be still, woman! *(in a friendly voice to NIKLAS)*
Come on, now, come to me!
You hear nothing but my voice!

(NIKLAS frees himself gently but firmly from MARTHA and approaches the DRAGON)

DRAGON: Yes, that's a good lad!
Come here, dog!
Come, slave!

(NIKLAS stands before the DRAGON, the DRAGON puts his arm around NIKLAS' shoulders with a friendly smile and walks slowly around in a circle with him. Their heads are very close together, but they do not look at one another. The DRAGON mumbles something unintelligible, as NIKLAS stares with wide, spellbound eyes)

MARTHA: *(to the DOE)*
What is he doing with my Niklas?
Please, Queen!

DOE: Though I am mighty,
I am powerless now!
He is under the Dragon's evil spell!
But my time will come and my chance as well!

(the DRAGON and NIKLAS stop next to the sword that NIKLAS had dropped when he fell down. The DRAGON takes NIKLAS' arm; NIKLAS bends down, picks up the sword, and slowly approaches the DOE with it. He stops in front of her, looks at her with crazed, glowing eyes, suddenly pulls her violently to him, holds her around the waist with both his arms. He is holding the sword by its hilt with his right hand and the end of the scabbard with his left.

The DOE is now caught between his breastplate and sword)

NIKLAS: *(brutally)*
>Doe, now you are mine,
>and you'll go with me!
>You'll be human from now on,
>and animal nevermore be!

MARTHA: Niklas, what are you doing?

JAKOB: *(despondent)*
>I want to go home, I can't stand this any longer!

DOE: *(suddenly fearful)*
>Let go of me, young man!
>This won't bring you happiness,
>you are under the evil spell of the Dragon,
>who wishes to ruin me!

NIKLAS: Quiet now! There is no other way, I must have you!
>We will share our bed and bread
>until the day we both are dead.

DOE: *(in despair)*
>Niklas, this isn't right!
>The choice is not yours to make!
>If I choose with human blood to unite,
>that step must be mine to take!
>And then it can never be for long!
>Between me and you there is a wall
>that cannot be torn down.
>And I can never tolerate a lord over me,
>or my power to help will be forever gone!

NIKLAS: Hah, why should I need fairies and elves?!
>I am a big, strong man,
>and I can help myself, I can!
>And now you'll come along with me,

or feel my wrath,
for I won't take no for an answer, you see!

SCHNECK: Somebody ought to kill this guy! *(to NIKLAS)*
Enough of this comedy!

MARTHA: Niklas! Let the fairy queen go, for the sake of
my love,
I beg you, do what I ask!

NIKLAS: But I don't want you any more!
Go away, be gone!
I don't want to see you again!
(holds the DOE tightly)
You, you, you are my desire!

DOE: *(in despair)*
Oh! Oh! The power is leaving my body!
I am lost! Lost!
Will no one help me in my hour of need?

DRAGON: Your world is coming apart now, indeed!
Aren't you amazed at what he can do,
the little iron man!

SCHNECK: *(to the DOE)*
I wish I could help,
but I don't know how!
I feel a bit weak in the knees just now!

DOE: His iron is what keeps me,
his armor and his blade!
And captive in this iron,
I feel my powers fade!

(SCHNECK has an idea. He jumps into the circle, concentrates, and mumbles)

DRAGON: *(grins)* Go on, clown, forget your tricks!

(sudden darkness, lightning and thunder. When the light returns, the sword in NIKLAS' hand has turned into a

snake. NIKLAS hurls it away, letting go of the DOE as he does so)

JAKOB: There's that thunder again!

DOE: *(places her hand on NIKLAS' forehead)*
Spell, be undone! Set him free!

(NIKLAS awakes and looks confused. The DRAGON is full of wrath)

MARTHA: Hurrah! Hurrah for Schneck!

SCHNECK: *(to the DRAGON)*
How's that for kicks?
Was that just tricks? *(to MARTHA)*
He isn't laughing now!

DOE: I thank you, Sorcerer Schneck!
I am deeply in your debt!

SCHNECK: *(waves her off with an "it was nothing" gesture)*

DRAGON: *(to SCHNECK)*
Just you wait, clown, you'll soon have nothing to smile about!

(SCHNECK begins to feel a little bit fearful)

NIKLAS: What happened?
I had a strange feeling . . .
A longing, a desire, a feverish dream . . .

MARTHA: *(goes over to NIKLAS)*
That was the Dragon's spell! *(hugs him)*
I almost lost you!

NIKLAS: There's a ringing in my ears
My limbs are all sore
I feel as if I'd fought
against a whole army or more
in a most terrifying battle.

(MARTHA hugs NIKLAS tightly)

DOE: *(to the DRAGON)*
> Well, Lord of the Night?
> What's your next move?

DRAGON: For the last time: Hand over the maiden!

DOE: The maiden is in my safe keeping!
> You must leave without her!

DRAGON: All right then, so be it!
> But I will show you yet
> what happens to those who
> oppose me at every turn!
> Prepare yourself, Doe,
> for your end is near!
> And your noble knight will not escape me,
> nor will the clown you hold so dear!

JAKOB: He didn't mention me, what a relief!

DRAGON: *(raises his arms heavenward)*
> Come, ye powers! Come storm and wind!
> I am your lord,
> you my servants all,
> and you must obey
> whenever I call!

(suddenly a storm arises, with wind, lightning, thunder, and rain. Leaves fly through the air. MARTHA is knocked down by the force of the gale. NIKLAS bends over her protectively. SCHNECK and JAKOB cower on the ground, covering their heads with their arms. The DRAGON and the DOE stand face to face)

DRAGON: *(shouts)*
> Lightning, strike,
> and burn her to ash!
> Wind, blow her away

with the rest of the trash!

(the storm increases to a gale. The DOE begins to stagger, sinks to her knees, struggles against the storm, then lifts her arms skyward)

DOE: Storm, I fear you not!
      Lightning, you touch me not!
      Water, you can do me no harm!
      Between us there is a strong bond:
      I am your sister, remember this!

(struggles to her feet and stands with uplifted arms)

      So, now put an end
      to your wild display,
      and you, sun, appear
      and let the Dragon suffer this day!

(the storm ceases. The sun comes out and shines down with great intensity. One beam of light is clearly visible, shining directly onto the DRAGON. The DRAGON appears wrathful and terrified at the same time. The others get up off the ground and look toward the DRAGON. JAKOB sits down, breathing a sigh of relief)

JAKOB: That was another close call!

DRAGON: *(begins to suffer from the heat)*
      Away! I need to get away from here!
      I can't stand it!

DOE: You'll stand still
      as long as I will!

(the DRAGON tries to move, but he is unable to escape the sunbeam. He wipes the sweat from his brow with a handkerchief)

DRAGON: This is as hot as a noonday blaze!
      I beg you, Doe, please make it end!
      I can cope with an entire regiment,

but not with the sun that you have sent!

DOE: You know that I cannot yield now!
　　It's time once again
　　that you step aside
　　while I turn the tide!

DRAGON: *(shouts)*
　　Let me go! Let me go!
　　I need to retreat to a place dark and cool!

SCHNECK: You know, it's too hot for me, here, too.
　　I'm going to go stand in the shade. *(he does)*

JAKOB: I'm half roasted as well!
　　Whew, what heat!

(the DRAGON tears off his coat, opens his collar, gasps for air, and sinks to his knees. He is turned away from the audience as he sinks down, his head disappears between his knees, his face is no longer visible)

DRAGON: *(in a very old voice)*
　　Oh, powers, help me,
　　dark night, come!

(he lifts his head. He now has an ancient face, and his body has the posture of a very old man)

　　Doe, I beg for mercy!
　　Let me go!

MARTHA: *(to the DOE)*
　　Listen to his pleas!
　　My heart is suddenly so afraid!

DOE: Be patient, it won't be much longer!

(the DRAGON rocks back and forth on his knees, weeping and wailing)

DRAGON: Young blood! Young blood!
　　I need young blood!

JAKOB: Will you listen to him?
    I'd much rather have a beer!

DRAGON: *(looks at MARTHA)*
    Maiden, I beseech you, come to me, come here!
    I am dying of thirst! Dying of thirst!

JAKOB: We couldn't care less!

(MARTHA instinctively tries to go to the DRAGON, but the DOE holds her back gently)

DRAGON: I need blood! Blood! *(breaks down)*
    Blood! Blood! Blood!

(NORG rushes onto the scene, sees the DOE, is scared, begins to flee, sees the DRAGON, looks at him shocked and frightened, hops over to the DRAGON, avoids stepping into the sunbeam, then looks from the DRAGON to the DOE.)

NORG: Damned fairy! *(despondently)*
    Oh, this is painful!
    What shall I do now, without my Lord?
    What shall I do, without the protection of his
    sword?

JAKOB: Starting to feel a little anxious, are we?
    Just you wait, your turn is next!

NORG: You'll have to catch me first,
    You blind simpleton!

DRAGON: *(rapidly fading away)* Blood! Blood! Blood!

(then the DRAGON is quiet, lies motionless. A moment of complete silence. NORG hops desperately around the edges of the sunbeam, reaches in with trepidation, as if he were touching hot water, jerks his hand back, reaches back in, shakes and tugs at the DRAGON, pulls his hand back out)

JAKOB: Is he gone, the demon?
    Lordy, if only I could see!

(the DOE walks over to the DRAGON, NORG runs away

and waits at a safe distance)

DOE: *(gently to the DRAGON)*
 Now you can go. You are free.

DRAGON: *(softly)*
 It's over. My beloved.

(the DOE helps him to his feet, they appear to embrace for a moment)

DRAGON: *(softly)*
 Don't leave me! Stay with me!

DOE: *(softly)*
 Go, dragon beast!
 All things must pass.
 Go on. Go.

(she pushes the DRAGON away gently, leads him for a few steps, cautiously lets go of him. He walks away shakily, but collapses after a few steps. NORG hops over to him, drags him along, puffing and panting, the DRAGON crawls a ways on all fours, collapses again. NORG looks at him, cannot resist the temptation, jumps up on him, presses a few times and grunts, looks furtively back at the others, jumps down, and drags him away. They disappear from view. The sunbeam has dissolved the moment the DRAGON left it, the sky now clouds over and thunder sounds in the distance. Suddenly one hears a cry of agony as the DRAGON dies and shortly thereafter the healthy wail of a newborn child. The sun breaks through; all is bright again)

DOE: The Dragon has been born again.
 And he will live eternally.
 I must turn him over to the wolves
 so that they may nurture him.
 Farewell, children of mankind!
 It pleases me to meet you, it pleases me to help you,
 but it also pleases me to return to the wood.

(turns to go)

NIKLAS: Wait! *(approaches her)*
>Queen! Fairy! Lovely lady!
>You are leaving us?

SCHNECK: I can't believe it!
>Here we go again!

NIKLAS: What do you mean? She said she liked me, and I
>. . .

(the DOE smilingly touches his lips with her hand, goes over to MARTHA, kisses her gently on the mouth, smiles at SCHNECK and walks over to JAKOB. MARTHA approaches NIKLAS and kisses him on the mouth. NIKLAS is bowled over. He runs his hands over his lips)

NIKLAS: What is that? Oh! Oh my, that tastes good!

MARTHA: *(smiling)*
>Yes, yes I believe it, you rascal!
>That's the taste of her lips, and her passion!

NIKLAS: *(beside himself)*
>Your lips! Your passion!
>*(hugs and kisses her)* Let me drink of your lips! Oh! Yes!

(meanwhile the DOE has removed the bandage from JAKOB's eyes. He winces, but then holds still. The DOE licks two fingers of her right hand and touches these to JAKOB's eyes. He can see again. He stares wide-eyed at the DOE and gets up off the ground)

JAKOB: I can see! *(louder)* I can see! *(shouts)* I can see!

(the DOE exits)

JAKOB: *(calls after her)*
>Lady, I thank you!
>I'll never forget this,
>I will revere you forever!

(he runs to NIKLAS and MARTHA and hugs them)

I can see again! Look, I can see again!

(MARTHA looks happy. NIKLAS pays no attention to JAKOB. JAKOB runs over to SCHNECK, hugs and kisses him)

JAKOB: I can see again, did you see? I can see again!

SCHNECK: *(smiling)* Yes, I see!

(MARTHA attempts to loosen the embrace of NIKLAS, but NIKLAS puts his arms right back around her)

NIKLAS: Martha! My beloved!

MARTHA: *(smiling)*
Calm down a little!
I feel like I'm back at the Dragon's!

(NIKLAS withdraws, a little embarrassed)

SCHNECK: Well, then, I guess I need to give you two a
wedding gift, don't I?

NIKLAS: *(happens to look over at JAKOB)*
Why, Jakob! You can see?

JAKOB: Yes, Sire, I can see! My eyeballs are like new, look
at them! *(shows NIKLAS his eyes)*

(meanwhile, SCHNECK has stepped into the circle, has covered his face with his hands, mumbles a magic formula. Darkness, lightning and thunder, smoke, then light again. In front of MARTHA and NIKLAS stands a giant bear, raising his front paws threateningly. MARTHA screams, NIKLAS reaches for his sword, but finds he isn't carrying one)

SCHNECK: Oh, darn!—Shin of lamb and beetle's ear,
get that bear away from here!

(darkness, lightning and thunder, smoke, then light again. Now there is an egg lying on the ground in front of MAR-

THA and NIKLAS. The two of them and JAKOB laugh. MARTHA picks it up)

MARTHA: Bravo, Schneck!
We'll enjoy this one!

SCHNECK: Damn, this is no fun!

(SCHNECK concentrates again, mumbles. Darkness, lightning and thunder, smoke, then light again. A beautiful cradle now stands before MARTHA and NIKLAS)

SCHNECK: Well? Satisfied?

JAKOB: Bravo!

NIKLAS: Schneck, there's no doubt about it!
You are the greatest sorcerer in the world!

(MARTHA walks over to the cradle, kneels down, and looks at it)

SCHNECK: Oh, goodness, no, not by a long shot!
But I feel my powers coming back!

MARTHA: *(surprised)*
There's a baby in the cradle!
A real baby!

(everyone looks astonished, all go to look into the cradle. MARTHA cautiously lifts the infant out. SCHNECK scratches his head)

SCHNECK: I wonder whose it is!

MARTHA: *(smiling)*
Well, not ours!
We haven't even begun to reproduce!

NIKLAS: *(with mock reproach)* Schneck!

SCHNECK: *(crushed)*
All right, all right, I'll make it go away!

(SCHNECK steps into the circle and concentrates again. MARTHA lays the baby back into the cradle, smiles,

and shakes her head. Then she stands back up and leans against NIKLAS. JAKOB reaches into the cradle and tickles the baby under the chin. Suddenly darkness, lightning and thunder, smoke, then light again. ALL have disappeared, including the cradle. After a few moments of silence, music begins to play, and the players come onto the stage to take their bows)

THE END

There's Not A Finer Country

Translated by

Robert Acker

"Those who do not remember the past are condemned to experience it again."

(George Santayana)

CHARACTERS:

STEFAN ADLER (55), cattle-dealer
MARIA (45), his wife
HANS (25), their son
ANNA (20), their daughter
RUDOLF HOLZKNECHT (50), innkeeper and mayor
OLGA (45), his wife
ERICH (20), their son
SEPP HOPFGARTNER (50), senior teacher and local branch leader
TONI (25), his son
FRANZ GRUBER (60), parish priest
ROSA (70), his sister and housekeeper
CHIEF OF POLICE
DISTRICT MAGISTRATE (40), a German
FIRST CRIMINAL INVESTIGATOR (later Gestapo)
SECOND CRIMINAL INVESTIGATOR (later Gestapo)
FIRST HEIMWEHR (right wing paramilitary group) MAN
SECOND HEIMWEHR MAN
A MARKSMAN
TWO HITLER YOUTH
DOCTOR
SS-HAUPTSTURMFÜHRER

STAGE SETTING:

*The village. In the foreground a part of the village square.
To the left a fountain, to the right a life-size crucifix. On the
left side of the village square is the house of Stefan Adler,
and to the right the inn "White Lamb" of the mayor. The living room of the Adler house and the main room of the inn
can be made visible by removing the front "walls." Between
both houses the village lane runs uphill. To the right and
left of it are other houses and in the background the church
tower. Behind all this are the mountains. It is always night,
or dawn or dusk. Scenes 1-9 take place in this setting,
scenes 10, 11 and 12 take place on an empty stage covered
with black cloth. Scene 13 takes place in front of the curtain.*

Scene I

*(Fall, 1933. Evening. The two rooms on the right and the
left are not visible, since the "walls" are in front of them.
Light is glimmering through the closed curtains of the living room on the left and the main room of the inn on the
right. Stars are flickering in the sky, the moon is shining,
the mountains are a black silhouette. Standing between the
two houses on the village square are ADLER, his wife,
MARIA, his daughter, ANNA, the mayor HOLZKNECHT,
the senior teacher HOPFGARTNER, his retarded son,
TONI, and the priest, GRUBER. The men have left their
hats in the inn, they have just run out to observe the specta-
cle that is described in the following. A few other inhabitants of the village are standing further up on the village
lane. All are looking at a mountain slope in the background
where a swastika is being formed by torches stuck in the*

*ground. One doesn't know at first what it is supposed to be-
come, first just the cross is visible and only at the end does
one see the hooks that belong to it. Two men are working on
this, each one is implanting torches to form one beam of the
cross. The people observe this procedure in silence. TONI
looks at it enthusiastically, sits down on the ground. His father sees this, gives him a kick, and motions for him to
stand up. TONI does.*

*Two HEIMWEHR MEN and the CHIEF OF POLICE come
from their rounds from the left. The HEIMWEHR MEN are
shoving bicycles and have rifles slung over their shoulders.
The three see the fire signal and know immediately that it
is going to be a swastika. The two HEIMWEHR MEN push
their way through the onlookers, glance up at the fire signal, get on their bikes and leave. TONI holds one of the men
back by grabbing his luggage rack, the man turns around
threateningly. HOPFGARTNER pulls his son back, the
HEIMWEHR MAN looks threateningly at TONI and his
father. HOPFGARTNER looks back coolly, the HEIM-
WEHR MAN gets on his bike again, leaves, follows his comrade, who is already riding up the village lane. At the top
they turn right around the corner and disappear. The PO-
LICEMAN has remained behind, smiles at the men, tips
his cap. All are looking at the fire signal, now two of the
hooks are visible. The POLICEMAN pulls out his pistol,
shoots twice into the air to warn the men setting the fire.
TONI is terribly startled, he jumps back. The MAYOR and
HOPFGARTNER acknowledge the warning with ap-
proval. ADLER smiles at the POLICEMAN too. For a moment the men stop working because they heard the shots,
then they continue to work quickly, they are in a hurry. The
other two hooks are completed. The swastika is finished. In
addition to ADLER, the POLICEMAN, and the PRIEST,
now everyone applauds and cries out "Bravo!" Even the
people further up applaud. TONI enthusiastically shouts
with joy and jumps up and down. HOPFGARTNER ex-*

tends his right hand to give the Nazi salute.)

HOPFGARTNER: *(bellows)* Sieg Heil!

(TONI imitates him in an exaggerated fashion.)

TONI: Heil! Heil, heil, heil!

(The others, except for ADLER, have to laugh at TONI. HOPFGARTNER thus hits him so hard on his out-stretched arm that TONI screams and hides his arm under his left armpit. OLGA goes back into the inn, the men follow. ADLER waves a friendly greeting to his wife and daughter who walk to the left into their house. ADLER follows the other men into the inn. The "wall" of the inn opens. On the back wall there is a picture of Dollfuß. The men went through the entrance way into the vestibule and now come through a door on the back wall into the main room. OLGA doesn't come in but goes from the vestibule to the stairs which lead to the second floor.)

OLGA: I'm going to bed. Good night everybody!

ADLER: Good night, Olga!

(The men go to their reserved table, where their half full beer mugs are still standing.)

MAYOR: *(to the POLICEMAN)* A beer, Robert?

POLICEMAN: Sure, make it a big one.

(The MAYOR goes to the spigot and pours a beer. In the meantime the men sit down at their places, TONI sits down beside his father on a bench which is somewhat distant from the table. His father gives him his beer mug.)

POLICEMAN: That was Hans and Erich, right?

ADLER: *(seemingly without emotion)* Probably. *(To the MAYOR:)* Isn't that right, Rudi?

MAYOR: *(seemingly proud)* Well of course!

POLICEMAN: Bravo, I say!

TONI: I say, bravo!

(HOPFGARTNER nudges TONI in the ribs, which makes him spill some of his beer. TONI constantly repeats every-thing, and his father would like to break him of his habit. He is despondent because his son is retarded and can't carry out courageous deeds like the other young men of the village. The MAYOR brings the POLICEMAN his beer and then sits down.)

POLICEMAN: OK, Prost, to your boys!

(All, except for HOPFGARTNER, hold up their glasses and then drink.)

HOPFGARTNER: If I had my way there would be a few
        other little fires, but with dynamite. I'd blow all the
        damn priests and Jews into the air!

TONI: *(breaks out laughing)* Air!

(TONI makes gestures and the sound of an explosion, his father nudges him in the ribs.)

PRIEST: So, that's the way it is?

HOPFGARTNER: Well of course. The damn Jews and
        priests are our greatest downfall.

TONI: *(mutters)* Downfall!

MAYOR: That's enough, Sepp. *Our* priest is OK.

(In Adler's house the light in the living room goes out and after a while the light in their bedroom (second floor, two windows in the direction of the inn) goes on, as does the light in the first window above the living room (Anna's room). After another short while the lights in both rooms go out, with a slight time difference between them.)

HOPFGARTNER: *(during all this)* What do you mean?
        Every black robe is the same.

(The PRIEST puts a coin onto the table, stands up and goes to the door.)

MAYOR: Come on, Father, stay here.

TONI: *(friendly)* Stay here!

(The PRIEST turns around.)

PRIEST: *(enraged)* I'm not going to let myself be put under the same roof with the Jews. Is that clear, Hopfgartner? I've been preaching to you for a long time that the Jews are our downfall. That they nailed our Lord Jesus to the cross. That they have spread out like the plague over the whole world. And are involved everywhere. And control everything. With their immorality. With their greed. You only have to come to church once and then you'll hear what I have to say about this topic!

POLICEMAN: Yes, we believe you. Now come on and sit down again.

PRIEST: No! I'm not going to be insulted like this!

MAYOR: *(to HOPFGARTNER)* Sepp!

HOPFGARTNER: *(to the PRIEST)* I'm really sorry. Excuse me!

TONI: Excuse me!

HOPFGARTNER: *(to the PRIEST)* I know that you don't belong to the same gang!

(The PRIEST comes back and sits down.)

HOPFGARTNER: You know, I've really had it! I can't stand it anymore. *(Raises his mug)* Come on, let's have a toast!

(The PRIEST toasts with great reluctance. They drink.)

POLICEMAN: You don't have to despair, Sepp! The most important people in the village are all on your side, are all in the movement. Rudi *(points to the MAYOR)*, the priest, Stefan *(points to ADLER)*, myself—what more do you want?

(On the mountain slope the torches go out, one after another (are being put out by the HEIMWEHR MEN).)

HOPFGARTNER: I want a commitment! A secret one at least! Why don't you join the Party?

MAYOR: That just won't work, Sepp! I can help you a lot

more if I am absolutely and without a doubt a member of the Conservative Party! And Robert *(points to the POLICEMAN)* likewise!

ADLER: I'll join!

HOPFGARTNER: What?

ADLER: I'll join!

HOPFGARTNER: Ah, that makes me happy! Well then, welcome to the club, Comrade Adler!

(HOPFGARTNER offers ADLER his hand, ADLER stands up and shakes hands with him.)

TONI: Comrade Adler!

HOPFGARTNER: *(to TONI)* Be quiet!

(HOPFGARTNER sits down again, ADLER reaches into his coat pocket, pulls out his wallet and gives HOPFGART-NER two bills.)

ADLER: There, that's a down payment for my membership dues. *(Sits down.)*

HOPFGARTNER: *(puts the money away)* Great, we can use every penny.

(Suddenly there is a tremendous deafening noise behind the Church, a flash of light illuminates the sky, glass shutters. They all prick up their ears, look at each other, get up, and go out on the street again. The "wall" closes. A few lights go on in the houses in the village. MARIA opens the window in the second floor of Adler's house, looks out in her nightdress.)

MARIA: What was that?

(ADLER looks up to her, shrugs his shoulders. ROSA comes running down the village lane from the rectory (which is in back of the church. She has put on a coat over her night-dress, her hair is a mess.)

ROSA: *(out of breath)* Help! Help! Franzi! Franzi!

(TONI nudges the PRIEST.)

TONI: *(seriously)* Help!

(ROSA arrives.)

PRIEST: Well, what's wrong, Rosa?

ROSA: Those brats! Those godless swine! What a rotten thing to do!

PRIEST: *(grabs her)* Well, what is it?

(Further up the street two people enter, look toward the rectory, and then look in the direction of the square.)

ROSA: They blew me to bits! The Antichrists! But I'll report them! *(To the POLICEMAN:)* Chief, do your duty! Right away!

MAYOR: *(grinning)* But you look pretty good for having been blown to bits!

ROSA: *(crying)* Now he's even making fun of me. Do I have to put up with all of this, Franzi?

PRIEST: Now just calm down! Did they fire one of those little party mortars?

ROSA: Of course, what do you think! Three windows are wrecked. And all my flowers! All my flowers are in ruins!

POLICEMAN: And who was it? Did you see them?

ROSA: Come on! I was asleep! And what a shock I got! It threw me right out of bed!

(HOPFGARTNER and the MAYOR grin.)

TONI: *(laughing)* Threw me out!

PRIEST: *(takes ROSA's arm)* Come on, let's take a look.

(He goes a few steps with ROSA, turns around.)

PRIEST: If something else like this happens one more time, then you're in for big trouble! And your brats too!

MAYOR: Who said it was ours? They could have come from someplace else!

PRIEST: Just one more time!

MAYOR: Now, come on, Father. You'll get paid for the damages! No matter whose fault it was! And if it was one of our boys, then he'll get a real thrashing!

PRIEST: I should hope so!

(He goes up the village lane with ROSA.)

ROSA: *(while leaving)* Am I ever worn out, Franzi! I just can't begin to tell you! The Last Judgement can't be any worse! Those brats! They don't have any respect any more! Just blow up the whole rectory! Where else would something like this happen? That never would have happened in the good old days, certainly not!

(The men have to grin because of ROSA. The PRIEST and ROSA disappear up around the corner. MARIA closes the windows and the drapes again.)

POLICEMAN: *(to the people who are standing further up along the lane.)* Go to bed! It's all over with!

TONI: Go to bed!

(The people go into their homes. Way at the end the two HEIMWEHR MEN appear on their bikes, ride down the village lane and stop.)

FIRST HEIMWEHR MAN: There was some noise someplace!

POLICEMAN: There certainly was! Were you guys sleeping, or what?

SECOND HEIMWEHR MAN: Sleeping! We were putting out the torches up there!

POLICEMAN: Very shrewd! And in the meantime the same people were probably throwing a mortar into the rectory!

FIRST HEIMWEHR MAN: Those swine! If I catch them!

POLICEMAN: Well, there's no more chance today. I already took a look. You can go home and go to bed.

FIRST HEIMWEHR MAN: Good! See you tomorrow!

(Both HEIMWEHR MEN tip their hats, get on their bikes, and leave to the left.)

POLICEMAN: *(to the MAYOR and ADLER)* Tell your boys to please leave the priest alone!

MAYOR: Sure, sure, if it really was them . . .

(The POLICEMAN tips his cap and leaves to the right.)

HOPFGARTNER: We're going too! Come on, boy! *(To the others:)* Good night!

TONI: Good night!

MAYOR: Take care, Sepp!

ADLER: Take care!

(HOPFGARTNER and TONI go up the village lane, TONI stumbles, HOPFGARTNER pulls him up impatiently, sets him down, continues, TONI trots behind him. To the right in the foreground HANS and ERICH appear, they are carrying back packs, press themselves against the wall of the house, listen.)

MAYOR: *(to ADLER)* Those were our boys, right?

ADLER: Presumably.

(The MAYOR wants to say something negative but he doesn't since he considers Adler to be a super Nazi.)

ADLER: Well, I have to get to bed. I have to transport some cattle tomorrow.

MAYOR: How's business?

ADLER: Not very good. I can't seem to sell the meat. The unemployed stuff themselves with potatoes. Thank God I still have a few lunchrooms.

MAYOR: I'm ready for the poor house too! What a pile of shit! But that's all going to change soon!

ADLER: Let's hope so! Well, take care!

MAYOR: Good night, Stefan!

(They turn away from each other and go into their separate homes. In the living room to the left the light goes on, HANS

and ERICH move out of the shadow of the house.)

HANS: *(softly)* Well: Sieg Heil!
ERICH: Wait a second!

(He goes to the side of Adler's house that is facing the public, picks up a little stone from the ground and throws it against the window in the second floor.)

HANS: What are you doing?

(ERICH takes off his back pack, takes out a bouquet of Alpine roses, and shows it to HANS.)

HANS: I'm going to give these to her!
ERICH: Oh no you don't. I'm going to do that myself!

(He throws another little stone against the window, the window opens and ANNA in her nightdress looks out. He throws the bouquet in the air. ANNA catches it and looks at it.)

ANNA: Mmm, these are beautiful! Thank you Erich!—
    Was that you two up there with the fire?
ERICH: Well of course! And we blew the priest's cook out of
    her bed!
ANNA: *(happily)* Rascals!

(She blows ERICH a kiss, closes the window, disappears. ERICH taps HANS on the shoulder, goes into the inn. HANS goes into Adler's house. Both of the "walls" open. On the left in the living room ADLER is sitting very lonely at the dining table, is staring into space. On the right in the inn the MAYOR is clearing glasses away from the reserved table, carries them to the cupboard. The MAYOR hears the door of the house, goes to the door of the main room, opens it, looks out into the vestibule, ERICH has already passed, the MAYOR follows him, appears again with ERICH, pulls him brutally by his arm into the main room, closes the door, looks at ERICH, boxes his ears.)

ERICH: *(perplexed)* What's that for?

(The MAYOR boxes his ears again, is about to do it a third time. ERICH puts his hands up to defend himself, steps back.)

ERICH: Stop that! What's that for, dammit?

MAYOR: Do you want me to lose my job, huh? Is that what you want?

ERICH: I don't get it. What do you want from me?

MAYOR: Just do that one more time! Just one more time! Then I'll throw you out, I swear it! You miserable little jerk!

ERICH: Hey listen, who do you think you're talking to? Want to pretend you're a big important man, or something? I'm a National Socialist! A fighter! I'm the future!

MAYOR: You're a little brat is what you are. Putting us all in danger. Go ahead and be a Nazi for all I care! I'm a Nazi! All of us are Nazis! But there's still another government in power!

ERICH: Not for long!

MAYOR: Well it's still there, you moron!

(ERICH looks angrily at his father, takes his back pack, goes to the bar, pours himself a beer, sits at the reserved table, drinks some beer, makes himself a cigarette, smokes. His father is nervous and angry, goes to the bar, begins to wash glasses.

At the same time when the MAYOR opens the door to the main room of the inn and goes out to his son in the vestibule, the door to Adler's living room opens and HANS looks in. He sees his father, who is sitting with his back to him at the table. ADLER doesn't turn around. HANS comes in, closes the door, takes off his back pack, removes his coat, hangs it up, gets a schnapps bottle out of the cupboard, takes a big gulp, puts the bottle back, sits down, takes off his hiking boots, goes in his stocking feet to the back pack, takes it, puts it on the table, opens it, takes out a pistol wrapped in a cloth, unwraps it, cocks and re-cocks it, observes it deliberately. (Even his father is against these actions.) ADLER glances up, looks at the weapon, looks at his son. HANS sits down, gets a box of cartridges out of his back pack, opens it, takes the magazine out of the pistol, shoves cartridges into the magazine. ADLER looks at him, then pulls the back pack over to his chair, looks in, reaches inside, takes out another pistol, unwraps it, looks at it, looks at HANS. After the last sentence of the MAYOR ("Well it's still there, you moron!") ADLER begins to speak.)

ADLER: Where did you get this stuff from?
HANS: What good would it do you if I told you?

(ADLER looks at HANS, puts the pistol down, stares into space, is quiet for a bit, then looks at HANS again.)

ADLER: I joined the Party today.
HANS: *(can't believe it)* What? Really?
ADLER: Yes, really.
HANS: *(is happy)* I can't believe it! That's incredible!

(HANS gets up, pulls up his father, hugs him.)

HANS: I'm so happy, Father! That's what I always wanted! That's incredible!
ADLER: *(smiling)* Okay, Okay! Just calm down! *(Separates himself from his son.)*

(The "wall" of the house again covers the living room. At this moment the MAYOR is drying his hands, goes over to the reserved table, sits down beside ERICH, looks at him, looks at the back pack, opens it, reaches inside, takes out a pistol, stiffens, unwraps the pistol, looks at it, wraps it up again, puts it back into the back pack, reaches deeper, takes out a package of wrapped up dynamite sticks, unwraps them, looks at them.)

MAYOR: That's why you were gone for three days! Visiting your German brothers, huh?
ERICH: *(stubbornly)* That's right!

MAYOR: Well our senior teacher and the illegal local branch leader will certainly be happy! *(Looks at the dynamite sticks:)* That's just what they wanted!

(In the window to the left of ANNA'S window the light goes on, goes off a moment later. HANS is going to bed. In the living room the light is still on. ADLER is still sitting there. ERICH doesn't answer, the MAYOR puts the dynamite sticks back into the back pack, closes it, broods.)

MAYOR: And Hans? Did he bring this kind of stuff along too?

ERICH: Well of course. Things are getting serious now.

(The MAYOR broods, takes his pocket watch out, looks at it, puts it back.)

MAYOR: You have to be clever, boy, if you want to survive in difficult times!

(ERICH doesn't answer. He despises his father.)

MAYOR: Go to bed now. It's late.

ERICH: Yes, I'm tired. *(Gets up.)* Six hours crossing the mountains! *(Points to the back pack:)* With that heavy stuff there! *(Takes the back pack.)*

MAYOR: *(stands up)* Come on, give it to me. I'll hide it in an empty wine barrel!

ERICH: Why do you want to do that? The Police Chief is one of us! He only searches your house if he lets you know beforehand!

MAYOR: Nevertheless! Safe is safe!

(The MAYOR takes the back pack from ERICH, who lets it go with a sigh, goes to the door.)

(The light in Adler's living room goes out. He is going to bed.)

MAYOR: Good night, boy!
ERICH: Good night!

(ERICH goes out, the MAYOR puts down the back pack

again, sits down at the table, broods. In the second floor the light in the first window on the side of the house facing the audience goes on and shortly thereafter goes out. ERICH is going to bed. The MAYOR stands up, picks up the back pack, takes it out to the kitchen through the door on the right, comes back in, looks at his pocket watch, leaves the main room, goes out onto the street, looks up the village lane, waits. In the second floor of Adler's house, on the side which faces the inn and where Adler's bedroom is, the curtain parts in a dark window, ADLER look down, sees the MAYOR, observes him. From far away one hears a car approaching slowly, the headlights pass over the houses, the motor dies, the lights go out, two criminal INVESTIGATORS in civilian clothes turn the corner, look around, the MAYOR approaches them, meets them, shakes their hands, all three come down the village lane, go into the inn and into the main room. ADLER, having observed that, disappears from the window.)

MAYOR: Please be seated!

(The policemen sit down at the reserved table.)

MAYOR: Do you want something to drink?
FIRST INVESTIGATOR: Do you have some coffee?
MAYOR: Not at this time of night. How about a little schnapps?

(ADLER comes out of his house, looks around, then goes over to the window of the inn, looks in from an angle through a crack in the drapes, listens.)

FIRST INSPECTOR: OK, fine.
SECOND INSPECTOR: For me too.

(The MAYOR pours out three schnapps glasses, sits down, lifts his glass.)

MAYOR: To your health!

(The INVESTIGATORS lift their glasses, drink, the

FIRST INVESTIGATOR lights up a cigarette.)

FIRST INVESTIGATOR: Well, Mr. Mayor. What can we do for you?

MAYOR: *(hesitates)* Well, first you have to promise me that I don't have to testify as a witness and that my name won't appear anywhere.

SECOND INVESTIGATOR: Why should we do that?

MAYOR: Because otherwise I'll be finished. They'll blow up my house. Or put a bullet through my brains. They're all over the place, the Nazis! In every village, in every position. They're even in the police department with you!

FIRST INVESTIGATOR: Sure, sure, maybe we're Nazis too . . . *(grins at his colleague:)* Right?

(The MAYOR gets afraid.)

SECOND INVESTIGATOR: *(grins)* Yes, could be!

FIRST INVESTIGATOR: That's a little difficult, Mr. Mayor. What are we supposed to do without witnesses? We can't do anything!

MAYOR: Well then I'm not going to cooperate. Either you leave me out of the whole mess or I'm not going to say anything!

SECOND INVESTIGATOR: Now what do you mean by that, Mr. Mayor? If you've seen something illegal then you have to report it! Otherwise you won't be a mayor much longer!

MAYOR: *(gets up)* If I testify,then I'm done for. You know that's not in your best interest! If nobody suspects me then I can give you information often. The people trust me. And besides that—in this case you don't need any witnesses. There's proof!

FIRST INVESTIGATOR: What kind of proof?

MAYOR: Weapons! Explosives!

(ADLER goes quickly back into his house, disappears. He goes to warn his son, but doesn't put any lights on.)

FIRST INVESTIGATOR: Well, that's different. Where are they?

MAYOR: Are you going to keep my name out of this?

FIRST INVESTIGATOR: We promise!

MAYOR: *(sits down)* There, right across the square! The son of the cattle dealer! He's an illegal Nazi! Hans Adler! He has a back pack full of weapons at home! Imported them fresh from the Reich!

FIRST INVESTIGATOR: *(gets up)* We'll get 'em! Come on, Willi!

(They both go to the door, the FIRST INVESTIGATOR turns around.)

FIRST INVESTIGATOR: And if you find out anything else—a phone call is enough!

(They want to leave.)

MAYOR: *(gets up)* Wait a minute!

(Both INVESTIGATORS turn around.)

MAYOR: You're going to interrogate him, right?

SECOND INVESTIGATOR: *(grinning)* We assume so!

MAYOR: Well . . . what's going to happen? Do people confess everything?

FIRST INVESTIGATOR: Usually.

MAYOR: Aren't there some stubborn types who don't give in no matter what you do?

FIRST INVESTIGATOR: Rarely.

(ADLER looks carefully out of the door of his house, motions towards the back. His son HANS comes out, he carries a back pack, shakes hands with his father, exits quickly to the left. ADLER goes back into his house.)

MAYOR: Well . . . you know . . . it's like this, my son . . . well, my son, he always hangs around with Hans Adler...

(Both INVESTIGATORS look at him in an astonished fashion.)

SECOND INVESTIGATOR: Well, you've got some nerve! *(To the FIRST INVESTIGATOR:)* Betrays his own son!

MAYOR: I'm not betraying him! But I just think that Hans Adler will mention him at the interrogation. I thought I better tell you that right off the bat.

FIRST INVESTIGATOR: Well fine, then we'll arrest your son too!

MAYOR: What? But—you can't do that!

FIRST INVESTIGATOR: My dear Mr. Mayor! Smuggling weapons is a crime! And it's not going to stop with smuggling, I assume!

MAYOR: *(despairing)* He won't do it. He won't do it any more. That was my plan! If his friend is arrested he'll get afraid!—Just wait and see!

(The MAYOR runs into the kitchen, gets the back pack, presses it into the hands of the FIRST INVESTIGATOR.)

MAYOR: That's my boy's back pack! Full of pistols and explosives!—Here, take it!

FIRST INVESTIGATOR: Well, I'm sorry Mr. Mayor! I have to arrest him!

MAYOR: Oh, please don't!—My God, what have I done!

SECOND INVESTIGATOR: *(conciliatory)* Mr. Mayor! Now just listen to me! This Hans Adler will betray your son! That's for certain! What do you think is going to happen if we don't arrest your son?

MAYOR: Well, what would happen?

SECOND INVESTIGATOR: Hans Adler will get out of jail one day and come home. And he will discover that his friend and companion isn't locked up. Although he gave the authorities his name. What will Hans Adler think?

MAYOR: *(panicked)* I have no idea!

SECOND INVESTIGATOR: He will think that your son spilled the beans and that's the reason why he isn't in jail. As a result he will tell everybody that your

son is a traitor. And he will possibly take revenge on
him.

FIRST INVESTIGATOR: Besides that we can't guarantee
that the two of us will interrogate this Hans Adler!
That could also be our colleagues! And then your
son will have had it anyway.

MAYOR: Please! I beg you! I will guarantee that my son
won't do anything anymore! And even if I have to
beat him to a cripple! I promise you!

FIRST INVESTIGATOR: Come on, just stop it!

SECOND INVESTIGATOR: Just trust us Mr. Mayor, your
son is better off in jail. Nobody can do anything to
him and he can't do anything to anybody!

MAYOR: *(gives up)* Can I at least take something out?

*(He opens the back pack, takes out two pistols and a pack-
age of dynamite, runs with them into the kitchen. The
FIRST INVESTIGATOR looks with a sigh at the second
one, who has to grin. The MAYOR comes back.)*

FIRST INVESTIGATOR: OK, where is he, your son?

MAYOR: On the second floor, first door to the right!

*(The FIRST INVESTIGATOR sets the back pack aside,
both of them go to the door, while going out the first one
draws his pistol, the second one takes out a rubber club.
They disappear in the vestibule to the right. The MAYOR
goes to the door, looks at them in despair, goes to the reserved table, sits down. For a long time one doesn't hear a
thing, then one hears the men clambering down the steps.)*

VOICE OF OLGA: Hey! What do you think you're doing?
Erich, Erich, what's wrong?

*(The INVESTIGATORS enter through the door, they are
carrying the unconscious ERICH, who is clothed in under-
shirt and underpants. Behind them is OLGA in her nightdress.)*

OLGA: Rudi! What are they doing?

(The MAYOR gets up, goes to them, looks at ERICH.)

FIRST INVESTIGATOR: He'll wake right up again!

(The FIRST INVESTIGATOR looks around, drags ERICH to some object or piece of furniture, where he can fasten him, takes out some handcuffs, puts one handcuff around ERICH'S wrist, fastens the other to the object or piece of furniture.)

FIRST INVESTIGATOR: Get him some clothes and something to wash him up with! *(To the SECOND IN-VESTIGATOR:)* Now we'll get the other one!

(Both INVESTIGATORS go to the door, OLGA kneels in front of ERICH, shakes him . . . The SECOND INVESTI-GATOR turns around.)

SECOND INVESTIGATOR: *(to the MAYOR)* You don't know by any chance where his bedroom is?

MAYOR: *(automatically)* On the second floor. Second room to the left.

SECOND INVESTIGATOR: Many thanks!

(Both INVESTIGATORS go out, OLGA runs into the kitchen, comes back with a wet cloth, moistens ERICH'S forehead. In the meantime the investigators cross the square to the door of Adler's house on the other side, try it to see if it's open, the door moves, they enter the house.)

OLGA: *(to the MAYOR)* What happened? Tell me!

MAYOR: Well what do think happened? There, take a look in the back pack! Full of weapons! I told him repeatedly, he should just stop all this!

(Across the way the light in Hans' room goes on. ERICH wakes up, grabs his painful head, wants to sit up, notices that he's fettered, looks horrified. Across the way the light in Anna's room goes on.)

VOICE OF ANNA: Papa! Papa! Pap . . .

(The voice is strangled. The light in the parents' bedroom

goes on.)

ERICH: What the hell? What's going on?

(The MAYOR goes to the window, shoves the curtain aside, looks at Adler's house. The light in Adler's living room goes on. The investigators are searching the house.)

OLGA: You've been arrested. On account of that crazy Nazi
    stuff! *(Begins to cry.)*

ERICH: What did you say? Arrested by who?

MAYOR: By the police! Who did you think?

ERICH: Shit! That can't be! Somebody must have ratted
    on me, some swine! Wait till I get a hold of him! I'll
    kill him! *(Pulls furiously at his handcuffs.)*

OLGA: I'll bring you something to put on. *(OLGA goes out.
    ERICH sees the back pack.)*

ERICH: My God, father, hide the back pack!

MAYOR: They've already seen it.

ERICH: How come? Didn't you hide it?

MAYOR: I didn't get around to it.

ERICH: Shit! Where are they now?

MAYOR: *(points)* Over at Hans' place.

ERICH: Somebody ratted on us.

(The MAYOR sits down resigned at the reserved table. OLGA comes in with some clothes for ERICH, helps him put on his pants, socks and shoes, she has to wait with his shirt and coat until ERICH is free of the handcuffs.)

(ADLER, MARIA and ANNA step out of Adler's doorway. They are scantily clothed. Behind them the two investigators. The second investigator has the rubber club in his hand. They all go over to the inn, come into the main room. The MAYOR looks astonished. ADLER also looks astonished at ERICH.)

ANNA: Erich! *(Wants to go over to him.)*

FIRST INVESTIGATOR: *(to ADLERS)* Sit down!

(ADLER, MARIA and ANNA sit down next to the MAYOR at the reserved table.)

FIRST INVESTIGATOR: *(to the MAYOR)* He already flew the coop!

(The MAYOR is panic stricken that it might come out that he betrayed his son and HANS.)

MAYOR: Who flew the coop?

FIRST INVESTIGATOR: What? *(Understands, mockingly)* Ah you don't know anything. Well, accordingly to our information your son was on the go with Hans Adler. His parents deny that.

MARIA: We don't deny anything! Hansi has been gone for three days. We don't know where he is. How many times do we have to tell you that?

(The SECOND INVESTIGATOR goes to ERICH.)

SECOND INVESTIGATOR: What's your name!

ERICH: Erich.

SECOND INVESTIGATOR: Good, Erich. Now tell us real nice if you were on the go with Hans Adler or not.

ERICH: I'm often on the go with Hans Adler. He's my best friend.

SECOND INVESTIGATOR: Maybe I didn't express myself clearly. I want to know, first of all, if you smuggled weapons with Hans Adler, and second, if you came home with him tonight.

ERICH: I didn't smuggle any weapons.

SECOND INVESTIGATOR: *(points to the back pack)* And I suppose there are pieces of candy in there, huh?

ERICH: I have no idea!

(The SECOND INVESTIGATOR suddenly hits ERICH in the head with the rubber club. He waits for a few seconds, then hits him again. OLGA rushes forward.)

OLGA: Stop! *(Pushes the SECOND INVESTIGATOR back.)*

FIRST INVESTIGATOR: That's OK, Willi! We'll find out
    at headquarters!

*(The FIRST INVESTIGATOR takes ERICH'S handcuffs
off the object, looks at OLGA, who helps ERICH put on his
shirt and coat, the first investigator hangs the back pack
around him, brings ERICH'S hands to his back, clasps the
second handcuff around ERICH'S wrist.)*

FIRST INVESTIGATOR: OK, let's go!

ERICH: Take care, father!

MAYOR: Take care, boy!

*(OLGA hugs ERICH, takes some water from the holy water
font beside the door, makes a cross on Erich's forehead,
mouth and breast, ERICH endures this unwillingly, turns
away. During all of this the FIRST INVESTIGATOR looks
at ADLER.)*

FIRST INVESTIGATOR: We'll see each other again. In
    the meantime say hello to your son for me!

*(ANNA gets up, goes to ERICH, hugs him tightly, kisses
him. The SECOND INVESTIGATOR takes ERICH by the
arm, leads him out, the FIRST INVESTIGATOR grins and
looks back at the MAYOR, tips his hat, closes the door.
OLGA looks at the closed door, ANNA sits down again,
ADLER looks at the MAYOR, who is staring into space. The
two INVESTIGATORS leave the house with ERICH, go up
the village street in the direction of the car. OLGA turns
around, looks at the others, goes to the bar, begins to wash
a glass, then stops and breaks out in tears.)*

MAYOR: *(to OLGA)* Maybe it's better like this Olga. This
    way he's out of trouble.

*(The INVESTIGATORS and ERICH disappear around
the corner, one hears the car doors closing, the motor is
started, the headlights come on and pass over the houses
when the car is turned, the noise of the car becomes fainter.)*

(Blackout.)

Scene 2

(May, 1938. Evening. Swastika flags are hanging from Adler's house and from the inn. On all the other houses towards the back likewise. A beautiful full moon is emerging from behind the mountains. Both "walls" of the houses are closed. There is no light in Adler's house, light is glimmering through the curtains of the main room of the inn. From the noises in the main room one can conclude that it is filled with inhabitants of the village. The German national anthem is being sung by many different voices, accompanied by a band. Two HITLER YOUTH (16 and 18) in uniform are standing next to the crucifix, pull it down, it crashes to the ground, they kick the figure of Christ, pull at it, pull it down, break its arms off. The song is finished. Cries of Bravo and Heil. The band begins to play dance music. The older HITLER YOUTH grabs the figure of Christ on the legs and swings it against the corner of the house several times so that the head breaks off. This is all done with great, calculated anger. The younger HITLER YOUTH kicks the head with his foot, plays soccer with it, the other drops the torso, steps back, the younger kicks the head to him, the older one catches it with his foot, kicks it back, both of them move across the square, one dribbles, the other one tries to steal the head away. The door of the inn opens, the two ex-HEIMWEHR MEN are thrown out. They are wearing swastika arm bands. The FIRST HEIMWEHR MAN falls down. Both HITLER YOUTH stop, look at him. HANS and ERICH come out behind the HEIMWEHR MEN. ERICH is wearing an SA uniform. HANS an SS uniform. The FIRST HEIMWEHR MAN picks himself up.)

HANS: *(to the HITLER YOUTH)* Piss off!

(Both HITLER YOUTH go into the inn. HANS and ERICH look at the two ex-HEIMWEHR MEN.)

FIRST HEIMWEHR MAN: What's going on?

HANS: *(calmly)* Take off his arm band!

FIRST HEIMWEHR MAN: What?

(ERICH goes over, tears off both arm bands, throws them to the ground.)

ERICH: *(to HANS)* Wait a minute!

(ERICH goes into the inn. HANS looks at both men calmly. ERICH comes back with his father, who is wearing a national costume with a swastika arm band. He has remained the MAYOR even under the new regime.)

ERICH: *(to his father)* How come they aren't locked up? How do you explain that?

MAYOR: Come on, calm down Erich! Half of the village was against us before! We can't simply lock up half the village!

ERICH: I was in jail for three years! And Hansi had to flee to the Reich. Didn't see his parents for five years! *(Looks at the HEIMWEHR MEN:)* Maybe you guys were the traitors!

SECOND HEIMWEHR MAN: No we certainly weren't! Please believe us! We didn't know anything about the weapons! We were just jerks. Because the Police Chief always covered for you!

HANS: *(has to grin)* That's for sure! You certainly were jerks! You couldn't catch us one single time! And we made such nice little fires! You worthless good-for-nothings! You'll never amount to anything!

MAYOR: Come on, let's go back in!

ERICH: *(to the ex-HEIMWEHR MEN)* Just wait and see what happens if we catch you acting like this again!

(The MAYOR, HANS and ERICH go back into the inn, the two ex-HEIMWEHR MEN go up the village lane.)

FIRST HEIMWEHR MAN: They think they're pretty tough! Arrogant bastards!

SECOND HEIMWEHR MAN: Time will change again!

(The HEIMWEHR MEN disappear. After a while the door of the inn opens, the senior teacher HOPFGARTNER, who is now the actual official Local Branch Leader, shoves out his son TONI. HOPFGARTNER is wearing the uniform of a Party leader with a swastika arm band, TONI is wearing an SA uniform with the lowest rank.)

HOPFGARTNER: A disgrace it is! A disgrace! Stand up straight! *(Hits him on the back.)* Stand up straight, I said! *(Hits him in the stomach.)* Stomach in, chest out! I really have to be ashamed of you! Do you know what the people are saying, do you know?— You only have a uniform on, so that everybody doesn't see when you shit your pants!—I am the Local Branch Leader, do ya understand?

TONI: No, don't shit in your pants!

HOPFGARTNER: *(steps back)* Stand still! Stand still, I say!

(TONI tries to click his heels, he doesn't do it correctly, his father kicks him in the shin.)

HOPFGARTNER: Feet together! Hands on the seam of your pants—the seam! Where is the seam?

(TONI stands there rigid, HOPFGARTNER steps back, stretches out his arm to give the Nazi salute.)

HOPFGARTNER: Heil Hitler!

(TONI stretches out his arm too high.)

TONI: Heitler!

HOPFGARTNER: Not Heitler! *(Emphatically:)* Heil Hitler!

TONI: Heitler!

HOPFGARTNER: Shit! Stand still!

(TONI stands at attention.)

HOPFGARTNER: Right face!

(TONI turns to the left.)

HOPFGARTNER: Right face, I said! *(Shoves him in the other direction.)* Forward march! Left two! Left two!

(TONI marches, but out of step.)

HOPFGARTNER: Stop!

(TONI stops, HOPFGARTNER goes over to him, grabs TONI'S left leg at the knee, moves it forward.)

HOPFGARTNER: That's left, you jerk! March!

(TONI marches.)

HOPFGARTNER; Left two! Left Two! Squad, halt!

(TONI stops, but with a delay.)

HOPFGARTNER: Practice marching for an hour every day! Every day! If you don't present a smart figure within a week, I am going to tear that uniform off of you!—Understand?

TONI: *(stands at attention)* Understood! *(Sticks out his arm to give the Nazi salute:)* Heitler!

(HOPFGARTNER puts his arm around him in a conciliatory fashion.)

HOPFGARTNER: Now, come on! Let's have another beer!

(HOPFGARTNER and TONI go into the inn. At the door they meet ERICH and ANNA. ANNA is wearing a festive dirndl dress. Both have a mug of beer in their hands. As soon as HOPFGARTNER and TONI disappear ERICH immediately kisses ANNA feverishly.)

ANNA: *(smiling)* Hey! Not so wild!

(ERICH pulls ANNA by the hand over to Adler's house, they enter. After a while there is light from the lamp on the

*nightstand in Anna's room. The PRIEST, his sister ROSA
and the MAYOR come out of the inn.)*

MAYOR: *(as he is leaving)* You always were a big help to us!
    Really! I really appreciate that! I hope that you're
    not mad at me if I have to tell you something! It
    makes me very uncomfortable, believe me!

PRIEST: What does?

MAYOR: I got orders from the Gauleiter. About the Corpus
    Christi procession . . .

PRIEST: Really?

MAYOR: It's like this. The people can't use any public
    streets for the procession.

PRIEST: What? No public streets?

MAYOR: That's right. Because it might interfere with traf-
    fic.

PRIEST: *(perplexed)* Interfere with traffic?

MAYOR: That's the way it is. I can show you the order.

PRIEST: You guys aren't in your right mind, are you?

MAYOR: Now look, the order doesn't come from me!

ROSA: Well, are we supposed to hold the procession in the
    air?

MAYOR: No, just use the paths through the fields!

PRIEST: We can't go through the village? Like we always
    did? Like we've been doing for hundreds of years?

MAYOR: No, not through the village. Just around the
    church and then to the path through the fields.

PRIEST: But that ends at the highway!

MAYOR: Well, then you'll have to turn around and go back
    the same way you came. I made a plan. I'll show it
    to you at the court house.

(The PRIEST looks at him angrily.)

MAYOR: Now look, I didn't have anything to do with it. I
    went to the Gauleiter's office and tried to get per-
    mission to use sixty meters of the highway so that
    you could get to the other path. They turned me

down. What am I supposed to do?

PRIEST: Anything else?

MAYOR: Yes, you can't carry any church flags or any flags
from the State of Tirol. The band and the marksmen can't march along. Well, not in uniform anyway. They can go as private individuals. I'll come
along too! I'll come along to make a point! Even
though they won't like it!

*(ROSA sees the cross lying on the ground and the broken
figure of Christ, lets out a scream, rushes forward, picks up
the Christ figure minus its head and arms, looks at it without comprehension. PRIEST and MAYOR also look at it.)*

PRIEST: *(to the MAYOR)* I want to talk with the Local
Branch Leader! Immediately!

*(The MAYOR goes into the inn, ROSA perplexedly holds
the Christ figure in her arms.)*

ROSA: I knew it! The Antichrist is here! Franzi, I told you
so!

*(The PRIEST goes over to her, looks at the figure of Christ,
looks around, sees the head lying on the ground, gets it. The
MAYOR and HOPFGARTNER come out.)*

HOPFGARTNER: What's wrong?

(The PRIEST holds the head in front of him.)

PRIEST: There! *(Points to the figure of Christ.)* Just look at
this!

MAYOR: Now that's going too far, Sepp!

HOPFGARTNER: That's none of my concern!

PRIEST: *(angrily)* What do you mean by that? What kind
of an age are we living in? People are leaving the
Church, they destroy the crucifix, they shit in front
of the altar!

HOPFGARTNER: You only have yourselves to blame! For
hundreds of years you damn priests oppressed the
people. Especially here in the so-called "Holy

Land." And now, when Church and State are finally separated, now, when you've lost all your power, now you're getting paid back for everything! And that's exactly what you guys deserve!

(ROSA turns away, leaves carrying the figure of Christ, turns around.)

ROSA: God will punish you, you Nazi pigs! Just wait!

HOPFGARTNER: Hey, you be careful, you old bitch! Or else I'll have you sent away!

ROSA: Yeah, do you think I'm afraid of you, you old windbag of a teacher?

PRIEST: Calm down, Rosa! Go home!

ROSA: You're swine! Swine! You take the kids and put them in a camp, away from their parents, so that they can do all kinds of swinish stuff! In their swinish little shorts! You should be ashamed!

PRIEST: You better go, Rosa!

(ROSA leaves with the figure of Christ.)

ROSA: *(To Christ)* See, I told you! I was right! They're just pigs, those guys in their little shorts!—Power through joy! *(Turns around.)* We always used to say: Power through suffering! *(Points to Christ:)* There, he showed us the way!

PRIEST: Are you going to leave, or what?

(ROSA leaves.)

ROSA: *(mutters)* My dearest God! All the things you have to endure . . .

PRIEST: I'm canceling the procession! Without any music, without any marksmen, without any flags, hidden someplace off the beaten path—I don't need that kind of procession!

HOPFGARTNER: Well, as long as we're talking about this: In the name of and by order of the Party I hereby declare the youth hostel in the rectory to be confiscated. The Hitler Youth is moving in there now!

PRIEST: So? The Hitler Youth in the rectory?

HOPFGARTNER: Besides that I forbid you to teach! In the future I will take over the religious instruction at school! From now on you will confine your activity to the church alone! To that building back there! Exclusively! Understand?

PRIEST: Well, that's what you think! Maybe you can do this with the Protestants out there, but not with our people. Certainly not! Others have tried that already! Our people are very attached to the Catholic religion, to Catholic customs. Even if a few opportunists are leaving the Church today, even if a few brats shit in front of the altar!

MAYOR: Now please stop you two! You know we have to stick together!

HOPFGARTNER: Now I want to tell you something, Mr. Gruber! Spiritual gentleman! National Socialism doesn't need the Catholic religion! National Socialism doesn't need any religion at all! National Socialism, Father, is a religion by itself! You never comprehended that, did you? Well, I'll tell you again: National Socialism is a great, noble German cult!

PRIEST: And the Führer is your God, right? No, thank you!

HOPFGARTNER: And another thing, Father! Jesus Christ is a Jew! Note that well! A damn Jew! Do you really think the German people can revere a Jew as God?

(The PRIEST looks at the head of Christ in his hands, looks at HOPFGARTNER, nods.)

PRIEST: Thanks for the lesson, Mr. Local Branch Leader! Now I know where I stand!

(The PRIEST leaves, sees an arm of Christ on the ground, picks it up, looks for the second one, picks that one up too,

*goes to the village lane, MAYOR and HOPFGARTNER
watch him leave.)*

MAYOR: I don't know, Sepp . . . If that was smart— He has
a great influence over the people!

HOPFGARTNER: He won't be here much longer!

*(STEFAN ADLER in national costume, without a swastika
arm band and his wife MARIA in her Sunday dirndl dress
leave the inn.)*

ADLER: A good night to the both of you!

HOPFGARTNER: *(without raising his arm, mechani-
cally)* Heil Hitler!

MARIA: *(smiles and stretches out her arm)* Heil Hitler!

MAYOR: Take care, good night!

*(ADLER and his wife go over to the door of their house,
HOPFGARTNER and the MAYOR turn to enter the inn.
The MAYOR turns around again, HOPFGARTNER goes
in.)*

MAYOR: *(calls after ADLER)* Stefan!

(ADLER turns around.)

MAYOR: Please don't forget to get your Aryan certifica-
tion! You are the last one!

ADLER: Oh, I forgot it again! I'll have it for you next week!

MAYOR: Fine, fine, I'm not in that much of a hurry!

*(The MAYOR goes into the inn. ADLER and his wife go into
their house. After a while there is light in the living room.
Inside of the inn music begins to play. A marksman in his
national costume comes down the village lane, he is carrying a huge swastika flag, the pole has been inserted into a
holder which he has fastened to his belt. The heavy pole
makes it difficult for the marksman, he totters back and
forth.)*

(Blackout.)

Scene 3

(June 1938. Evening. The cross is standing in its previous location, the figure of Christ is still missing. The decorative flags on the houses are gone. The "wall" of the inn is closed. The "wall" of the living room of Adler's house has been pulled away. On the wall is a picture of Heinrich Himmler. STEFAN ADLER, his son HANS in an SS uniform and ERICH in an SA uniform are sitting at the dining table. ERICH made himself very natty for this evening, he is well shaved, his hair has been combed with pomade. They have all just eaten, ANNA and MARIA are cleaning off the table, carrying the dishes into the kitchen. They are drinking red wine. ERICH takes out a tin cigarette case, opens it, offers it to ADLER, who shakes his head smilingly and takes out his pipe, holds it up, takes out a pouch of tobacco, fills his pipe, then smokes. ERICH offers HANS a cigarette, HANS takes one, ERICH takes one himself, lights his and HANS' cigarettes. All three smoke. ANNA comes back, sits down, sees that the wine glasses are half empty, fills them up for the men. MARIA also comes back, sits down, smiles at ERICH invitingly.)

ERICH: Well, Mr. Adler . . . *(stands up)*

ADLER: Well, what's this all about? Since when are we on such a formal basis?

ERICH: *(grins)* Ahem . . . this is the momentous occasion, right?

HANS: *(grinning)* Go on! You're usually not so slow!

ERICH: OK, here goes! Mr. Adler, Anna and I, we've liked each other for a long time, and so I would like to ask you, your wife of course too, whether I, whether we can get married?

(MARIA smiles, ADLER is terribly depressed, he just doesn't show it. He hesitates. All look at him expectantly.)

ERICH: I know that we don't have much, our inn still has

a lot of debts, but now things are starting to improve!

MARIA: Oh, stop! As if that were important!

(They all wait for ADLER'S answer.)

ERICH: And then there's something else, I have to say that right away too—Anna, Anna is gonna have a baby from me.

ADLER: So?

MARIA: She's only known it for a few days, Stefan. We thought we should talk about all this at the same time. That doesn't matter, does it? We're not such bigots, right Stefan?

ADLER: No, that we're not.

MARIA: Besides that, it won't be born until after the wedding.

(There is silence for a while, all look at ADLER.)

ADLER: *(to ERICH)* Sit down, Erich!

(ERICH sits down amazed, ADLER gets up, looks at everyone, goes to the window, looks at the closed curtain, turns around to face the others.)

ADLER: I'm a Jew.

All freeze, for a while deadly silence.

MARIA: *(softly)* What are you?

ADLER: A Jew. A full-blooded Jew.

(Again silence for a while.)

ANNA: *(suffocating)* That's not true.

ADLER: Yes it is. I'm sorry, child!

MARIA: How can that be? You were born here!

ADLER: My grandparents came from the East. To Vienna. My parents came here from there.

MARIA: But you're Catholic.

ADLER: That doesn't make any difference to Hitler! A Jew is a Jew!

(For a while silence. Suddenly HANS gets up, goes to his father, knocks him to the floor with a single blow from his fist.)

MARIA: *(crying out)* Don't!

(MARIA and ANNA get up and go to ADLER, who is lying unconscious on the floor, kneel down beside him. ERICH remains seated as if turned to stone. HANS stands there trembling, suddenly goes to the door and leaves, slams the door behind him, goes out in front of the door, looks around, goes to the well, submerges his head under water, throws it in the air, lifts himself erect again, sits down despondently on the edge of the well, hides his face in his hands, begins to cry. ERICH suddenly get up, takes his cap, and also goes out.)

ANNA: *(sees this)* Erich!

(ERICH has already gone, comes out of the house, looks around searching, sees HANS at the well, goes over to him, looks at him helplessly. In the meantime MARIA gets some brandy out of the cupboard, goes to ADLER, massages his forehead and temple with it, he wakes up. ANNA gets up and also goes out of the house, looks around, goes to ERICH and HANS. MARIA helps ADLER get up, leads him over to the couch, sets him down, sits down beside him, looks at him despondently, he stares into space. Outside ANNA stands behind ERICH, looks at him. He stands with his back to her.)

ANNA: *(crying)* Erich! I'm so sorry! I didn't know that! Really not! Please forgive me. You don't have to marry me! I'll understand!

(ERICH turns around to her, is at wits end, doesn't know what to say, then goes over to her, embraces her. HANS looks up, looks at them, gets up, pulls his pistol out of the holster, ANNA sees it.)

ANNA: Hansi!

(ERICH looks, sees it too, HANS cocks and re-cocks the pistol, wants to place it next to his head, ERICH rushes forward, fights with him for the pistol, is able to pull it away from him, throws it in the well, embraces HANS.)

ERICH: Hansi, you're like a brother to me. Really, believe me! It's always been like that!

(HANS pulls himself loose.)

HANS: I'm a Jewish swine! A Jewish swine!

(ADLER hears that inside, turns over on the couch to face the wall, HANS looks at his SS uniform, takes off the belt, tears off his jacket, throws it away. Inside MARIA reaches for the shoulder of her husband, turns him towards her, takes his hand, kisses it, gets up, goes out of the house to the others.)

MARIA: Please come inside, all of you. I have something I want to say.

HANS: I'm never going to go in there again!

(MARIA picks up the jacket from the ground, takes HANS by the arm.)

MARIA: Please, Hans! I know a way out!

HANS: There is no way out!

MARIA: *(firmly)* You just come! Do you hear?

(MARIA goes first, ANNA and ERICH follow her. HANS watches them leave, then follows as well. They all come again into the living room.)

MARIA: Everybody sit down!

(The three sit down at the table, MARIA hangs up the SS jacket, gets out the schnapps bottle and a glass, fills it up and takes it to her husband.)

MARIA: Here, drink.

(ADLER sits up, drinks.)

MARIA: Are you OK?

(ADLER nods.)

MARIA: Come.

(She helps ADLER stand up, leads him to the table, he sits down, HANS doesn't look at him, MARIA sits down too, looks straight ahead for a while, it's difficult for her to say what she wants.)

MARIA: *(looks at HANS and ANNA)* Your father is not your father!

(All look at her without comprehension.)

ADLER: *(softly)* What are you saying? That's not true, Maria!

MARIA: Yes it is!

HANS: *(gets hopeful)* Can you swear to that?

MARIA: *(after a while)* Yes, I can swear to that!

(Blackout.)

Scene 4

(June 1938. The next evening. The figure of Christ is not hanging on the cross. The "wall" of Adler's house is closed, the "wall" of the main room of the inn is open. Instead of Dollfuss there is now a picture of Hitler hanging on the wall. ADLER, MARIA, ANNA, HANS (in civilian clothes), ERICH (in SA uniform), the MAYOR, and HOPFGART-NER (in uniform) are sitting at the reserved table. TONI (in an SA uniform) is sitting somewhat to the side on a bench and is sitting very erect so that he will not anger his father again. OLGA, standing behind the bar, has stopped washing glasses, is listening. HOPFGARTNER is holding an official document in his hand, in which the lineage of ADLER is described. He reads it, gives it to the MAYOR,

who reads it also.)

HOPFGARTNER: *(to ADLER)* And you swine even joined
our Party, even though you knew that you were a
wretched Jew! I think that's a particularly disgusting type of infamy!

ADLER: I could kick myself for that!

*(The MAYOR has finished reading, looks at the document,
shakes his head, looks at ADLER.)*

MAYOR: I just don't get it! I just don't get it! That's all I
needed. A damn Jew in our village. In the whole
country there's maybe eighty Jews left, and there
has to be one here of all places! Well, that really
does me in!

HOPFGARTNER: *(to HANS)* Good that you've already
taken off your uniform! Otherwise I would have
had to lock you up! *(To the whole family:)* All of you
are of course banned from the Party immediately!

MARIA: Not so fast, Sepp! Don't be too hasty!

HOPFGARTNER: Mr. Local Branch Leader, if you please!

TONI: Please!

MARIA: *(to HOPFGARTNER)* Hey, don't act so important!
Don't you remember that we used to play doctor, up
there in the raspberry thicket?

HOPFGARTNER: *(gets up)* Who do you think you're talking to?

OLGA: That gal is pretty daring!

MARIA: *(ignores Olga's statement)* And later, you wanted
to marry me! But I didn't want you. You were too
treacherous for me.

HOPFGARTNER: Just do me a favor and keep your filthy
mouth shut. You Jewish whore, you!

TONI: *(gets up)* Jewish whore!

HOPFGARTNER: *(to TONI)* Sit down! Or I'll knock your
block off!

(TONI sits down again, MARIA looks at TONI, then at

HOPFGARTNER again.)

MARIA: Boy, am I ever glad that I didn't take you!

HOPFGARTNER: *(saw MARIA looking at TONI)* That's not my fault! I come from a healthy stock! I have a doctor's testimony to that fact. Why do you think my wife killed herself? Because she had a bad conscience!

MARIA: You should be the one having the bad conscience! You treated her like a piece of dirt!

HANS: Let it go, mother, please!

HOPFGARTNER: So that's what you think!

MARIA: Well of course! She was constantly coming to me in tears!

ANNA: *(despondent)* Mama! Please!

HOPFGARTNER: No! No! I don't have to take that from you! Not from a Jew bitch! *(Goes to the telephone behind the bar.)* I'm going to call the Gestapo now! I'm going to have you all thrown in jail! For insulting a leader of the Party! *(Picks up the receiver.)* You're going to get a nice little surprise!

HANS: *(perplexed to MARIA)* My God, mother, what are you trying to do?

(MARIA gets up, goes to HOPFGARTNER, who is dialing and wants to shove MARIA away, she pushes his hand away, whispers something in his ear, HOPFGARTNER freezes, puts the receiver back, stares at her.)

HOPFGARTNER: What? —What?

MARIA: Come, sit down again!

(MARIA goes to the reserved table, goes past TONI.)

TONI: Jewish bitch!

(MARIA doesn't pay any attention to him, sits down, HOPFGARTNER comes slowly to the table, looks at MARIA, also sits down.)

MAYOR: Now what's going on?

MARIA: *(to the MAYOR)* Hansi is Sepp's boy.

MAYOR: What?

MARIA: Hansi's father is the Local Branch Leader!

(All are amazed.)

HOPFGARTNER: I don't believe that! That's a Jewish trick!

MARIA: Come on, don't act so dumb! Just figure it out! Hansi is now twenty-five.

(HOPFGARTNER looks at HANS, calculates in his head.)

ADLER: You mean you actually . . . with him . . . ?

MARIA: Yes, Stefan. I'm sorry. He absolutely wanted to have me. He wouldn't even let me alone after our wedding. And then one day he got me, right after church, when you were on the road.

HOPFGARTNER; Yes, maybe that's right . . . That was about that time.

(HOPFGARTNER looks at HANS, suddenly feels a certain pride rising up within himself, because HANS—as opposed to TONI—is healthy and strong. TONI looks with misgivings back and forth between HANS and his father.)

MARIA: And Anna, she isn't Stefan's child either.

MAYOR: Now wait just a minute!

MARIA: Anna is the child of the railroad signalman. He wanted to have me too. And how! He's still single today! *(She takes out an envelope, opens it, lays a letter down in front of the MAYOR and HOPFGARTNER.)* This notarized oath is from him! Confirmed by the county judge!

(The MAYOR reads the paper, HOPFGARTNER looks at it.)

OLGA: *(behind the bar)* What a shameless hussy!

MAYOR: *(to MARIA)* Well, you're a fine one! *(To ADLER:)* And you put up with this?

(STEFAN doesn't answer, he is confused. ANNA is also confused, can't quite believe it. HANS wants to believe it.)

MAYOR: In your case I would give my wife a good beating. I really would!

OLGA: I could understand that!

MARIA: Well, you know Mr. Mayor, that isn't quite so easy with a man who isn't able to have children himself. Who only sleeps with me at the most twice a year. I should say: used to sleep with me. But that's a long time ago too!

OLGA: Oh, please spare us! We've had enough of your dirty laundry! This is unbelievable!

HOPFGARTNER: *(looks at STEFAN)* A typical Jew! Either horny as hell or impotent! Then they're greedy for money, to compensate!

(STEFAN begins to tremble, grinds his teeth together, can no longer control himself out of despair and anger. ANNA casts a tormented glance at her father, she feels sorry for him.)

ANNA: *(softly)* Papa!

(HOPFGARTNER looks at HANS, gets up.)

HOPFGARTNER: Well, I have to go! *(Shakes his hand.)* Take care, boy!

HANS: *(embarrassed)* Take care!

TONI: *(jealous)* Jewish swine!

HOPFGARTNER: Shut up!

(ADLER suddenly gets up with a jerk, his chair flies back, he grabs HOPFGARTNER, pulls him over to himself, boxes his ears, then holds him with both hands on his collar.)

ADLER: I was born here! *(Boxes his ears.)* I grew up here! *(Boxes his ears.)* I worked here.

(The MAYOR has gotten up, wants to help HOPFGARTNER. ADLER pushes him away. MARIA hides her face in

her hands.)

ADLER: I paid my taxes! *(Boxes his ears.)*

(TONI rushes over to ADLER, who pushes him away so that he falls down. HANS has gotten up, pulls his father away, holds him firmly.)

ADLER: *(to HOPFGARTNER)* I went to war for this country! I'm a Trolian! Do you understand that, you Nazi shithead?

(ADLER pulls himself away from HANS, goes out, goes over into his house, then the light in the living room goes on. TONI gets up, sits down again. HOPFGARTNER puts his uniform in order, looks at the others, goes to the telephone again. MARIA runs after him, takes the receiver in her hand, he rips it loose, she takes it again.)

MARIA: Come! I have to tell you something! *(Pulls him to the door.)* Come!

(She pulls HOPFGARTNER out of the door. The MAYOR goes to the bar, pours himself a beer.)

OLGA: She's a shrewd one, I can tell you that!

(HANS sits down again with ANNA and ERICH at the table. MARIA and HOPFGARTNER come out of the inn. The "wall" of the main room closes.)

MARIA: I've lived together with that man for such a long time! Please leave him alone! He's going to have it hard enough!

HOPFGARTNER: No! I'm going to deliver him to the Gestapo! He's going to a camp! Right away today!

MARIA: Listen a minute, Sepp! You always wanted to have me! I know, I'm not young anymore, but if you want . . . I'll get a divorce right away! Then we can get married, I'll move to your place with Hansi, with your son, and then we'll be a family! I'll even take care of Toni promise you!

(HOPFGARTNER considers. He wishes he had a wife, a family, he feels lonely, he's unhappy with TONI, he's happy that he suddenly has a healthy son by the name of HANS.)

HOPFGARTNER: *(softly)* You really hurt me back then . . . For years I never got over your rejection. —OK, fine, I agree. BUT—I can't protect your husband forever. There are laws. It would be best if he left. He should emigrate. Like the other Jews are doing.

MARIA: Good, I'll tell him that.—Take care, I have to leave!

HOPFGARTNER: Take care!

(MARIA goes back to her house, HOPFGARTNER watches her leave and goes back into the inn. ANNA is just coming out, follows her mother. The "wall" of the living room opens. The picture of Himmler isn't there any more. ADLER is sitting at the table, staring into space, the door opens. MARIA looks in, ANNA appears behind her, they both enter, sit down at the table with ADLER. For a while there is silence. ADLER doesn't look at his wife. ANNA is totally confused. Across the way the MAYOR comes out of the inn, departs to the right in the direction of the Court House.)

ADLER: *(looks up)* I suppose they'll be picking me up any second.

MARIA: *(sadly)* No, I've prevented that. But at a heavy price! Because you can't control yourself!

ANNA: *(to MARIA)* But you were constantly provoking him yourself!

MARIA: I can afford to do that.

ADLER: What's the price?

MARIA: I'm going to marry him. The Local Branch Leader.

(ADLER looks at her, he gets extremely angry again.)

MARIA: *(despondent)* Well, what was I supposed to do, huh?

ADLER: Did you really go to bed with that swine?

MARIA: Yes, I did. And I regret it to this very day! But—I just want you to understand: he is not Hansi's father. That wouldn't have been possible. He just doesn't remember exactly anymore, when we did it . . . Thank God!

ADLER: And the guy from the railroad?

MARIA: Ah, I never had anything with him! He's just an acquaintance! A socialist! He likes to give it to the Nazis! *(To ANNA:)* But that's our secret, Anna! And for heaven's sake, don't ever tell Hansi! Just let him believe that Sepp is his father. You saw how he reacted! And at least both of you are protected!

ANNA: OK, fine.

ADLER: What a disgrace! What a disgrace!

ANNA: *(perplexed)* I would so much like to marry Erich!

(For a while there is silence. HANS leaves the inn, goes to Adler's house, comes into the living room, looks at the family, sits down on the couch.)

HANS: *(after a pause to his mother)* Is that right? Is that really true?

(MARIA nods.)

ADLER: Get out my sight, boy! I never want to see you again! Never again!—Go to your Local Branch Leader. You two belong together! Nazi swine!

(HANS gets up, goes out. Goes up to his room.)

MARIA: *(after a pause)* You should emigrate, Stefan.

ADLER: Sure, anything else?

MARIA: Stefan, believe me, bad times are coming for you!

ADLER: Be quiet, I don't want to hear anymore!

MARIA: Stefan, I implore you . . .

ADLER: *(angrily)* You should be quiet, I said!

(The MAYOR arrives with a file folder from the Court House, goes into Adler's house, knocks on the door.)

MARIA: Come in!

(The MAYOR enters.)

MAYOR: May I sit down?

MARIA: Please!

(The MAYOR sits down, opens the folder in front of him, looks at the group, looks at STEFAN.)

MAYOR: Please don't get mad again, Stefan! Or else I'll have to get the police! There are a few things I have to take care of, and it won't do you any good, if you try to fight it, that will just make everything worse!

(STEFAN looks at the MAYOR, looks at the folder.)

ADLER: *(points at it)* Am I in there?

MAYOR: Yes, so to speak. Some regulations have arrived. Naturally I never paid them any heed, because I thought that our village was free of Jews!

(He opens the folder, thumbs through it, stops at one page.)

MAYOR: This comes from the Aryanization Office. From County Economic Advisor Duxneuner. Following regulations *(reads excerpts)*: "Any wealth above 5000 Reichsmarks is to be reported to the Federal Property Office ... Trade and selling licenses are to be canceled. Real estate is to be confiscated and turned in ... " *(Looks up, looks at ADLER.)*

(Silence for a while. ADLER gets up slowly.)

MAYOR: *(fearful)* You'll control yourself, won't you? I have to do this, I have my orders!

ADLER: *(softly)* You want to take my money away? My house? My business?

MAYOR: Yes, what am I supposed to do?

(ADLER goes to the weapons case, takes out a hunting rifle. The MAYOR stands up terrified.)

ADLER: Here, try this out!

MARIA: *(gets up)* Please, Stefan! You can't fight against the whole world!

ADLER: So, you don't think I can? Well I'll show you! Even
  if I get bumped off! I'll still kill a few of you! *(Cries)*
  I'm not going to let my whole life be ruined! Just because my father didn't have a foreskin! —I'm not a
  sheep that you can lead to slaughter! *(He looks at
  the MAYOR, something occurs to him, he suddenly
  becomes quite calm.)* Why am I getting all excited?
  There's another way of doing this! *(Puts the rifle
  back, looks at the MAYOR, smiles grimly, yells at
  the MAYOR:)* Sit down!

*(The MAYOR sits down, so does MARIA. ADLER looks at
the MAYOR, who is becoming restless. At this moment
HANS leaves the house in his SS uniform. He is carrying a
large suitcase and goes over to the inn.)*

ADLER: That was a few years ago. You still weren't in
  power. I mean, you were already in power! Because
  you, you were always in power! You change like a
  weather vane in the wind!

MAYOR: Be careful! Don't insult me! Because otherwise
  you'll really be in for it! I can do a lot of other things
  besides confiscating your property!

ADLER: That I believe! But—you won't! You are going to
  be real nice and leave me in peace!

MAYOR: *(screams)* I can't do that!

ADLER: Just you wait! Well, I'm going to start my story
  again: A few years ago, when you were still in the
  conservative party, a really conservative mayor,
  some criminal investigators came here one night.
  And they arrested your son. They wanted to arrest
  mine, too. —Oh, excuse me, he isn't my son any
  longer! —At any rate, my quasi-son, but he had already flown the coop!

(The MAYOR feels a little precarious.)

ADLER: Somebody spilled the beans on those two! But
  who, the whole village wanted to know! Who was
  the swine? Ha, what do you think?

MAYOR: I have no idea!

ADLER: So, you have no idea? Are you sure?

MAYOR: *(gets up)* Now look, I don't have any time for this crazy talk! Just come to the Court House tomorrow! Then you'll find out the rest!

(The MAYOR goes to the door.)

ADLER: You were the one!

(The MAYOR stops abruptly, but doesn't turn around.)

ADLER: You were the traitor!

(The MAYOR turns around, is frightened to death.)

MAYOR: You're really nuts, you know?

ADLER: I heard it! You understand? I heard it! I saw it! Through the window! I was standing over there, during the night. somebody like myself, Mr. Mayor, always has to be careful! Always has to know what's going on! I've still got that in my blood, you can't take it out of me! That's the only thing I've still got! Distrust! Watchfulness! (Quotes:) "Well, first you have to promise me that I don't have to testify and that my name won't appear anywhere!"—Right? You Judas?

(The MAYOR begins to totter, goes to the table, braces himself, sits down.)

ANNA: *(to the MAYOR)* But—you wouldn't have betrayed Erich! Your only son! That can't be! Why would you do that?

ADLER: No, no, he certainly just wanted to betray our Hansi! In order to ingratiate himself, to protect himself. He's always trying to protect himself from all sides—But the jerk obviously got tricked by the police!

MARIA: What a rotten thing to do! That is really the last straw. *(To ADLER:)* Why didn't you tell us about that?

ADLER: Everything in good time!

MARIA: But that has to be known! That's not right! Somebody who betrayed the Nazis can't be a Nazi mayor!

ADLER: Yes, you're right. That really should be made known. Then the mayor will be gone before me! *(To the MAYOR:)* Ha, and what do you think Erich is going to say about all this? Think he'll say "Thank you very much, Father, that you were responsible for bringing me to jail!" Huh?

(The MAYOR slides from the chair onto his knees.)

MAYOR: I beg of you!

ADLER: *(coldly)* Get up! You don't have to be afraid! We'll make a little deal!

(The MAYOR sits down again, ADLER sits down too, fills his pipe, lights it, smokes. HOPFGARTNER, HANS (with suitcase) and TONI leave the inn, go up the village lane, TONI trots behind them at a little distance, is displeased. HOPFGARTNER puts his arm around HANS.)

ADLER: It's real simple. You leave me in peace, and for that I'll keep quiet.

MAYOR: *(perplexed)* Well, how's that supposed to work? I'm not alone, you know! Don't forget the Local Branch Leader!

MARIA: I'll take care of him. He now has a healthy son, and I'm going to become his wife.

MAYOR: *(perplexed)* But I just called up the district magistrate!

At his home! I talked with him personally!

(ADLER breathes out, shakes his head.)

MAYOR: I'll do everything, Stefan! Everything! Really! But only in the realm of the possibilities that still exist!

(ADLER gets up, walks around, ponders.)

MAYOR: I can't stop the confiscation, Stefan! That's already in the works!

(For a while there is silence.)

MARIA: You have to transfer everything to Hansi, Stefan! That will work because Hansi is now an Aryan!

ADLER: Why sure! Anything else? That SS clown is not going to get anything from me! Not a penny! So that he can fatten up his new father at my expense, eh? If I transfer everything to Anna, then he'll get it *(points to the MAYOR)*!

ANNA: Why is that?

ADLER: Because you're going to marry his boy!

MAYOR: Don't be silly! If I want to have it, I'll get it anyway!

(ADLER looks at the MAYOR.)

MAYOR: Yes, naturally! The confiscated properties are sold in a preferential way to Party members. And especially cheap! Unless, of course, the State wants to have them!

(For a while there is silence.)

ADLER: *(to the MAYOR)* Just leave. I have to think about it! Then I'll tell you my decision!

(The MAYOR looks done in, takes his folder, goes out and over to the inn. ADLER sits down beside MARIA and ANNA, stares into space.)

MARIA: I have to tell you again, Stefan: emigrate!

ANNA: *(angry)* Yes, and what's Mama supposed to do? Huh? Didn't you hear about that? She's sacrificing herself for you! She's going to marry this horrible person! If you leave, she doesn't have to do that!

ADLER: Who knows . . . ? Maybe it isn't such a big sacrifice . . .

MARIA: *(makes a sigh halfway between a laugh and a sob)* Oh!

ADLER: *(calmly, coldly)* Everybody out of here! None of

you belong to me anymore!

(MARIA gets up, goes out, ANNA looks at her father sadly.)

ADLER: What's wrong? Go over to your Nazi boy!

(ANNA gets up, goes to the door, turns around.)

ANNA: *(calmly)* If you weren't a Jew, you'd probably also
be a Nazi.

(She leaves. ADLER sits alone.)

(Blackout.)

Scene 5

*(November 12, 1938. Late in the night. It is cold, there is
snow on the mountains. The repaired figure of Christ is
hanging on the cross again. The left house "wall" is closed,
no light is coming out of the ADLER house, the "wall" of the
main room of the inn is open. HANS (in civilian clothes),
ERICH (in civilian clothes), the CHIEF OF POLICE, the
two ex-HEIMWEHR MEN (in civilian clothes) and the
MARKSMAN from scene 2 (also in civilian clothes) are sitting at the reserved table. TONI is sitting in his SA uniform
in a stiff posture on the bench beside them. The MARKS-
MAN has a horse-whip, is playing with it. HOPFGART-
NER (in uniform) and the MAYOR are standing at the
telephone, HOPFGARTNER has the receiver in his hand.
All are looking at the telephone.)*

HOPFGARTNER: *(on the telephone)* The boiling soul of
the people, yes sir!—yes sir!—yes sir!—That's what
I said! All in civilian clothes! Yes, yes, they are all in
civilian clothes. —Yes sir, he's here too! The Chief of
Police is here!—I'll tell him—Yes sir!—Without a
sound! Yes sir!—Then I'll give a full report!—Yes

sir! Heil Hitler, Herr Sturmführer!

(HOPFGARTNER hangs up, he and the MAYOR come to the reserved table.)

HOPFGARTNER: Well! You probably know it already, a Jew murdered a member of the German consular staff in Paris. As a result the people's soul has begun to boil all over in the German Reich! It was also boiling yesterday in Innsbruck. The synagogue and several apartments have been destroyed, and a few of the Jews departed this life. Naturally we can't be behind the times here! We don't have to kill him; but he should be taught a little lesson!

ERICH: What's that? Are we supposed to play the boiling soul of the people?

HOPFGARTNER: Yes, I can't get the whole village boiling so quickly! In Innsbruck it was the SS that did it!

ERICH: Well, I'm not going to go along.

HANS: Me, neither. You can't ask us to do that, Sepp!

HOPFGARTNER: Oh yes I can!

HANS: No, dammit! I have a conscience, you know!

HOPFGARTNER: Come on, give me a break! This whole idea of conscience is a Jewish invention! There is only one thing that matters—duty!

HANS: *(gets up)* That's not my duty to beat up the man who raised me!

(ERICH looks at HANS, HANS remembers that he did indeed beat up his father. He sits down depressed.)

HOPFGARTNER: *(to the ex-HEIMWEHR MEN)* Then you do it! You owe me a little test of your worth anyway.

FIRST HEIMWEHR MAN: Good, We'll light a little fire under him!

(The ex-HEIMWEHR MEN get up, the MARKSMAN as well.)

MARKSMAN: *(grinning)* I'll go along too!

HOPFGARTNER: *(to the POLICEMAN)* And you stay here! You hear nothing and you see nothing.

(The POLICEMAN nods.)

FIRST HEIMWEHR MAN: *(looking at the horse-whip of the MARKSMAN)* I could use something like that!

HOPFGARTNER: *(to the POLICEMAN)* Give me your rubber club!

(The POLICEMAN hesitates for a short time, but then doesn't dare to contradict, pulls out his rubber club, gives it to the FIRST HEIMWEHR MAN. The SECOND HEIMWEHR MAN makes his right hand into a fist and points at it with his left index finger.)

SECOND HEIMWEHR MAN: *(grinning)* I'll take this along!

MAYOR: But don't destroy anything!

HOPFGARTNER: What?

MAYOR: Well . . . I just mean . . .

(HOPFGARTNER gives him a contemptuous glance.)

HOPFGARTNER: *(to the men)* Well, off you go!

(The three men go out the door, TONI watches them go, gets up, follows them.)

HOPFGARTNER: Stay here, boy!

(TONI turns around.)

TONI: Just look!

HOPFGARTNER: OK, fine, go ahead! You can learn a little something about harshness!

(TONI goes out. The three men come out of the door of the inn, go over to the ADLER house, TONI follows them, the MARKSMAN sees him, pushes him back.)

MARKSMAN: Beat it, piss off!

(TONI goes a few steps back, the MARKSMAN goes over to the other two. The FIRST HEIMWEHR MAN tries the door

knob, the door is locked. HOPFGARTNER and the MAYOR walk to the window of the inn, look out between the curtains. HANS, ERICH and the POLICEMAN remain seated at the table. The POLICEMAN is angry, that he had to let himself be ordered around by HOPFGARTNER. The MARKSMAN goes to the first window of the living room, breaks a pane with the handles of the horse-whip, reaches in, opens the lock, opens the window, climbs in, the two ex-HEIMWEHR MEN climb in after him, TONI watches and then also climbs in, after the men have disappeared. Up above in the bedroom the light goes on. ADLER awakens at the sound of the breaking glass. After a while one hears noise in the bedroom, a window pane splinters, furniture is being destroyed. The MAYOR angrily contorts his face. He would like to take control of everything and is not interested in destruction. On the second floor of the inn a light goes on in the room that is directly across from the ADLER house, the curtain is shoved aside, ANNA opens the window, looks out in her nightdress, looks over to the bedroom of her father. OLGA appears in back of her, also in a nightdress. After a while the door of the house opens, the unconscious ADLER is dragged out by the two ex-HEIMWEHR MEN. He's wearing pajamas and is bleeding from his mouth and nose. In Adler's living room the light goes on, furniture and dishes are being broken to bits. The MARKSMAN is doing that. TONI emerges from behind the HEIMWEHR MEN, is irritated and excited as he follows the events. On the one hand he likes the destruction, on the other hand he has pity for ADLER. The HEIMWEHR MEN drag ADLER to the well, dip his head repeatedly into the water. TONI finds that very funny, and he has to laugh. ANNA disappears from the window, OLGA leans over the window sill and continues to look on curiously. ADLER wakes up gasping for air, tries to tear himself loose, he is dipped in the water again. ANNA comes running out of the inn, she has put on a coat over her nightdress and is wearing rubber boots. She rushes over to the two ex-HEIMWEHR MEN.)

ANNA: Get away! Leave him alone! Get away!

(ANNA is pushed away by the SECOND HEIMWEHR MAN, goes back again, pulls the SECOND HEIMWEHR MAN back, he grabs her and leads her forcibly into the inn. ADLER tears himself away from the FIRST HEIMWEHR MAN, pushes him into the well, so that he ends up with his whole body in the water. TONI starts to laugh uncontrollably, he rolls around on the ground from laughter. During all this the SECOND HEIMWEHR MAN pushes ANNA into the main room of the inn.)

SECOND HEIMWEHR MAN: *(to ERICH)* Hold onto her, dammit!

(The SECOND HEIMWEHR MAN slams the door shut, goes out again, ANNA wants to go to the door again, ERICH gets up, pulls her back, she defends herself vehemently, he forces her down onto a chair, she remains seated, covers her face with her hands and cries. During all this the MARKSMAN has come out of the ADLER house, looks around, ADLER wants to flee at this moment to the door of his house, the MARKSMAN steps over to him, hits him with the horse-whip, ADLER protects his face with his hands, the FIRST HEIMWEHR MAN finally manages to get out of the well trough, rushes over to ADLER, starts thrashing him with the rubber club. The SECOND HEIMWEHR MAN comes out of the inn, doesn't do anything, but only observes. TONI has stopped laughing, looks on as the men beat ADLER. ADLER collapses to his knees, the blows hail down on his head and back. TONI gets up and suddenly rushes over to the MARKSMAN, pulls him back and down to the ground, sits on him and begins to strangle him.)

HOPFGARTNER: *(cries through the window)* Toni! Stop! Toni!

(The SECOND HEIMWEHR MAN goes to TONI, pulls him up by his hair, tears him away. ADLER totally collapses, the FIRST HEIMWEHR MAN stops beating him, looks down at him. TONI tears himself away from the Heimwehr man, runs away a short distance. The MARKS-MAN staggers up, grabs his throat breathing heavily, looks at TONI.)

MARKSMAN: You just wait, I'll get you yet! Then I'll beat
the ass off of you!—What a jerk!

(The FIRST and SECOND HEIMWEHR MEN look at ADLER, who is lying motionless on the ground.)

SECOND HEIMWEHR MAN: He's had enough!

(The FIRST HEIMWEHR MAN looks down at himself.)

FIRST HEIMWEHR MAN: Shit! I'm totally soaked!

(The FIRST HEIMWEHR MAN goes to the village lane. The SECOND HEIMWEHR MAN drinks some water from the well, the MARKSMAN is already going into the inn, the SECOND HEIMWEHR MAN follows him.)

HOPFGARTNER: *(screams through the window)* Toni!
Get over here!

(TONI doesn't react, he's looking at ADLER. The MARKS-MAN and the SECOND HEIMWEHR MAN enter the main room of the inn.)

MARKSMAN: Well! I guess we earned some free beer!

(ANNA wants to get up and go outside, ERICH takes her wrist, pushes her down.)

ANNA: Let me go!
ERICH: You stay here! You finally have to learn where you
belong!

(He forces ANNA down, she pulls her hand loose, but remains seated. In the meantime the MAYOR goes to the bar, pours out two beers, the two thugs sit down, light up ciga-

rettes.)

HOPFGARTNER: *(softly, he means TONI)* I'll teach you to obey me!

(HOPFGARTNER turns away from the window, looks at the reserved table, looks at the MAYOR, goes over, takes the two beers that have been poured out.)

MAYOR: Do you want one too?
HOPFGARTNER: Yes, if you would be so kind!

(The MAYOR pours another beer, HOPFGARTNER brings the two mugs to the SECOND HEIMWEHR MAN and to the MARKSMAN.)

HOPFGARTNER: Prost! Hope you enjoy it!

(The two men take the mugs, drink a big gulp. During all this TONI goes slowly over to ADLER outside, walks around him carefully, nudges him with the tip of his shoe, pulls back his foot horrified, looks around, goes into the inn. The MAYOR brings HOPFGARTNER his beer, TONI enters.)

HOPFGARTNER: Get over here!

(TONI comes to him, HOPFGARTNER gets up, boxes his ears, TONI lets him do it without flinching, HOPFGART-NER points to the next table, TONI sits down there, the MARKSMAN looks at him with the expression "Just wait!" HOPFGARTNER sits down again, drinks some of his beer. Outside ADLER tries to get up, but he doesn't succeed. HANS and ERICH sit there depressed. ANNA looks at ERICH.)

ANNA: *(calmly)* I never should have married you!
ERICH: Well I didn't take part in any of his, Anna!
ANNA: To let it happen is the same thing!
ERICH: Come on, he isn't even your father!
ANNA: *(gets up)* He's a human being! A human being!

(She goes out, leaves the inn, looks around, sees her father lying on the ground, runs over, helps him up, sets him down on the edge of the well, takes a handkerchief out of her coat pocket, holds it under the stream of water which is coming out of the pipe, washes the blood out of the face of her father.)

ANNA: *(crying)* Go away! I beg you, go away! They'll finish you off! You must believe me!

(ADLER doesn't answer.)

(Blackout.)

Scene 6

(End of November, 1938. Night. Both "walls" are closed. Both of the broken windows in the ADLER house are not repaired. There is no light in the ADLER house, light is glimmering through the windows of the main room of the inn. Someone is playing the zither in the inn. After a while HOPFGARTNER, MARIA, HANS and TONI exit through the inn door. Behind them are the MAYOR and OLGA. HOPFGARTNER is wearing his Party leader's uniform with highly polished boots, MARIA a wedding dirndl, HANS his SS dress uniform, TONI the SA uniform, the MAYOR a national costume, OLGA a dirndl.)

OLGA: My goodness! When I look at you—you make quite the lovely couple!

MAYOR: And their children do too! *(Laughs raucously.)*

(MARIA looks up to her former bedroom, HOPFGARTNER sees her glance.)

HOPFGARTNER: *(to the MAYOR)* What's going to happen to him now?

(Points to the ADLER house.)

MAYOR: Well, everything is going according to instructions!

HOPFGARTNER: Yes, well what?

MAYOR: Well, on the nineteenth an instruction came from the Gestapo Chief that all Jews are to be transported to Vienna. Yesterday they rescinded the order. But we are supposed to continually urge them to emigrate!

HOPFGARTNER: Yes, and are you doing that?

MAYOR: Sure, sure, I'm doing that! You don't have to worry about that! He'll soon be gone!

HOPFGARTNER: And the house?

MAYOR: *(lies)* Yes . . . That, that he's giving to Anna.

HOPFGARTNER: Well, then you achieved your goal!

MAYOR: Listen, that has nothing to do with me! Besides that—he could just as well have signed it over to Hansi!

HANS: I don't want a single thing from him!

HOPFGARTNER: But I want something! His car! How does that look when the Local Branch Leader drives around on a motorcycle? And he doesn't need it anymore!

MAYOR: *(grins)* And besides that it's getting cold, right? OK, fine! You'll get it!

MARIA: I'm cold! Let's get going! *(Turns to leave.)*

OLGA: Well, much happiness and many roses to the young couple!

(MARIA, HOPFGARTNER, HANS and TONI go up the village lane, the MAYOR and OLGA watch them go. The zither player stops playing.)

OLGA: *(disdainfully)* That's a fine little group!

(OLGA enters the inn, the MAYOR looks over at the ADLER house, goes over, tries the door handle, it is locked, uses the door knocker. Nothing moves. The MAYOR walks over to

the broken window of the living room.)

MAYOR: *(calls softly)* Stefan! Stefan! Open up, please! I have to talk with you about an urgent matter!—My God, how am I supposed to help you if I can't even get a chance to talk with you?

(The light in the living room goes on, the MAYOR goes to the door of the house and waits, the door is opened, he goes in, the door of the house closes. The "wall" of the living rooms opens. The furniture is destroyed, the cupboard is open, is partially ruined, a radio, a file folder and a drawer area lying on the floor, the contents of the drawer are partially strewn about, a broken hunting rifle is lying on the floor, broken pieces of plates and glasses are lying about, the dining table is lying on its side, one leg is broken off, also partially broken chairs are lying about. One intact chair is standing by the couch, on the couch is a pillow and a wrinkled blanket. On the chair is an overflowing ash tray, a pipe, a tobacco pouch, a pipe cleaner, a lighter, a half empty schnapps bottle, a schnapps glass. ADLER and the MAYOR enter through the door. ADLER is wearing a coat, pants, a shirt, a pullover, a scarf, winter socks, looks in poor shape. He goes to the couch, lies down, covers himself with the blanket.)

MAYOR: *(sees the chaos)* My God, this can't be true. I made a special point of telling them they shouldn't break anything!

(He looks for an intact chair, takes it, sits down next to ADLER.)

MAYOR: I had nothing to do with all of this, Stefan! I swear it! *(Looks at the broken window.)* You should have the window fixed. It's really cold in here! *(Looks at ADLER.)* Are you sick, or what?

(ADLER doesn't answer.)

MAYOR: I wanted to come earlier, you know! But the Local Branch Leader, he's always watching me. He doesn't trust me! Because he knows how good-natured I am!—By the way—today he married your wife!

(ADLER doesn't react, stares into space.)

MAYOR: Yes, Stefan, you finally have to decide what's going to happen to your possessions! I have been named the administrator and I am supposed to get a move on!

ADLER: I'll give it to Anna!

MAYOR: *(is happy)* Well fine, wonderful!—Say, I noticed that somebody came over here . . . Wasn't that the notary?

ADLER: That's right. Once again you saw correctly! *(Takes an envelope from under the pillow and gives it to the MAYOR.)* There's the present. To my ex-daughter.

MAYOR: Well, wonderful! You did the smart thing, Stefan! The best solution! *(Fits the envelope in his pocket.)* Yes, Stefan . . . Now we still need the documents. Books, business papers and so on!

(ADLER points to one of the drawers on the floor. Papers have fallen out. The MAYOR goes over, looks fleetingly at the papers, gathers them together.)

ADLER: *(during all this)* In Innsbruck there's a whole load of pigs that have been waiting for three days! You better take care of that!

MAYOR: Good!

ADLER: At least twenty farmers are waiting for me. Butchers and restaurants in half of the district are waiting for me. There are delivery obligations. If you don't service them, the business will be ruined within a month!

MAYOR: *(hectically searching around)* My goodness, I just don't know my way around!

ADLER: Anna knows what's going on. She always kept my books and handled all correspondence!

MAYOR: I see! Well, good, fine! —Erich is also going to

have to get involved!

ADLER: *(points)* The file folder under there is also part of it.

(The MAYOR collects together several file folders, pushes everything into a big pile, sits down again on the chair panting.)

MAYOR: Yes . . . It's like this, Stefan, by the 15th of March 1939 the province has to be free of Jews! That means that by then you either have to emigrate or move to Vienna!

ADLER: You will prevent that!

MAYOR: Now that's a good one!

ADLER: I mean it, you will prevent that!

(The MAYOR stares into space, there is a turmoil within him.)

MAYOR: *(after a pause)* By the way, I got a new instruction. I have to take in your car! For the Local Branch Leader!

ADLER: *(grins grimly)* You people are really robbers!

MAYOR: Now listen, that is totally legal! Aryanization for Party use! That is covered by the law!

ADLER: Yes, I'll believe that! You sure make the right laws for yourselves!

(Silence for a while.)

MAYOR: *(mutters darkly)* A hole in the head, then there would be peace!

ADLER: *(understands quite well)* Come on now! You don't want to commit suicide? That would really be a shame!

MAYOR: *(jumps up)* I mean you! You should get a hole in the head you unabashed Jewish swine, you!

ADLER: I would think about that matter with a hole, if I were you, Mr. Mayor! I've already made my statement, you know!

MAYOR: What?

ADLER: I wrote down everything about your treason. At a lawyer's! In case of my death it is to be given to the Gestapo! In case of my deportation the same thing will happen!

MAYOR: That is sheer madness! That's madness! I can't keep you here for years! Can't you understand that?

ABLER: Your problem!

MAYOR: They won't ever believe you! Who is going to believe a Jew?

ADLER: The Gestapo investigates everything! Everything! You should know that!

(The MAYOR looks despondent, goes to the door, comes back again, gathers up the papers and the file folders, goes out.)

(Blackout.)

Scene 8

(September 1939. Dawn. Both of the "walls" are closed. Now all the windows of the ADLER house are broken. In the second floor the curtains are closed, in the ground floor all the windows have been covered with planks from the inside. Light is glimmering through the curtains of the main room of the inn. The MAYOR, OLGA, ANNA, HOPFGART-NER (in civilian clothes) and TONI are standing between the houses. ANNA is carrying her 10 month old child wrapped in a blanket, it is still sleeping. TONI is wearing a Sunday suit with shirt and tie, is cleanly washed and combed, is afraid. HANS, ERICH and the SECOND

*HEIMWEHR MAN are going up the village lane. ERICH
and the SECOND HEIMWEHR MAN are wearing mountain hunter uniforms, HANS an SS uniform. ERICH turns
around, raises his cap, lets out a cheer, HANS and the SEC-
OND HEIMWEHR MAN also turn around, laugh and
raise their hands in greeting. Their family members match
them leave, the young men disappear above around the corner. ANNA turns around sadly, goes into the house with her
child.)*

MAYOR: *(happily to TONI)* And what's with you, huh? Not
   fighting?

TONI: Cut off prick!

MAYOR: What?

(HOPFGARTNER boxes TONI's ears.)

HOPFGARTNER: Be quiet! *(to MARIA:)* Where did he get
   that from?

MARIA: I have no idea!

*(OLGA looks curiously, the MAYOR amazed. TONI moves
back in the direction of the village lane.)*

TONI: Me war! No cut off prick!

OLGA: What's wrong with him?

HOPFGARTNER: *(to TONI)* Will you come here! Come
   here, I said!

*(TONI falls further back, turns around wants to run after
the soldiers, HOPFGARTNER runs after him, grabs him
by the collar, drags him back.)*

HOPFGARTNER: What are you talking about? Where did
   you get such stuff? Nothing is going to happen to
   you!

TONI: Yes! Cut off prick! *(Breaks out in tears.)* I don't like!

HOPFGARTNER: *(to MARIA)* Did you say something to
   him?

MARIA: I didn't say anything to him. He probably heard it
   someplace! At the examination! Or at the court!

He's not as stupid as you think!

MAYOR: Well, tell me, what's it all about?

MARIA: They are gonna sterilize him, sterilize Toni!

HOPFGARTNER: *(to MARIA)* Do you have to say that? Everybody doesn't have to know that!

OLGA: *(mockingly)* My goodness, Sepp, that isn't a disgrace!

(TONI tries to tear away again, HOPFGARTNER fights with him, finally takes him in a headlock.)

HOPFGARTNER: *(panting to the MAYOR and OLGA)* Now please just go inside! Or do you like watching?

(The MAYOR and OLGA go into the inn, OLGA glances knowingly at her husband.)

HOPFGARTNER: *(to TONI)* Are you going to give in, huh?

TONI: *(crying)* No, don't cut off! Please, don't cut off!

MARIA: Come on, Toni! They aren't going to cut anything off. Believe me! That's just a small little operation!

HOPFGARTNER: *(presses harder)* Are you going to give in?

TONI: Yes, give in!

(HOPFGARTNER lets go of TONI, who straightens himself out, stands there perplexed, HOPFGARTNER runs his fingers through Toni's hair, puts them in order.)

HOPFGARTNER: *(suddenly gentle)* Now come on, let's get it over with!

(HOPFGARTNER takes TONI by the arm, leaves with him, TONI looks in a perplexed fashion back at MARIA, they disappear. MARIA looks over at the ADLER house. The MAYOR comes out of the inn, goes over and stands beside MARIA, also looks at the ADLER house.)

MARIA: Since when has he nailed everything shut?

MAYOR: Oh, months ago! After they broke all his windows!

MARIA: Who? Who did that?

MAYOR: Yuh, how should I know! Everybody who passed by in the night probably threw a stone in!

MARIA: *(shakes her head)* What a horrid thing to do! *(To the MAYOR:)* He always paid them the best prices for their cattle! And always in cash, always on time! He advanced them the fodder! Loaned them money in difficult times! And now they break in his windows! A nice way of saying thanks!

MAYOR: *(fearful)* I hope he's still alive!

MARIA: What?

MAYOR: Anna always puts something to eat in front of his door, you know! For three days now he hasn't removed it!

MARIA: Well how come you haven't looked in on him?

MAYOR: We did! We banged against the door. He shouted that we should leave him alone! Insulted Anna! How come you don't look in on him?

MARIA: You know very well, that he doesn't ever want to see me again! He threw me out, after all! For having sacrificed myself!

MAYOR: My . . .

MARIA: Yes, I have my pride! He doesn't have to be jealous of the senior teacher! I did it for him! Only for him!

(The MAYOR looks at the house.)

MAYOR: It's madness! Look at how the house is going to pot! That just won't do!

MARIA: No, it can't really go on like this! *(After a while.)* He must work again! Absolutely!

MAYOR: He's not permitted to!

MARIA: Oh, don't be silly!

MAYOR; No, that's not possible. It's forbidden!

MARIA: Yes, yes, that would suit you just fine, if he met his end. Then you'd be rid of a very unpopular witness! But I'll guarantee you one thing: If he dies, then I'll reveal your treason!

MAYOR: *(perplexed)* If he dies, then it's going to come out anyway! He's written it all down!

MARIA: *(understands)* Ah, that's why you're so concerned about him! I always was amazed!

(The MAYOR looks at MARIA, goes to the first broken window, drums on the boards.)

MAYOR: Stefan! Stefan!, open up! Open up, I say!

(Nothing moves, the MAYOR looks at MARIA, who also goes over.)

MARIA: Stefan! It's me, Maria! Open up, please! —Stefan, please! I'm worried about you!

(Nothing moves, the MAYOR continues to drum against the boards.)

MAYOR: Stefan! My God, now let us in! My but you're a thankless person! I did everything for you! I even went extra to the district magistrate at the county seat! I stressed all your positive accomplishments! I managed to get a delay for you! What else do you want?

(Through a crack between two boards a rifle barrel comes out, almost touches the mayor's eye, the MAYOR steps back startled, steps to the side to the wall so that he won't be hit in case something happens.)

MAYOR: *(to MARIA)* He's crazy! He's totally crazy!

MARIA: *(angry)* OK, fine, then don't! But I'm not going to come again, Stefan! I can promise you that!

MAYOR: Now listen, Stefan! I want you to work again! To practice your trade again! Did you hear me?

(The MAYOR looks out of the corner of his eye at the window, the rifle barrel disappears, the MAYOR steps to the window again.)

MAYOR: Did you hear what I said?

MARIA: Stefan!

(They wait for a reaction, suddenly the house door is opened. The MAYOR and MARIA go in, go into the house. The "wall" of the living room opens. There is still the same disorder, nothing has changed, just that there are additional pieces of clothing lying around on the floor. ADLER comes in by the door. He is now totally shabby, has been wearing the same clothing for months, has obviously not bathed for the same amount of time. Now he doesn't have a coat on. MARIA and the MAYOR enter behind him. It is still dusky, there is no light in the room. ADLER sits down on the couch, MARIA sits down on the second chair and looks at ADLER, the MAYOR looks for another intact chair, brings it to the others, also sits down.)

MARIA: *(to ADLER)* You look terrible!

ADLER doesn't answer.

MARIA: There's a war. Hans and Erich have reported for service.

(ADLER nods indifferently.)

MARIA: *(indignantly)* You just can't lie there on the couch year in and year out. Take a bath, eat something, go out into the fresh air!

ADLER: *(to the MAYOR)* Well: what do you have to say to me?

MAYOR: You heard me already! You should go to work for me!

ADLER: So? For you?

MAYOR: My goodness, OK then for Anna! The business belongs to her! And Erich is in the war! I can't do it all by myself! Now just come and help me!

MARIA: You should really be thankful for the offer, Stefan!

MAYOR: That's what I think too! Because it's not permitted! I can get in a lot of trouble! I guess I'll have to say that you are doing forced labor for me! Otherwise they'll get me!

(ADLER looks at them both. Naturally he would very

much like to work again. He is going to pot here, is so alone and without anything to do.)

ADLER: *(after a while)* Good! I agree!

MAYOR: Well, finally! You'll see, we two will be good partners. You do the purchasing, Anna and I will do everything else!

MARIA: Now I'm really happy, Stefan! That will certainly be good for you when you are among people again!

ADLER: Yes! I've been among people my whole life! I can't imagine a better job! *(Smiles.)* I can still remember how I got started. I was thirteen years old. My father gave me some money and said: Go to the market and buy a sheep—That night I came home, with a sheep, and gave my father the money back again. I got slapped right away!—What, did you steal the sheep?—No, I said, I didn't steal it! First of all I bought one sheep for the money, then I sold it immediately again, bought a new one—and in the evening I simply had both: the sheep and the money!—*(Looks at the MAYOR.)* He didn't believe me, my father! He went asking around. But my story was right!—Then my father gave me the sheep and the money to boot! And so I started my business. In the year 1897!

(Blackout.)

Scene 8

(December 1941. Twilight. Both "walls" are closed. The windows in the ADLER house are repaired. On the windows of the houses there are black room-darkening shades as a protection against air attacks. Therefore there is no light coming from the main room of the inn. ANNA comes

*down the village lane, she is in mourning attire, wears a
dark coat. The two HITLER YOUTH are going up the lane,
the younger one is carrying a collection box.)*

FIRST HITLER YOUTH: Winter Aid! Winter Aid!

*(They meet ANNA, the one HITLER YOUTH holds the col-
lection box toward her, ANNA takes a coin out of her purse,
throws it into the box, the HITLER YOUTH continue on.)*

FIRST HITLER YOUTH: Winter Aid! Winter Aid!

*(From the left comes HANS with his traveling bag. He is
wearing an SS uniform, on top of that a uniform coat, he
has become a Sturmführer. They both see each other, ANNA
runs over to him, embraces him.)*

ANNA: *(softly)* Erich has died!

*(HANS presses ANNA to his chest. He is totally petrified.
He does terrible things on the Eastern front.)*

ANNA: *(looks at him)* At least you are still alive! *(Embraces him again, then separates herself from him,
takes him by the hand:)* Come in!

HANS: *(shakes his head)* I'm going home!

ANNA: Is something wrong?

*(HANS only looks at his sister sadly, goes up the village
lane and away.)*

ANNA: *(calls after him)* His cross is in the church! From
Erich! Maybe you can take a look at it!

*(ANNA goes into the inn, but not into the main room. The
"wall" of the main room opens. There is already a light on.
The MAYOR, HOPFGARTNER, the CHIEF OF POLICE,
the PRIEST and the DISTRICT MAGISTRATE are sitting
at the reserved table. The DISTRICT MAGISTRATE is a
North German, late 30s, wears an elegant national costume. OLGA is dressed in mourning clothes and is standing behind the bar. The MAYOR is wearing a black
mourning arm band.)*

MAGISTRATE: *(to HOPFGARTNER)* You are quite right, Local Branch Leader! *(to the MAYOR)* It can't go on any longer! I can no longer take the responsibility!

(The MAYOR makes a gesture of hopelessness.)

MAGISTRATE: *(to the MAYOR)* Did you know that people have already been sent to concentration camps on account of "friendliness to Jews"?

(The MAYOR looks worried.)

MAGISTRATE: *(to the PRIEST)* And now to you, Mr. Gruber! *(To the POLICEMAN:)* The document!

(The POLICEMAN takes a paper out of his jacket pocket, gives it to the magistrate.)

MAGISTRATE: *(reads aloud)* Complaint—filed by Local Branch Leader Hopfgartner. Sermon from 8th of December on Matthew, Chapter 11, verses 2 to 10. In connection with the idea, that one should fear no man, Father Gruber also spoke about the supposed persecution of those who think differently and said, I quote: "Be courageous, do not be afraid, God does not want cowardice, on the contrary, God wants us to protect our fellow bothers and sisters from the dominion of the devil incarnate!" Father Gruber also spoke about the education of children and said thereby among other things, I quote: "Today's youth are being raised to be children of Satan, to be traitors and denouncers of their own parents and brothers and sisters!" *(The MAGISTRATE looks up.)* This is a serious violation of Paragraph 130a of the Reich's Penal Code of Law. Misuse of the pulpit! And naturally it is also a violation of the Law against Treachery! How do you justify yourself?

PRIEST: I only have to justify myself before the Lord God, not before you!

MAGISTRATE: You are not very smart, Mr. Gruber! Do you know that I really don't have to talk with you at all? That is not my job! On the contrary—it is the job of the police to pass this complaint on to the Gestapo immediately!

(Outside ADLER comes from the right. He is again healthy and well-groomed, is wearing breeches, a native jacket, a native hat, a woolen coat, in his hand he has a well worn briefcase. He goes into the inn.)

MAGISTRATE: *(while all this is going on, continues)* But a few people put in a good word for you! And so I want to give you one last chance! I am not a fanatic like you, Father!—If you are prepared to publicly recant your sermon, in the church, and to excuse yourself, then we'll let the whole matter rest!

PRIEST: *(shakes his head)* That I cannot do!

(ADLER comes into the main room of the inn, all look at him, the MAYOR is startled, motions secretly to him that he should leave again. The MAGISTRATE sees the gesture, the MAYOR, embarrassed, stops.)

MAGISTRATE: *(to ADLER)* Who are you?

(ADLER hangs up his hat, takes off his coat, hangs it up.)

ADLER: *(during all of this)* Who are you?

MAGISTRATE: I am the district magistrate!

ADLER: Stefan Adler, cattle dealer.

(ADLER sits down at another table.)

MAGISTRATE: What? Are you him?

ADLER: Right! Olga, bring me a tea!

(OLGA doesn't do it.)

MAGISTRATE: *(gets up)* Hey, are you mad?

ADLER: What do you mean?

MAGISTRATE: You just think you can go walking proudly through the countryside, or what?

ADLER: Why not?

(The MAGISTRATE goes over to him.)

MAGISTRATE: Just look at how you're dressed!

(ADLER looks at himself.)

ADLER: It's normal, isn't it?

MAGISTRATE: Don't you know that Jews are forbidden to wear local national costumes or parts thereof?

ADLER: No, that's news to me!

MAYOR: I must have overlooked that. Were there some instructions about that?

(The MAGISTRATE looks at ADLER.)

MAGISTRATE: Show me your food rationing card! Right now!

(ADLER reaches into the inner pocket of his coat, takes out the rationing card, gives it to the MAGISTRATE, who looks at it.)

MAGISTRATE: That's what I thought! *(To the MAYOR:)* You obviously don't seem to worry about anything, Mr. Mayor! *(Tears a coupon from the card:)* No meat, *(tears out the second coupon)* no milk, *(tears out the third coupon)* no cheese! *(Looks at ADLER:)* Regulations! For Jews! *(Gives the card back to ADLER.)* And now get out!

(ADLER sticks the card back into his pocket, gets up, goes over to his coat. The MAGISTRATE sits down again, drinks some of his beer. All are looking at ADLER, who puts on his coat and hat and takes his brief case and goes to the door.)

MAGISTRATE: *(he remembers something)* What a minute!

(ADLER turns around.)

MAGISTRATE: Come here! Right now!

(ADLER approaches him, he's boiling with rage. The MAGISTRATE gets up, taps on ADLER'S left chest.)

MAGISTRATE: There's something missing here, right?

ADLER: What?

MAGISTRATE: *(to the MAYOR)* Why isn't this man wearing the Jewish Star?

MAYOR: Well, I don't know anything about that! Nothing ever came! Certainly not, Mr. Magistrate!

MAGISTRATE: *(to ADLER)* From now on you will wear a Jewish Star! Is that clear?

ADLER: And what does that look like?

MAGISTRATE: Now he doesn't know what a Jewish Star is! —A six pointed star of yellow cloth, in the middle the black letters "Jew"! *(Taps on Adler's left chest.)* Sew it on here! Did you understand?

ADLER nods.

MAGISTRATE: OK, then beat it!

(ADLER has to control himself, so that he doesn't hit the MAGISTRATE, the MAYOR folds his hands in a pleading fashion, motions for Adler to leave, ADLER turns around, goes out, goes over to his house.)

MAGISTRATE: Unbelievable, how unabashed this pack of Jews is! *(Sits down again, looks at the MAYOR.)* That man is going to disappear! I'll take care of that personally!—And as far as you're concerned, Father, the complaint will be passed on! *(To the POLICEMAN:)* Do you understand?

(The POLICEMAN nods, the PRIEST gets up, takes his coat, goes out.)

MAGISTRATE: *(to HOPFGARTNER)* It's a good thing that you called me! This is really a pigsty here . . . ! *(Stands up.)*

(OLGA is totally at wits end, because her husband made such a bad impression, at the same time she is furious at HOPFGARTNER.)

MAYOR: *(to the MAGISTRATE)* But you're probably not going to be driving home now, are you? You can certainly stay here with us, Magistrate!

(The "wall" of the main room of the inn closes. The PRIEST comes out of the inn, puts on his coat, looks over to the ADLER house, goes over there, tries the door, it is open, he goes in. The "wall" of the living room opens. The room is now cleaned up again. The light is on. ADLER is standing at the cupboard, has poured himself a schnapps, and drinks. There is a knock at the door.)

ADLER: *(unwillingly)* Yes?

(The door opens, the PRIEST comes in.)

PRIEST: Hello, Stefan!

ADLER: Oh, the great clergyman!

PRIEST: *(depressed)* Not so great any more!

ADLER: *(unfriendly)* Well, what do you want?

PRIEST: May I sit down?

ADLER: By all means! In this house anybody can do whatever they want! Nothing belongs to me any more!

(The PRIEST sits down, ADLER pours himself some more schnapps.)

PRIEST: I have to apologize to you!

ADLER: How come? You didn't do anything to me!

PRIEST: Yes, but I helped to prepare the groundwork! And I never stood by you!

ADLER: My goodness. That doesn't make any difference! Nobody stood by me!

PRIEST: The mayor is standing by you. I heard myself, how he defended you!

(ADLER begins to giggle, it turns into laughter, he can hardly contain himself. The PRIEST looks amazed, ADLER takes a second glass, fills it, brings it to the PRIEST.)

ADLER: Here, have a drink!

(ADLER has to keep on laughing, takes his glass and the

bottle, sits down next to the PRIEST at the table. The PRIEST raises his glass, drinks.)

ADLER: *(grinning)* Don't you know some tailor? For a Jewish star? I'm not very good at sewing! And I don't have a wife any more!

PRIEST: I'm serious, Stefan! I was always agitating against the Jews! Even from the pulpit!

ADLER: That doesn't make any difference! *(Pours himself another glass, drinks.)*

PRIEST: Oh yes it does!—You know, it's real easy to revile against people you don't know! But I know you! And because of that fact, I really didn't want to admit it for a long time, but it's true, because of that fact my prejudices collapsed!

ADLER: Why's that? After all I'm a real nice kind of Jew! So what? There are certainly other kinds too! Bloodsuckers, swindlers, rapists!

PRIEST: The same kind of people exist among Christians as well!

ADLER: Wall Street capitalists, Bolsheviks, ritual murderers!

(The PRIEST lowers his head.)

ADLER: That's OK, Father! I'm not mad at you! I just don't understand how you can sit at the same table with such people!

PRIEST: That wasn't voluntary! I was subpoenaed there!

ADLER: How come?

PRIEST: Oh, because of a sermon! But I don't care! They can stuff their swastikas! —It just can't continue like this! You have to consider each word three times before you say it! Spies are lurking everywhere! In the school the children ripped every crucifix from the wall. And while they were doing that they screamed, under the direction of the Local Branch Leader: "Without Jews, without Rome, we can build Germany's dome!"

(ADLER fills the priest's glass, the PRIEST drinks.)

PRIEST: "The free magnificent beast of prey," that's what they wanted to make out of the youth! Now they are at the front, the beasts of prey, and are being shot to bits! *(Looks straight ahead, there is silence for a while, ADLER fills his pipe, lights it.)* I don't get any more flour to make the hosts. Just to get me mad they won't give any! And next week they are going to take my church bells and make cannons out of them!

(The PRIEST is terribly sad, ADLER looks at him, has sympathy with him. The PRIEST looks up, looks at ADLER.)

PRIEST: You have to disappear, Stefan! The best thing to do would be to go down to Switzerland, over the mountains! You know your way around there!

ADLER: *(as if it were a matter of fact)* No, I'm not going to go away!

PRIEST: They will come and take you by force!

(ADLER doesn't answer.)

PRIEST: They say that all the Jews are being taken to a private settlement area in the occupied East. Is that where you want to go?

(ADLER doesn't answer.)

PRIEST: And who knows if that's right . . . Maybe they have something a lot worse planned . . .

ADLER: *(after a while)* What am I supposed to do in Switzerland! What am I supposed to do in America? What should I do in Palestine? My home is here! *(Softly:)* This is a fine country! I don't know a finer!

(Silence for a while, the PRIEST gets up, gives ADLER his hand, ADLER stands up, shakes his hand.)

PRIEST: Take care! May God be with us!

(The PRIEST goes out, ADLER sits down again, HANS (in

*uniform) comes down the village lane, the PRIEST leaves
the house, goes up the village lane, meets HANS.)*

PRIEST: Hello, Hansi!

*(HANS doesn't answer, goes past the PRIEST without look-
ing at him. The PRIEST watches him go by, then continues
on, HANS remains standing in front of his father's house,
ponders for a while, then goes in. He knocks on the door.)*

ADLER: Yes?

*(HANS comes in, ADLER looks, gets up slowly, HANS
comes towards him, looks at ADLER.)*

ADLER: Some schnapps?

*(HANS nods, ADLER gets a glass, fills it, gives HANS the
glass.)*

ADLER: Have a seat!

*(HANS sits down, drinks the schnapps in one gulp,
ADLER fills both glasses again, sits down, drinks, looks at
HANS. HANS stares into space, looks at his father, would
like to talk, can't, gets up, goes to a window, stares at the
curtain. ADLER looks at him.)*

ADLER: Don't you want to take off your coat?

*(HANS doesn't answer, after while his shoulders suddenly
begin to tremble, he has to cry, suppresses with great effort
his sobbing, ADLER gets up, goes over to him, looks at him,
puts his hand on HANS' shoulder, HANS can no longer
control himself, sobs terribly, ADLER looks on helplessly,
then turns HANS to face him, embraces him, HANS wants
to surrender, then he suddenly tears himself loose, races
out, goes quickly to the village lane, ADLER stands in the
room lost. The "wall" of the living room closes.
HOPFGARTNER and the POLICEMAN step out of the
inn. The POLICEMAN tips his cap, leaves to the right,
HOPFGARTNER goes up the village lane. The "wall" of the
main room of the inn opens. The MAGISTRATE and the*

MAYOR are still sitting at the reserved table. The MAGIS-TRATE is drinking a fresh beer, is smoking a cigarette. OLGA is standing behind the bar and is washing glasses. The MAYOR is sitting there like a scolded schoolboy. Embarrassing silence. OLGA wipes her hands on her apron, comes over to them, looks at the magistrate, sits down next to her husband.)

OLGA: Now I have to tell you something, Magistrate! My husband has always done his duty! Always! And during the time when the Party was forbidden, he constantly held his protective hand over the Party comrades! Our son Erich was in jail! Because he smuggled weapons for the movement! And now he has been killed, our Erich, at the front! Near Moscow! The Local Branch Leader doesn't have to act in such a way!

MAYOR: Just mind your own business, Olga!

OLGA: No, it has to be said! The Local Branch Leader is making a laughing fool out of the Party! Is making a laughing fool of the SA!

MAGISTRATE: Express yourself more clearly!

OLGA: Gladly! He has a boy, who isn't quite right up here *(taps on her forehead)*! He's retarded! A total idiot!

MAGISTRATE: Is that right? I didn't know that!

MAYOR: *(gets involved)* The moron is a member of the SA! Can you imagine that? His father stuck him in an SA uniform! And this is the way he walks! *(Stands up, contorts his face, imitates TONI.)*

MAGISTRATE: *(shakes his head)* The things that don't go on!

(The MAYOR sits down.)

MAGISTRATE: Does he have sexual ambitions?

MAYOR: *(doesn't understand)* What?

MAGISTRATE: Does he chase after girls?

OLGA: Why, certainly, he has the same drives as other men do! But—I mean, in the meantime he's been castrated!

MAYOR: It's called sterilized!

OLGA: Oh, I see! Sterilized! Well, at least he can't make any moron children!

MAGISTRATE: A mentally ill person in an SA uniform— No! That doesn't present a good image! I must say!

(Blackout.)

Scene 9

(January 1942. Dawn. The "wall" of the living room of the ADLER house is open. On the dining table there is a piece of bread, an onion, a yellow Jewish star and a needle with thread. There is no light on. The door to the living room opens, ADLER is pulling on a dusty black trunk by a handle. In his other hand he is holding a petroleum lamp. His electricity has been turned off. ADLER is dressed differently from the previous scene, he isn't wearing any kind of national costume. He drags the trunk to the front, puts the petroleum lamp next to it, investigates the lock of the trunk, goes out, comes back with a hammer and a crowbar, kneels down, breaks open the lock, opens the trunk, takes the petroleum lamp, illuminates the inside, reaches in with the other hand, takes out a black book (Jewish Book of Psalms), puts the lamp on the floor, blows the dust from the book, thumbs through it, stops on one page, reads a bit, puts the book on the table, reaches into the trunk again, takes out a stiff black hat (like the Orthodox Jews wear), puts it on the table, then takes out a old black kaftan, then a black pair of pants and worn boots, puts everything beside the trunk, reaches in again, takes out a prayer shawl, unfolds it, a red silken little sack falls out, he puts down the prayer shawl, takes the little sack, opens it, reaches in, takes out prayer

bands, looks at them, puts them back in the little sack, puts the little sack on the table, stands up, takes the kaftan and the lamp, puts the lamp on the table, sits down on a chair with the kaftan, takes the Jewish star, holds it on the left breast of the kaftan, takes the needle, begins to sew on the star, stops, opens the Book of Psalms, looks at the place which he found (Psalm 59).)

ADLER: *(reads)* Deliver me from my enemies, O my God, protect me from those who rise up against me, deliver me from those who work evil, and save me from bloodthirsty men. *(He continues to sew, continues to say the psalm by heart as if in a dream.)* For, lo, they lie in wait for my life; fierce men band themselves against me. For no transgression or sin of mine, O Lord, for no fault of mine, they run and make ready. Rouse thyself, come to my help, and see! Thou, Lord God of hosts, art God of Israel. *(He has sewn on the star, puts the needle away, observes the star, continues to pray.)* Awake to punish all the nations; spare none of those who treacherously plot evil. Each evening they come back, howling like dogs and prowling about the city. There they are, bellowing with their mouths, and snarling with their lips—for "Who," they think, "will hear us?" But thou, O Lord, dost laugh at them; thou dost hold all the nations in derision. O my Strength, I will sing praises to thee; for thou, O God, art my fortress. My God in his steadfast love will meet me; my God will let me look in triumph on my enemies. Slay them not, lest my people forget; make them totter by thy power, and bring them down, O Lord, our shield! For the sin of their mouths, the words of their lips, let them be trapped in their pride. For the cursing and lies which they utter, consume them in wrath, consume them till they are no more, that men may know that God rules over Jacob to the ends of the earth. Each evening they come back, howling like dogs, and prowling about the city.

They roam about for food, and growl if they do not get their fill, But I will sing of thy might; I will sing aloud of they steadfast love in the morning. For thou hast been to me a fortress and a refuge in the day of my distress. O my Strength, I will sing praises to thee, for thou, O God, art my fortress, the God who shows me steadfast love.

(While ADLER is still praying, one hears a car coming from above, the circles of light of the headlights pass over the houses, the motor dies off, the headlights go out, car doors bang, two men turn around the corner, come down the village lane. These are two criminal investigators from 1933, now members of the Gestapo. From the left ROSA comes from the church to the lane, watches the men, disappears again. When the GESTAPO MEN have arrived between the houses, ADLER is finished with the psalm. The GESTAPO MEN turn towards the inn, pull the door bell cord beside the entrance, a little bell rings softly inside, ADLER listens. The "wall" of the living room closes. The MEN ring the bell again. After a while the door opens, the MAYOR looks out, has put on a winter coat over his nightgown, he is wearing slippers on his feet. Light is coming out of the vestibule.)

MAYOR: What do you want?

FIRST GESTAPO MAN: Gestapo! *(grins)* We know each other! Right, Mr. Mayor?

(The MAYOR looks more closely, recognizes them.)

MAYOR: You are the . . . Didn't you arrest my boy back then?

FIRST GESTAPO MAN: Right!

SECOND GESTAPO MAN: *(friendly)* How are you, anyway?

MAYOR: He's been killed!

SECOND GESTAPO MAN: Oh! Sorry to hear that!

MAYOR: Yes, but . . . How is that possible? How come you are now with the Gestapo?

FIRST GESTAPO MAN: *(grinning)* We have a question for you: How come you are still mayor?

SECOND GESTAPO MAN: Come on! First we need something to drink!

(The two GESTAPO MEN enter with the MAYOR, who closes the door.)

VOICE OF THE MAYOR: Olga! Olga! Get up! —Just go into the room! I'll wake up my wife! *(Bellows:)* Olga! Make some coffee!

(After a few seconds the MAYOR rushes out of the house, runs over to the ADLER house and goes in (the door is not locked). The "wall" of the living room opens, ADLER, in the meantime, has put on the black pants, the boots and the kaftan, is just buttoning it up. The prayer shawl is in the trunk again, the cover is closed. The MAYOR storms in.)

MAYOR: Hurry up! Get out of here! The Gestapo is here!

(ADLER doesn't pay any attention to him.)

MAYOR: Don't you hear what I'm saying? The Gestapo is over at my place!

(ADLER takes the bread and the onion from the table, puts both into his pocket, also puts in the Book of Psalms, takes the little red silken sack, also puts that into his pocket, puts on his hat. The MAYOR just now sees how ADLER is dressed, looks at him in an amazed fashion.)

ADLER: *(very calmly and clearly)* Now here, in the coming year in Israel; now servants, in the coming year free men. *(Quotation from a blessing for Passover.)*

MAYOR: *(hectically)* My God, get out of here, please!

ADLER: You don't have to be afraid. I haven't written down any testimony. There is nothing at a lawyer's.

MAYOR: What? There is nothing?

ADLER shakes his head.

MAYOR: Are you sure?

ADLER: I'm sure!

MAYOR: Ah, Thank God!—What a relief!—*(Not at all
angry:)* You bastard, you swine!—Well, then do
what you want to!

*(The MAYOR storms out again, runs over into the inn.
ADLER looks around, says farewell to the room, blows out
the petroleum lamp, goes out of the room. The "wall" of the
living room closes. ADLER comes out of the house, closes
the door slowly, looks around, then goes to the well, takes a
drink from the water pipe, sits down on the edge of the well,
waits. From the church the PRIEST suddenly appears,
comes running down the village lane. He is in all of his vestments, since he is celebrating the early mass. He wants to go
into the ADLER house, but sees ADLER sitting at the well,
goes to him.)*

PRIEST: Rosa said that somebody came. Probably the police!

ADLER: Yes, I know.

*(The PRIEST looks at ADLER, sees, that it is no use to talk
with him about fleeing, sits down panting next to him on
the edge of the well. ROSA and MARIA come running down
from above, arrive.)*

MARIA: Stefan!

PRIEST: *(to MARIA)* It's no use, Maria! The stubborn man
can't be budged!

MARIA: *(to ADLER)* I'll go with you!

ADLER: *(shakes his head)* No, Maria! This path I have to
go down alone! *(Smiles.)*
It's only meant for me!

(ADLER get up, looks at his wife, embraces her.)

MARIA: *(crying)* Let me go! Please!

ADLER: Don't make it so hard for me!

MARIA: *(softly)* I can't stand it with him!

ROSA: Poison him! You should poison him!

PRIEST: Rosa!

ROSA: No! You have to poison somebody like that! The Lord God understands that!

(The door of the inn opens, the GESTAPO MEN appear, are holding coffee cups in their hands, the FIRST GESTAPO MAN is eating bread and butter, they listen. Behind them appear the MAYOR and OLGA. The SECOND GESTAPO MAN looks back to them, puts his finger to his lips. OLGA looks on curiously. In the meantime ADLER separates himself from his wife's embrace, looks at her.)

ADLER: Please forgive me that I didn't tell you that I'm a Jew. Birds of a feather should stay together, that's probably the way it is.—And forgive me that I accepted your sacrifice and was even jealous in addition!

MARIA: *(sobs)* Stop! That wasn't such a sacrifice! I wanted to save the children, yes! But I also wanted to save myself! I was afraid! I was terribly afraid of what would happen!—And—with the senior teacher, you were probably right! That wasn't such a big sacrifice!

ADLER: Let it be, Maria!

MARIA: No, I have to say it! Somehow, Stefan, I was always attracted to him! And at the same time I hated him! *(Looks at ADLER.)* I can't stand it any longer, Stefan!—Please, let me go along!

(ADLER shakes his head.)

PRIEST: Stefan, I beg you! Take your wife and go with her to a hut in the woods. I'll take care of you!

(ADLER shakes his head.)

FIRST GESTAPO MAN: Hey! Kaftan-Jew!

(All look at the GESTAPO MEN, ROSA crosses herself. Both GESTAPO MEN finish their coffee, give the cups to OLGA, approach slowly. The MAYOR and OLGA remain

standing by the door.)

FIRST GESTAPO MAN: *(to ADLER)* You look wonderful!

SECOND GESTAPO MAN: *(to ADLER)* You don't even have to change your clothes—for the East!

FIRST GESTAPO MAN: *(to ADLER)* OK, come on, let's go!

(MARIA embraces ADLER again, doesn't want to let go. He separates himself gently but powerfully from her, looks at her, kisses her on the mouth, shoves her delicately away from himself, looks at the PRIEST, shakes his hand.)

FIRST GESTAPO MAN: You don't have to say good-bye to each other! The damn priest is coming along!

(The PRIEST looks at the FIRST GESTAPO MAN, ROSA looks horrified, the FIRST GESTAPO MAN pulls out an arrest warrant, looks at it.)

FIRST GESTAPO MAN: *(to the PRIEST)* This is a whole litany! *(Reads:)* Misuse of the pulpit, treachery, radio crimes, undermining military discipline, friend to Jews and opponent of the Führer! *(Grins.)* My compliments! That certainly paid off!

(ROSA rushes over to the FIRST GESTAPO MAN, hits him, he grabs her on the upper arm, grins and pushes her away, she kicks him in the shin, now he gets angry and shoves her away so that she falls to the ground. The PRIEST helps her get up.)

SECOND GESTAPO MAN: *(grinning)* That's a lively old bat!

(ROSA looks despairingly at the PRIEST, the FIRST GESTAPO MAN puts handcuffs on one of Adler's wrists, the PRIEST takes off his stole, kisses it, gives it to ROSA, takes off his vestments, gives them to her, gives her a blessing with a short movement of his right hand, caresses her cheek. ROSA begins to sob.)

PRIEST: *(softly)* Don't cry sister! We'll soon see each other again!

*(The FIRST GESTAPO MAN pulls ADLER with the hand-
cuffs over to the PRIEST, puts the second handcuffs on the
PRIEST, so that the PRIEST and ADLER are locked to
each other. The SECOND GESTAPO MAN gives ADLER a
shove.)*

SECOND GESTAPO MAN: OK!

*(ADLER and the PRIEST start out, the two GESTAPO
MEN behind them.)*

FIRST GESTAPO MAN: *(to the MAYOR)* Where does the
      moron live? *(They already talked about that in the
      inn.)*

MAYOR: Up there, in the school building! Behind the
      church, to the left!

*(The four men go up the village lane, MARIA, ROSA, the
MAYOR and OLGA watch them leave.)*

MAYOR: *(mutters)* Finally! Now we'll have some peace!

*(Suddenly ANNA (coat over her nightdress) comes quickly
out of the door of the inn, looks around, sees the men walking up the lane.)*

ANNA: *(screams)* Papa!

(Blackout.)

Scene 10

*(The stage is black and empty. In the middle is an operating
table, covered in plastic, TONI, naked, lies tied to it. A
DOCTOR in a white coat is standing next to him, is getting
rid of the air in an injection needle. TONI looks at him with
fear and with eyes wide open. The doctor smiles at him in a
friendly manner, puts the needle on Toni's lower arm, sticks
it in, pushes the contents into the vein.)*

(Blackout.)

Scene 11

(The stage is black and empty. The PRIEST is hanging on two iron hooks upside down. He is wearing the pants of a concentration camp prisoner, his upper body is naked, a large cross was cut into his chest with a knife, around his ankles are chains by means of which he was hung on the hook. Beside him stands an SS-HAUPTSTURMFÜHER with a club in his hand, he looks at the PRIEST, after a while he nudges him with the stick, the PRIEST swings slightly, shows no sign of life.)

(Blackout.)

Scene 12

(The stage is black and empty. ADLER—in the uniform of a concentration camp prisoner—is carving a heavy stone. The uniform is torn and filthy, he himself is emaciated and totally worn out. He stops, grasps the stone anew with great effort, continues, collapses, the stone clatters to the ground. ADLER remains kneeling, puts his forehead to the stone. After a while an SS man comes over, it is HANS, Adler's son. HANS sees the prisoner kneeling on the ground, stops in back of him.)

HANS: Hey!

(ADLER doesn't move. HANS kicks him in the hips with his foot, ADLER falls to his side, looks slowly up at HANS,

recognizes him, closes his eyes in disgust, lowers his head, slowly stands up, picks up the stone again, gives great effort not to show his face to HANS, because the shame seems unbearable to him. HANS continues on. (Note: Since HANS doesn't recognize his father immediately, ADLER must now have such a changed appearance that the audience doesn't recognize him immediately either.) HANS stops after a few steps, doesn't move for a while, then turns slowly around, looks at his father, who stands motionless with the stone and has lowered his head and closed his eyes. HANS goes back, looks at his father, who feels his look and slowly raises his head and looks at HANS. They look at each other for a long time.)

HANS: Father?
ADLER: Son?

(HANS stands there motionless, takes the stone out of his father's hands, puts it slowly on the ground, looks at his father again for a while, then slowly embraces him, pulls him toward himself. After a while the father also raises his arms, also embraces his son. Then HANS opens his pistol case with his right hand (he continues to hold his left hand around his father), takes out the pistol, shoves it between his and his father's chest, points it at his father, pulls the trigger, the shot is fired. ADLER drops his arms and collapses, but HANS continues to hold him firmly, so that he can't fall down, HANS kisses the dead father on the cheek, presses him intimately to himself, points the pistol to his own chest, pulls the trigger, falls down, with him the father. They both lie on the ground in an embrace.)

(Blackout. Curtain.)

Scene 13

(Light on the curtain, the audience begins to applaud because they believe that the play is over. After a while the MAYOR comes out from between the curtain. He is wearing a national costume with a red-white-red arm band. The MAYOR smiles and motions for the applause to stop.)

MAYOR: Thank you, thank you, thank you! *(Applause dies down.)* Fellow citizens, friends, Austrians! Thanks to the confidence that our American friends have shown in me, I am now once again your mayor! This confidence is not without reason, I believe! You know yourselves that I helped many people in this difficult time. Many! Irrespective of social standing or views, always trying to achieve unity and harmony!—Friends, we have all experienced terrible things! Many of our sons—even my son—many of our fathers died for an idea, in which they believed with every fiber of their being! Therefore let us honor those who fulfilled their soldierly duty—in the tundras of the North, in the snow covered fields of Russia, in the hot desert sands of Africa! Even though some things may have happened which are now given too much importance and exaggerated endlessly by some—war, my dear fellow citizens, is just not a scoop of honey. No one should be given reproach! None of our brave countrymen, none of those who fought the economic battle on the home front in want and hunger, none who represented law and order in the government! For no one, no one of us knew, that we were being led by a mad man! All of us, all of us were misused, they exploited our most noble feelings, exploited our idealism, our faith, our devotion!—Dear fellow citizens, I know that there was hate and dissension and malevolence in our village in this difficult time. Let us forget that now, I appeal to you! Let us obliterate this time, let us extinguish it in our hearts and in our minds! Let us forget bickering and discord and petty revenge! For now, friends, we must start with rebuilding; and only with a united effort will we be able to make this rebuilding work! Therefore I ask you: Let's all stick together, let us with new courage, with new strength, with a new creative impulse build up together the new Austria of the future!—I thank you!

(The MAYOR bows, disappears between the curtain, the light on the curtain goes out.)

THE END.

Afterword

In 1817 an actor by the name of Karsten offered the court theater in Weimar, which was directed by Goethe, a performance of a play whose main protagonist was a poodle. The poet considered the presence of a dog on the stage incompatible with the dignity of the institution that had been in his care for a quarter of a century and indignantly refused. The mistress of the Duke of Weimar, however, Caroline Jagemann, wanted to see Karstens' trained poodle perform, used her influence on the Duke and had her will. The play was put on, and in the resulting fracas, Goethe, who was not paid for this job anyway, lost the directorship.

It is interesting to note that Karstens' home ground was a suburban theater in Vienna, the Theater an der Wien. In that city there was no dearth of theaters that did not stand on their dignity and on the stages of which the presence of a dog was not out of place. Ever since the eighteenth century, theaters in the suburbs of Vienna had competed with the staid and stately court theaters with their repertoire of opera and heroic tragedy by offering a lighter fare, burlesques, farces, operettas and comedies that dealt with the concerns of the bourgeoisie and the lower classes and had thus attracted an audience that found their offerings more relevant and the price of admission more affordable. Gradually changing in character, this tradition of "popular plays" (*Volksstücke*) performed in "popular theaters" (*Volkstheater*) culminated in the nineteenth century with the plays by Ferdinand Raimund (1790-1836) and Johann Nestroy (1801-1862), who adapted the genre to the serious discussion of social and political problems. In the twentieth century the quality of the *Volksstücke* declined, and as the genre was exploited for chauvinistic, "blood-and-soil" propaganda by the Nazis, it was held in low esteem after

1945. In the sixties and seventies it was revived by such playwrights as the Bavarians Franz Xaver Kroetz and Rainer Werner Faßbinder and the Austrians Wolfgang Bauer, Peter Turrini and Felix Mitterer, who used it as a vehicle of–frequently very bitter–social criticism. Among this group of interesting and rewarding contemporary writers of *Volksstücke*, Mitterer stands out for the range, variety and power of his plays, which have attracted international attention and acclaim.

Felix Mitterer was born in Achenkirch in the Tyrol in 1948 and was brought up by foster parents who made a living as farm laborers. He began to write stories when he was twelve and, on the recommendation of a teacher who recognized the boy's talent, was sent to a teachers' training school when he was fourteen. An ardent reader and passionate movie fan, he took little interest in his formal education, failed his examinations and, in 1966, found himself a job at the customs office in Innsbruck. In the early seventies he began to write radio dramas, and in 1977 he achieved his breakthrough: in rapid succession he published his first book (a story for children), a script of his was filmed for television, and his first play was performed. He could now resign from the customs office and become a full-time writer.

This first play, *Kein Platz für Idioten* (*No Room For Idiots*),[1] tells the story of a retarded boy who is maltreated by his mother and bereft of every opportunity to develop. When he is put in the care of an old man who offers him love and companionship, the boy rapidly improves, but he is still not accepted by the community. The old man takes the boy to the local pub on Sundays to treat him to hot dogs and a soft drink, but on the instigation of a guest who argues that the boy, who does not look "normal," will scare away tourists, he is forbidden to come back. When, out of sheer ignorance, he commits an insignificant sexual misdemeanor, he is committed to an asylum to rid the community of his embarrassing presence.

Kein Platz für Idioten (*No Place For Idiots*) sets the tone for Mitterer's plays in many ways. It deals with Mitterer's central concern–the fate of the outsider, who is hated, feared, maltreated, despised, neglected or exploited in our society. The powerful portrayal forced the audience to become aware of what we do to our fellow humans whose only crime is that they are different. It tells the story of such an outsider in a dramatically effective but straightforward way; none of Mitterer's works has the complex plot with the intrigues and counter-plots of traditional "literary" plays, and this simple structure brings them much closer to real life. The dialogue is couched in the Tyrolian dialect, which is, however, toned down sufficiently to create no serious difficulties for South German and Austrian audiences and readers.

Last but not least, while the play, like so many others by Mitterer, unflinchingly exposes the viciousness that seems to be such an ageless characteristic of the human race, it does not depict a hopeless world: the old man who befriends the retarded boy shows us that there is an alternative to selfishness and brutality. This is particularly worth pointing out as so many of the contemporary *Volksstücke* by other authors depict a world that is wholly depraved.

While *No Place for Idiots* is set in the present, *Stigma* takes us one and a half centuries into the past. It was written for a season of popular plays to be staged in Hall, Tyrol, but the mayor of that town would not have it, whereupon the whole venture moved to Telfs, some twenty miles west of the Tyrolean capital, Innsbruck. There has been an annual season of folk plays in Telfs ever since.

The linearity of the plot of *Stigma* is emphasized by its division into "stations," a designation that clearly refers to the stations of the cross. Moid (dialect for Maria) not only sees herself as Christ's chosen bride, but she herself is also a Christ figure, and the play clearly displays

analogies to that time-honored version of the *Volksstück*,
the passion play.[2] Nonetheless, or perhaps for that very
reason, the first performances of *Stigma*, in August 1982,
were accompanied by demonstrations and bomb threats.
As is so often the case, most of the protesters had neither
seen nor read the play they condemned, but in some respects the play is indeed incendiary. As long as Moid
(Mady in the English translation) seems to strengthen vil-
lagers in their faith, she is tolerated, particularly as she
provides her employer with a rich source of additional in-
come. The turning point comes when one of the people
who approach her for help and advice, a woman who has
worked hard all her life and in her old age is reduced to
begging, asks Mady to help her to die, and Mady, driven to
desperation by a cruel comment on the old woman's request, bursts out:

> "Woe unto you, you wealthy of the earth,
> you'll have no consolation! Woe unto you,
> you gluttons, you'll starve! . . .

> Oh, God! Oh, God What shall I do? . . .You
> said, blessed are the poor for they shall
> inherit Heaven! Heaven! . . . I want jus-
> tice to reign here and now, on earth, and
> not just afterward in Heaven!

Having challenged the social order, Mady's fate is
sealed: the farmer has no use for a servant who pillories
his exploitation of the farm-hands, and the Church has no
use for a saint who wants justice now, on earth, and not
merely in the life to come. The commission that is sent to
the village to examine her proclaims her to be a fraud and
hysteric; she is excommunicated and–accidentally–killed.
      The four one-acters that form *Visiting Hours (Be-
suchszeit)* are adaptations of radio plays that Mitterer
wrote in the course of the seventies. The cycle was first

produced in 1985 in Vienna and has become Mitterer's most widely performed work. The man in the old-age home, the woman in jail, the farmer in the psychiatric ward and the dying woman in the hospital are all shown to be prisoners, robbed of their freedom and their dignity; but their visitors are also prisoners, trapped in the strait-jacket of social constraints and at the mercy of social forces they do not understand. Communication between the visitors and the visited is so painfully inadequate that it is most appropriate that one of the playlets should have been rewritten as a monologue. This second version, *Siberia* (*Sibirien*), presents the old man in far greater detail and is even more impressive in its evocation of his environment and the people he has to deal with. First performed in Telfs in 1989, it was a great success in Vienna and Berlin and is rapidly achieving international recognition.

Dragon Thirst (*Drachendurst*), first performed in Telfs in 1986, taps into a very old sub-genre of the *Volksstück*, the féerie. Plays and operettas in which supernatural beings mingle with humans and which owe a large part of their appeal to stage effects have always formed part of the repertory of the popular theaters. The most famous Viennese work of this kind is undoubtedly *The Magic Flute*, made immortal by Mozart's music. Mitterer's fairy play is by far the most light-hearted of his works, but it too makes comment on real life. As the playwright himself has remarked, the time of action is "the past or the future or a timeless time, where in another dimension–i.e., in us ourselves–an eternal battle rages, the battle of good against evil, black against white, money against bread, love against hatred, life against death . . . In the end, as in all fairy tales, good is victorious, but evil is immediately reborn, the cycle begins again, the play never ends." [3]

As I have mentioned earlier–and as must be obvious to any reader of this volume–Mitterer has been preoccupied in his writing with the fate of the outsider, who is victimized for no better reason than that he is different. Now the exemplary, representative outsider in the Christian world has been, for many centuries, the Jew, and it was therefore to be expected that Mitterer should sooner or later take up this topic. He did so in *There's Not a Finer Country (Kein schöner Land)*, first performed in Innsbruck in 1987. The play is based on a real person, Rudolf Gomperz, who was born in Vienna in 1878 and settled in St. Anton in the Tyrol in 1905, where he substantially contributed to the development of the tourist industry. While he was of Jewish descent, he married a non-Jew, and his sons became enthusiastic Nazis. In 1938 almost all of the citizens of St. Anton, in spite of the services he had rendered the community, turned against him. So as to save the sons, Frau Gomperz invented the story that their father was not Gomperz, but an "Aryan" with whom she had had an affair. Gomperz was deported in January, 1942 and disappeared in a concentration camp.

Stefan Adler, the main protagonist of *There's Not a Finer Country*, is modelled on Gomperz, but his fate is in some respects atypical. Unaware of his Jewish ancestry, he joins the NSDAP (National Socialist German Workers' Party) in the fall of 1933. When he discovers that his grandparents were Jewish and is ostracized and humiliated by the very people who used to celebrate him as the "most respected person in the whole village," he refuses to leave St. Anton. The overwhelming majority of the six million Jews who died in the gas chambers had no opportunity to save themselves. In one important respect, however, Adler fits the popular stereotype of the Jew only too well: he is a dealer in farm animals, and he talks with pride of the skill in buying and selling he had already when he was all of thirteen. Needless to say, Mitterer had no intention of denigrating Adler by inserting this episode in his text. In fact, he had the story of the boy's sheep trading from a non-Jewish cattle dealer. Unfortunately, however, the uncanny business acumen displayed by Adler as a mere stripling corresponds exactly to the widespread prejudice in Austria that no Christian can compete with Jews when it come to money matters.[4]

But one should not focus too much on Adler when reading this play. Its evocation of the history of a typical Austrian village from 1933 to the immediate postwar years—of the enthusiasm with which so many Austrians embraced the Nazi creed in the thirties, the uncanny speed with which so many others switched their allegiance to the Nazis after the Anschluss, the brutalities that counted as patriotic deeds and the fate of the few who dared resist—meets the facts, and as Austria has not been very successful in coming to grips with its past, Mitterer's play is timely and important.

In addition to his activities as a playwright, Mitterer has shown himself to be a gifted actor, and he is the author of highly successful TV series. Writing for television is of course very attractive: it is not only far more rewarding financially, but it reaches incomparably larger audiences than the theater. As Mitterer is deeply committed to drawing attention to social abuses by his pen, reaching a wide public has to be important to him. There is no doubt, however, that he will continue to write for the stage, and as there are excellent plays by him that could not be included in the present selection, it is to be hoped that a second volume of his plays in English translation will be published in the not too distant future.

Hans Eichner
University of Toronto

Notes

1.   For the English version see *Anthology of Contemporary Austrian Folk Plays* (Riverside: Ariadne Press, 1993), pp. 269 ff.

2.   Herbert Herzmann, "The Relevance of the Tradition. The Volksstücke of Felix Mitterer," *Modern Austrian Literature*, Vol. 24, No. 3/4, p. 175.

3.   Felix Mitterer, *Stücke*, vol. I (Innsbruck: Haymon, 1992), p. 23.

4.   According to a survey conducted in Austria in 1973, 57% of those asked claimed never to have met a Jew, but 65% of them felt that "where Jews control business activities, no non-Jew has a chance." (Bernd Marin, "Umfragebefunde zum Antisemitismus in Österreich 1946-1982." SWS-Meinungsprofile aus: *Journal für Sozialforschung*, Vol. 23 (1983), in: John Bunzl and Bernd Marin, *Antisemitismus in Österreich* (Innsbruck: Inn-Verlag, 1983) pp. 225 ff.

ARIADNE PRESS

Translation Series:

February Shadows
By Elisabeth Reichart
Translated by Donna L. Hoffmeister
Afterword by Christa Wolf

Night Over Vienna
By Lili Körber
Translation by Viktoria Hertling
& Kay M. Stone. Commentary by
Viktoria Hertling

The Cool Million
By Erich Wolfgang Skwara
Translated by Harvey I. Dunkle
Preface by Martin Walser
Afterword by Richard Exner

Buried in the Sands of Time
Poetry by Janko Ferk
English/German/Slovenian
English Translation by H. Kuhner

Puntigam or The Art of Forgetting
By Gerald Szyszkowitz
Translated by Adrian Del Caro
Preface by Simon Wiesenthal
Afterword by Jürgen Koppensteiner

Negatives of My Father
By Peter Henisch
Translation and Afterword
by Anne C. Ulmer

On the Other Side
By Gerald Szyszkowitz
Translated by Todd C. Hanlin
Afterword by Jürgen Koppensteiner

The Slackers and Other Plays
By Peter Turrini
Translation and Afterword
by Richard S. Dixon

The Baron and the Fish
By Peter Marginter
Translation and Afterword
by Lowell A. Bangerter

I Want to Speak
The Tragedy and Banality
of Survival in
Terezin and Auschwitz
By Margareta Glas-Larsson
Edited and with a Commentary
by Gerhard Botz
Translated by Lowell A. Bangerter

The Works of Solitude
By György Sebestyén
Translation and Afterword
by Michael Mitchell

Krystyna
By Simon Wiesenthal
Translated by Eva Dukes

Deserter
By Anton Fuchs
Translation and Afterword
by Todd C. Hanlin

From Here to There
By Peter Rosei
Translation and Afterword
by Kathleen Thorpe

The Angel of the West Window
By Gustav Meyrink
Translated by Michael Mitchell

Relationships
An Anthology of Contemporary
Austrian Literature
Selected and with an Introduction
by Adolf Opel

Three Late Plays
By Arthur Schnitzler
Translation and Afterword
G.J. Weinberger

Professor Bernhardi and Other Plays
By Arthur Schnitzler
Translation G.J. Weinberger
Afterword Jeffrey B. Berlin

Translations:

The Bengal Tiger
By Jeannie Ebner
Translation and Afterword
by Lowell A. Bangerter

Three Flute Notes
By Jeannie Ebner
Translation and Afterword
by Lowell A. Bangerter

*Farewell to Love and Other
Misunderstandings*
By Herbert Eisenreich
Translation and Afterword
by Renate Latimer

The Sphere of Glass
By Marianne Gruber
Translation and Afterword
by Alexandra Strelka
Preface by Joseph P. Strelka

A Man Too White
By György Sebestén
Translation and Afterword
by Michael Mitchell

The Green Face
By Gustav Meyrink
Translated by Michael Mitchell

*The Ariadne Book of Austrian Fantasy
The Meyrink Years 1890-1930*
Edited and translated
by Michael Mitchell

Walpurgisnacht
By Gustav Meyrink
Translated by Michael Mitchell

On the Wrong Track
By Milo Dor
Translated by Jerry Glenn
and Jennifer Kelley

Night Train
By Friederike Mayröcker
Translation and Afterword
by Beth Bjorklund

Memories With Trees
By Ilse Tielsch
Translation and Afterword
by David Scrase

Return to the Center
By Otto von Habsburg
Translated by Carvel de Bussy

View from a Distance
By Lore Lizbeth Waller

Five Plays
By Gerald Szyszkowitz
Translated by Todd Hanlin, Heidi
Hutchinson and Joseph McVeigh

*Anthology of Contemporary Austrian
Folk Plays*
By Veza Canetti, Peter Preses &
Ulrich Becher, Felix Mitterer, Gerald
Szyszkowitz, Peter Turrini
Translation and Afterword
by Richard Dixon

The Condemned Judge
By Janko Ferk
Translation and Afterword
by Lowell A. Bangerter

*Thomas Bernhard and His
Grandfather: "Our Grandfathers
Are Our Teachers."*
By Caroline Markolin
Translated by Petra Hartweg

The Convent School
By Barbara Frischmuth
Translated by
Gerald Chapple and James B. Lawson

The Calm Ocean
By Gerhard Roth
Translated by Helga Schreckenberger
and Jacqueline Vansant

Remembering Gardens
by Kurt Klinger
Translated by Harvey I. Dunkle

ARIADNE PRESS

Studies in Austrian Literature, Culture and Thought